CUSTOMER RELATIONSHIP MANAGEMENT

INTEGRATING MARKETING STRATEGY AND INFORMATION TECHNOLOGY

WILLIAM G. ZIKMUND
Oklahoma State University

RAYMOND McLEOD, JR.
University of Texas at Austin

FAYE W. GILBERT
University of Mississippi

WILEY

www.wiley.com/college/zikmund

Acquisitions Editor *Jeff Marshall*
Marketing Manager *Charity Robey*
Production Manager *Lari Bishop*
Designer *Shoshanna Turek*
Illustration Editor *Jennifer Fisher*
Copy Editor *Karen Thompson*
Indexer *Lorretta Palagi*
Cover Design *Jennifer Fisher*
Cover Images *Copyright © 2002. Jayme Odgers*

This book was set in Minion and printed and bound by Malloy, Inc. The cover was printed by Phoenix Color Corp.

This book is printed on acid free paper.∞

ISBN 0-471-27137-3

Printed in the United States of America

10 9 8 7 6 5 4 3 2 1

Bill, you left us too soon.
Your cheerful laugh will always be with us.

Contents

Preface

The purpose of this book is to describe elements of Customer Relationship Management as they relate to marketing strategy and to information technology. We explore the practical idea that information about past, present, and future customers should form the heart of strategic plans. The basic premise is that successful executives must understand both marketing concepts and information system architecture in order to successfully acquire and use a comprehensive, reliable, and integrated view of the customer base over time.

Practically speaking, the book is written to serve as an introductory course in customer relationship management/marketing at the undergraduate or graduate levels of course work. Further, this text may be beneficial as an additional reading for most business courses, particularly marketing management, sales management, principles of marketing, or management information systems as the content focus is on the intersection of marketing concepts and information systems technology. The cross-functional blend of marketing and information systems can be an effective way to:

- provide a central focus for a course in customer relationship management or marketing;
- foreshadow a research or data analysis experience by providing information about the development and usage of the MIS infrastructure required to answer basic market segmentation questions;
- complement an executive or managerial continuing education course for those who must balance the costs of CRM systems with the expected benefits in reaching defined customer segments;
- support an information technology or data mining course where an understanding of user applications could provide practical insight; and,
- stimulate discussions in an organizational environment where managers and employees could use the information as a source of ideas.

ORGANIZATION OF THE BOOK

The book begins and ends with fundamental marketing management theory as it presents concepts as they relate to understanding and satisfying customer needs. The text covers the development of the information system and provides students with a roadmap of how to acquire information about customers over time. The chapters and their primary concentrations are as follows:

CHAPTER 1: THE NATURE OF CUSTOMER RELATIONSHIP MANAGEMENT

Defines CRM as a process and as a hub of learning for the organization, and outlines costs and benefits of the CRM system for organizations and customers

CHAPTER 2: UNDERSTANDING CUSTOMER DIFFERENCES

Begins with a basic view of market segmentation and concludes with aspects of using CRM systems in B2B markets.

CHAPTER 3: INFORMATION TECHNOLOGY AND COLLECTING CUSTOMER DATA

Profiles the CRM architecture, contact points for data input, data storage, methods of arranging data to facilitate retrieval, the concept of closed-loop marketing, and sources for collecting customer data.

CHAPTER 4: THE CRM DATA WAREHOUSE

Begins by defining the data warehouse and its architecture; identifies the components of the warehouse data repository, metadata repository, and the types of metadata; concludes with information on navigation and security.

CHAPTER 5: CUSTOMER LOYALTY

Defines loyalty as behaviorally or attitudinally based; the chapter then outlines factors that affect loyalty in a positive and negative direction.

CHAPTER 6: CUSTOMER RETENTION STRATEGIES

Describes the evolution of relationship marketing programs and methods of retaining customers throughout the customer life cycle, as well as ideas for responding to customer complaints.

CHAPTER 7: WINBACK AND ACQUISITION STRATEGIES

Offers ideas for identifying why customers are about to leave the organization and potential actions to take to acquire and to reconnect with customers.

CHAPTER 8: SALES FORCE AUTOMATION AND AUTOMATED CUSTOMER SERVICE CENTERS

Outlines the tasks for sales force automation systems, reasons for resistance to implementation, and an overview of customer service centers.

CHAPTER 9: THE BASICS OF DATA MINING, ONLINE ANALYTICAL PROCESSING, AND INFORMATION PRESENTATION

Defines and describes concepts of data mining, its functions, and relational online analytical processes.

CHAPTER 10: MEASURING CUSTOMER SATISFACTION AND LOYALTY

Offers a review of the basic steps in conducting surveys, as well as examples of measures to assess quality, brand loyalty, and e-loyalty.

CHAPTER 11: ISSUES FOR IMPLEMENTING CRM SYSTEMS

Concludes the text with reminders of the need for phased development for CRM systems, supporting and challenging forces for its implementation, and the potential rewards for CRM implementation.

PEDAGOGICAL FEATURES AND WEB SITE SUPPORT

Each chapter begins with an example from the real world that illustrates the content to follow. Each chapter includes a list of key terms as well as a set of discussion questions for review and critical thinking. The Instructor's Manual (available online) then provides suggested answers to these questions and suggestions for other assignments or activities. Instructional resources also include a test bank with a generous number of multiple choice questions for each chapter, along with a reference for each question to the specific pages in the text it covers.

SUMMARY

An academic colleague of one of the co-authors asked, "How can anyone write a book about customer relationship management (CRM) when many are still debating the basic definition of the term?" Have we defined CRM in this first attempt to combine marketing and information system concepts? We hope you find that we have at least begun to help you frame the discussion of the intersection of these fields and the implications for the future of business practice.

OUR FRIEND, BILL

While it has been a pleasure to work on completing this text, many of the central concepts are due to the artful prose of Bill Zikmund. Part of his legacy to education is found in his analogies and examples. Hopefully, Bill's skillful twist of a phrase is still obvious throughout the revisions to this text and will remain an obvious anchor through future revisions as well. The notion of blending marketing and information system theory with authors from disparate disciplines is also due to Bill's drive and to his curiosity about new ways to view the art of business. With much gratitude and fond remembrance, this text is dedicated to the life and consummate skill of William G. Zikmund.

ACKNOWLEDGEMENTS

Thanks go to Tobin Zikmund for writing the Test Bank.

We would like to thank the creative and production teams at Leyh Publishing, who have been terrific: Rick Leyh, Lari Bishop, Jennifer Fisher, Jaye Joseph, and Camille McMorrow.

Rick Leyh has had the pleasure to know Bill Zikmund as a friend through many successful textbook projects. Giving Leyh Publishing the opportunity to contribute to this groundbreaking text in our small way is an example of Bill's generosity.

Susan Elbe, Jeff Marshall and Charity Robey at John Wiley and Sons were supportive and encouraging to us in this breakthrough project from the beginning.

Feedback from a number of our colleagues has been essential to the development of this text:

Scott Bonifield, University of Central Florida

Harold F. Koenig, Oregon State University

David Paradice, Florida State University

David Strutton, University of North Texas

Dennis N. Bristow, St. Cloud State University

About the Authors

William G. Zikmund

A native of the Chicago area, William G. Zikmund lived in Tulsa, Oklahoma. He was a professor of marketing at Oklahoma State University. He received a Bachelor of Science degree in marketing from the University of Colorado, a Master of Science degree in marketing from Southern Illinois University, and a Ph.D. in business administration with a concentration in marketing from the University of Colorado.

Before beginning his academic career, Professor Zikmund worked in marketing research for Conway/Millikin Company (a marketing research supplier) and Remington Arms Company (an extensive user of marketing research). Professor Zikmund had also served as a marketing research consultant to several business and nonprofit organizations. His applied marketing research experiences ranged from interviewing respondents and coding questionnaires, to designing, supervising, and analyzing entire research programs.

During his academic career, Professor Zikmund published dozens of articles and papers in a diverse group of scholarly journals ranging from the *Journal of Marketing* to *Accounting Review* to the *Journal of Applied Psychology*. In addition to *Essentials of Marketing Research*, Professor Zikmund has written *Exploring Marketing Research, Business Research Methods, Marketing, Effective Marketing,* and a work of fiction, *A Corporate Bestiary.*

Professor Zikmund was a member of professional organizations including the American Marketing Association, the Academy of Marketing Science, the Association for Consumer Research, the Society for Marketing Advancement, the Marketing Educators' Association, and the Association of Collegiate Marketing Educators. He served on the editorial review boards of the *Journal of the Academy of Marketing Education, Marketing Education Review,* the *Journal of the Academy of Marketing Science,* and the *Journal of Business Research.*

Raymond McLeod, Jr.

Prior to accepting an appointment as assistant professor at Metropolitan State College in Denver, Ray worked in industry with IBM, Recognition Equipment Inc., and Lifson, Wilson, Ferguson, and Winick, a management consulting firm. In 1973 he accepted a faculty position at Texas Christian University and in 1980 joined the faculty at Texas A & M University. In 1998 he joined the management science and information systems faculty at the University of Texas at Austin, where he now serves as adjunct professor, teaching courses in Marketing and MIS.

Findings of Professor McLeod's research have appeared in such journals as California Management Review, MIS Quarterly, Journal of Management Information Systems, Decision Sciences, IEEE Transactions on Engineering Management, and Communications of the ACM. He is co-author with George Schell of Management Information Systems, Eighth Edition (Prentice-Hall, 2001) and Management Information Systems Case Book, Sixth Edition (Prentice-Hall, 1995). He is author of Information Systems Concepts (Macmillan, 1994), and Introduction to Systems Analysis and Design: An Organizational Approach (Dryden, 1994).

Dr. McLeod has served on the editorial boards of the Journal of Management Information Systems, Data Base, Information Resources Management Journal, and Journal of Information Technology Management. He is past chair of the ACM Special Interest Group for Computer Personnel Research (SIGCPR), and holds a Certificate in Data Processing, awarded by the Data Processing Management Association (DPMA). He is presently serving as editor of the International Journal of Information Technology Education.

Faye W. Gilbert

Faye W. Gilbert is a Professor of Marketing and Pharmacy Administration at The University of Mississippi where she is also currently serving as the Associate Dean for the MBA program. With a 1988 Ph.D. from the University of North Texas, Faye has published her work in the Journal of the Academy of Marketing Science, the Journal of Retailing, the Journal of Business Research, Psychology and Marketing, the Journal of Marketing Theory and Practice, the Journal of Research in Pharmaceutical Economics, Marketing Education Review, and the Journal of Marketing Education, among other journal and conference proceeding outlets. Faye has also written supplementary materials to accompany several texts. She has served as president of the Society for Marketing Advances and as a founding member of the Ole Miss Women's Council for Philanthropy. She is the recipient of the outstanding teaching award, the Elsie M. Hood, for The University of Mississippi, as well as two commendations from the Mortar Board Honor society.

The Nature of Customer Relationship Management

When Joann Idleman arrives at the airport in Las Vegas, a sleek white limousine is waiting to whisk her off to Harrah's hotel and casino.[1] She doesn't bat an eyelash as she passes Caesars Palace and the Mirage, two showy resorts where the 67-year-old entrepreneur from California was once a regular. Now she wouldn't dream of staying anywhere but Harrah's.

Upon arriving at the hotel, she is greeted with a big smile by her personal host, Gary Ernst, who makes her hotel reservations and books her seat at concerts and boxing matches. In her suite, she finds fresh-cut flowers, cookies, chocolate-covered strawberries, cold drinks in the fridge and a welcoming voice mail from the concierge. If she goes to Harrah's on her birthday, there's cake in the room. "I think they know my whole life history," says Idleman. "Whether it's a birthday or an anniversary, there's always something in the room to acknowledge that, and that, to me, is special."

Idleman has been gambling at Harrah's since 1995; in 1998 she started staying at the hotel exclusively. The year before, the company had rolled out a loyalty card program called Total Rewards, which tracks customers' gaming activity and gives them rewards to encourage them to spend more money at the slots and tables. Although Idleman says it was the service—not the player card—that made her a Harrah's devotee, the company would not have been able to provide its high-caliber service without the card. And thanks to that service, Idleman's spending increased by 72 percent from 1997 to the present. Now, she spends between $5,000 and $10,000 on gaming per visit. Ernst and company better treat her like a VIP.

This customer's experience illustrates a perfect company-customer relationship for a high-value customer. This book will attempt to show how large and small companies try to establish and maintain similar customer relationships. This chapter defines customer relationship management and how it benefits both customers and companies.

THE CONCEPT OF RELATIONSHIP MANAGEMENT

At the broadest level, the function of an enterprise's marketing activities is to bring buyers and sellers together, to create customers. While getting customers is fundamental to business success, keeping customers is more important. Successful firms work to build long-term relationships with their customers. The term **relationship management** (or **relationship marketing**) communicates the idea that a major goal of a business enterprise is to engage in interactions with customers over the longterm.

Consider the local butcher of years ago. When a female customer walked into the shop, the butcher said hello and called the customer by name. The butcher knew how the customer wanted her steaks and chops trimmed. He knew her family always grilled hamburgers on the weekend and that they preferred ground sirloin over ground chuck. Although he specialized in meats, he also stocked hamburger buns so his customer needed to make only one stop. She appreciated the personalized service she received. Both the butcher and the customer profited from this loyalty relationship.

The old-fashioned butcher understood his customers and promptly responded to their needs. In recent years, contemporary marketers have realized that they can learn a lot from shopkeepers of the past. Contemporary marketers recognize that, once a sale occurs, the firm must stress managing relationships that will bring about additional exchanges. Making a sale should not be viewed as the end of the marketing process, but rather as the start of the organization's relationship with a customer.

> The relationship between a buyer and seller seldom ends when a sale is made.
> In a greatly increasing proportion of transactions, the relationship actually
> intensifies subsequent to the sale. This becomes the buyer's critical factor in
> the buyer's choice of a seller next time around.... The sale merely con-
> summates the courtship. Then the marriage begins. How good the marriage
> is depends on how well the relationship is managed by the seller.[2]

A principle thesis of this text is that customers who receive more than they expect from an organization are pleased and satisfied. Satisfied customers who develop a history of positive interactions and who want to purchase the same product or a related item will return to the organization that has treated them well in the past. As firms strive to treat customers in a manner that encourages repeat sales, they maximize the lifetime value of customer relationships.

Successful small firms, such as the traditional butcher, have to be relationship oriented.[3] They know that their customers—buyers who purchase promises of satisfaction—prefer to do business repeatedly with people and organizations they trust.[4] They know that establishing relationships with customers can increase long-run sales and reduce marketing costs.[5] They know that not all customers want the same products and services. They know that two individuals may buy the same product for different reasons. They know that marketing to existing customers to gain repeat business provides benefits to both the organization and the customer. In summary, a business enterprise, organization, or firm must focus on both getting and keeping customers. It is the marketer's job to use the resources of the entire organization to create, interpret, and maintain the relationship with the customer.[6]

It seems important to note that academic and practitioner-oriented experts see a gap between the theory of relationship management and its practical application.[7] Philosophically, relationship management addresses the heart of marketing and, hopefully, the heart of any organization—its desire to profitably meet the lifetime needs of customers better than the competition does. At a tactical level, when inappropriately applied, relationship management uses information technology to spawn short-term loyalty schemes that are often opportunistic and may create loyalty to the incentive (i.e., frequent flyer points), as opposed to the provider (the airline). Thus, it is important to understand both the philosophy and the tactics of customer relationship management.

CUSTOMER RELATIONSHIP MANAGEMENT

A **customer relationship management (CRM)** system, by its simplest definition, is a process to compile information that increases understanding of how to manage an organization's relationships with its customers. In this simple view, a CRM system consists of two dimensions, analysis and action.[8] More formally, **CRM** is a business strategy that uses information technology to provide an enterprise with a comprehensive, reliable, and integrated view of its customer base so that all processes and customer interactions help maintain and expand mutually beneficial relationships. CRM is thus a technique or a set of processes designed to collect data and provide information that helps the organization evaluate strategic options. A CRM strategy should help organizations improve the profitability of their interactions with current and potential customers while at the same time making those interactions appear friendlier through individualization and personalization.[9] The purposes of a CRM system are to enhance customer service, improve customer satisfaction, and ensure customer retention by aligning business processes with technology integration.

A CRM system brings together lots of pieces of information about customers, customer characteristics, sales transactions, marketing effectiveness, responsiveness, and market trends.[10] For example, consider the United Services Automobile Association (USAA), a company that offers insurance and financial services to more than 3.3 million customers who share a mutual background: the military.[11] (Nearly 90 percent of all active duty military officers are members, and less than 1 percent ever leave.)

USAA's CRM approach relies on information technology to emphasize personalized service, mainly via the company's 32 telephone call centers, where nearly 10,000 customer service representatives field over 400,000 calls each day. When a call comes in, the employee requests the member's account number and then opens a screen listing a chronology of all previous contacts and purchases. As the conversation proceeds, the USAA customer service representative might access the firm's Enterprise Needs-Based Sales and Service tool, which generates a customized profile of services that the member might find useful. For instance, if the member lives in a flood plain yet doesn't have flood insurance, the service representative can inform the customer about the benefits of flood insurance.

An effective CRM system describes customer relationships in sufficient detail so that all aspects of the organization can access information, match customer needs with satisfying product offerings, remind customers of service requirements, know what other products a customer has purchased, and so forth.[12] A bank's CRM should give a service representative in its telephone call center the ability to retrieve a complete record of a customer's company interactions seconds after the customer provides identification information. Many CRM systems allow customers themselves to directly access information about their transactions with a company.

THE CRM SYSTEM AS A HUB OF APPLIED LEARNING

In essence, the CRM approach represents another step in the development of the traditional **concept of marketing**—a philosophy or a way of envisioning an organization as an integrated system where all aspects work to satisfy customer needs, at a profit, within society's long-term best interests. Integrated systems require access to information that cuts across all functional areas of the firm. Satisfying customer needs implies a necessity to acquire information before, during, and after the sale. While not-for-profit organizations may prefer terms such as "donations" to the term "profit," the issue remains one of comparing costs to the benefits of alternative actions. A charity should enhance the proportion of funds used to benefit others (its profit) as opposed to spending all the donations on administrative functions. And, as organizations consider the long-term best interests of a society, they tend to choose actions that benefit the economy, ecology, and people who are behaving in an ethical manner.

Throughout this book, the term "organization" will be used to represent a firm, business, association, or business enterprise that must rely on exchanges for its existence. Churches, hospitals, IBM, and lemonade stands are thus seen as "organizations" in this broader sense of the word.

Exhibit 1.1 illustrates that information technology within a CRM system is a continuous process. The firm recognizes its lack of knowledge and begins to learn about customer segments and their distinct needs before the first sale is made. From purchases databases, mailing lists, e-mail referrals, and other sources, organizations can acquire mountains of data about potential customers and thus begin to tailor promotional messages, product features, and options. With the first sale or transaction, a new customer is acquired and a relationship should begin.

If satisfied with the first transaction, the customer learns to trust the organization or to believe it will deliver on its promises. The organization learns a bit about the customer's needs, and a circular process begins as the firm collects and analyzes data about customer transactions and preferences that is converted into information for different functional areas. This is a simplified view of the process. Segmentation is the topic of Chapter 2, while Chapters 3 and 4 will provide additional details about the IT process within CRM approaches, and Chapter 5 will explore the concept of customer loyalty.

What is not evident in Exhibit 1.1, but clearly implied, is the danger of abuse with CRM systems. "Early returns from companies as diverse as Pizza Hut, Holiday Inn, Sears, American Airlines and MCI suggest that a good customer database can provide a substantial competitive edge. But good technology without good psychology is a loser's formula."[13] If an organization becomes too enamored with phone calls, e-mail drives, and direct mail promotional schemes, it may erode its image in search of CRM implementation success. Customers want to be sure that their **privacy** is intact and, at the same time, customers want organizations to call them by name and to remember their history with the firm.

EXHIBIT 1.1	THE CRM PROCESS AS A HUB OF APPLIED LEARNING

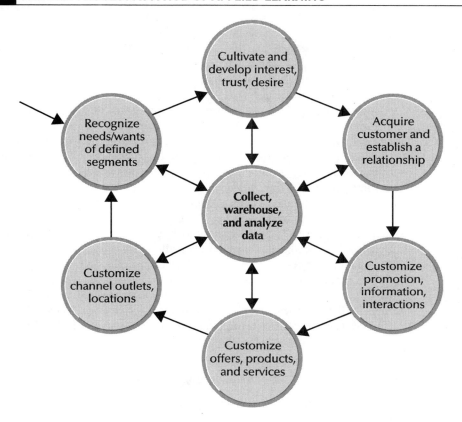

The basis for building effective CRM systems and strategies is to build profitable relationships in the long term that are mutually beneficial and that fulfill promises as customers experience the product or service offering.[14] However, many organizations experience difficulties in building information and e-commerce initiatives since implementing the new technology requires a complex array of skills to capture data from dynamic processes. Further, organizations must balance the need for security with the goal of increasing personalization.[15] People often find it difficult to change traditional approaches and to grasp the information needed to plan effective strategies.

In recent years, advances in information technology have led to vast improvements in CRM systems. As many organizations have discovered, it is a mistake to think about CRM systems *exclusively* in technological terms. A **customer focus** without accurate information is similar to attempting to circumnavigate the planet without a map. Investing in information technology without relevant questions or a plan for applications can lead to the development of very expensive toys that offer no return on investment. While the technological components of the business processes associated with CRM are a primary aspect of this book, we begin not with a discussion of technology, but with a discussion of the strategy of building and enhancing customer relationships.

POTENTIAL RETURNS OF CRM SYSTEMS

Proponents of CRM systems and the traditional concept of marketing view the customer as the pivotal point around which the business revolves. A fundamental principle of marketing is that customers are different. Some customers cost a great deal to attract and require a great deal of service while others require very little service and seem anxious to learn about your organization. A basic tenet is that different customers represent different levels of profit for the firm.[16]

Successful organizations attempt to define characteristics of the best customers, to then estimate the *lifetime value* of such customers, and to adjust marketing strategy accordingly. Best customers represent a proportion of all customers in an industry who provide profitable interactions, cost little to care for, and who tend to spread positive word-of-mouth information about the organization. Calculating value over time as a return on the firm's investment in acquiring the customer requires a comparison of revenue and costs—how much did we spend to achieve a given level of revenue?

As shown in Exhibit 1.2, there are potential benefits as well as costs associated with CRM systems for both organizations and customers. Organizations, or the CRM champions within the organization, tend to think of all the benefits of the system—the promise of increased revenues and lowered costs. Customers, in contrast, may first think of the costs associated with the system and have to be reminded of some of the benefits. For example, if the customer orders one product from a supplier on the Internet and there are suddenly 2,000 messages from firms that sell related goods, the customer may think twice before placing another order on the Web or with that organization. Thus, it can be helpful for organizations to consider the benefits and disadvantages of CRM systems as they invest in their development.

POTENTIAL BENEFITS OF CRM SYSTEMS TO THE ORGANIZATION

The satisfaction of consumers' needs and wants is the justification for an organization's existence. An effective CRM system is a way for the organization to develop a customer focus that has impact, that allows the organization to hear the customer's voice. A customer focus means that the organization is ready to view the purchasing process from the customer's

EXHIBIT 1.2 **POTENTIAL COSTS AND BENEFITS OF CRM SYSTEMS**

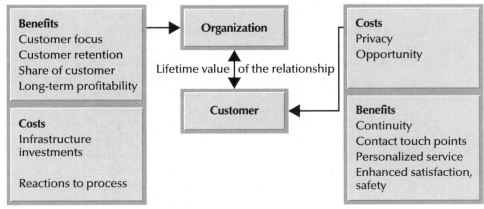

Benefits
Customer focus
Customer retention
Share of customer
Long-term profitability

Costs
Infrastructure investments

Reactions to process

Organization

Lifetime value of the relationship

Customer

Costs
Privacy
Opportunity

Benefits
Continuity
Contact touch points
Personalized service
Enhanced satisfaction, safety

point of view, to empathize with the customer's feelings, and to treat the customer's information with great care. If organizations can learn enough about individual customers, then the customer should be more satisfied, trusting, and willing to talk positively to others about the organization's wonderful approach—the systems should enable the organization to retain regular customers as it acquires new ones.

Retaining customers and establishing customer loyalty are major objectives of CRM approaches. The cost of acquiring a customer can be high. An old business adage says, "It costs six times as much to get a new customer as it does to keep an old customer." Although the figures vary by industry and increase with each passing year, the point is valid. There are no acquisition costs for existing customers who tend to buy the same items again and who seek other related products or services from trusted organizations. Higher customer retention rates will generally increase revenues and, in most cases, reduce costs. **Customer retention** simply means that the firm satisfies customers and/or offers variety such that the customer comes back and repeats transactions with the same organization.

"The first purchase is only a trial," is another relevant saying.[17] Suppose a telephone company has six million customers using a call-waiting feature that costs five dollars a month.[18] During the course of a year, a certain percentage of these customers cancel their service for some reason during the trial period. If the firm could, through personalized promotional messages, stop just 1 percent of those customers—or 60,000 accounts—from canceling, it would retain $3.6 million in annual revenue.

The development of CRM systems leads to a different kind of thinking about the nature of a business. Historically, marketers have thought in terms of a single product, and their goal has been achieving a high share of the market—more customers than their competitors have. In relationship management, the company objective often is to achieve a high share of customer.[19] The company tries to sell an individual customer as many goods and services as it can over the lifetime of that customer's patronage. In essence, **share of customer,** or **share of wallet,** means that the organization wants to please customers to the point that they want the organization to sell them something else. For example, Wal-Mart specializes in lower priced goods, and through its supercenters it increases its share of customers from its regular line of products to include groceries and automobile repairs. CRM systems attempt to make individual customers more profitable by recognizing the initial sale and recommending related items or services to enhance the customer's experience. Thus, *cross-selling* and *up-selling* can be fundamental outcomes of effective CRM systems.

Cross-selling is the marketing of complementary products to existing customers. A retail bank that has a checking account customer may market a safety deposit box or a car loan to its customer. Over time, it may be able to get the customer's home mortgage and equity loan business. One aspect of cross-selling is **bundling,** in which a combination of products is sold as a bundle at a price lower than the total of the individual prices. For example, Southwestern Bell Telephone's local telephone service offers The Works—Call Return, Call Blocker, Call Forwarding, Call Waiting, Caller ID, and several other offerings for one low monthly rate. **Up-selling** is the marketing of higher value products to new or existing customers. An insurance company may convince a customer to upgrade coverage, a credit card company may try to persuade a customer to upgrade to the platinum card, or a furniture store may attempt to convince a customer to purchase the more expensive version of a table or couch.

As organizations experience the benefits of a customer focus—retention of loyal customers and greater share of customer—the long-term profit picture should also improve.

Since it is less costly to retain a customer than to attract a new one, CRM systems that actually enhance loyalty reduce expenses. As sales of related products and services increase, revenues rise. The beauty of the customer focus is the emphasis it places on the way that organizations collect and use information as a fundamental tool in creating value for customers.[20] However, to calculate the return on investment in CRM systems, organizations must also consider costs.

POTENTIAL COSTS OF CRM SYSTEMS TO THE ORGANIZATION

The authors of this book will have a great deal to say about how an effective CRM system allows a company to adjust strategies for different customer segments. For now, we will simply say that a major benefit of an effective CRM approach is that it allows marketers to send the right messages about the right offers to its best customers at the right time. Achieving that level of quality from a CRM system may require a significant investment in the organization's **information technology (IT) infrastructure** (server-based systems, software licenses and updates, firewalls for security, personnel to install and maintain systems, training for system users in different disciplines, etc.) The IT infrastructure is the processing capacity required to fulfill customer needs.

The concept of building a technology infrastructure can apply to cities and towns as well as to firms. With significant Web-based processes, the system must be available 24 hours each day for 7 days of each week for 365 days of each and every year. If the organization is located in an area that experiences intermittent power outages, it may lose credibility, customers, and the possibility of future repeat sales unless it invests in battery support and failsafe back-up systems.

Another significant cost in developing an effective CRM system is the price of process change. **Process change** implies an alteration in the habitual pattern for accomplishing a task. Implementing new systems and changing traditional thought patterns may both be very difficult to accomplish. If the CRM approach is viewed, for example, as simply a way to provide financially based incentives, customer loyalty may not develop, and, in fact, the firm may damage its brand image as customer anger develops. As competitors match the financial incentives, the entire industry may experience higher operating costs for the same level of sales—a decline in profitability. "It takes a much deeper philosophy of relationship development based on added value delivery to sustain relationships at an affective level."[21] And relationships with an affective, or emotional, tie tend to be the most profitable over a lifetime of interactions.

Despite the best efforts of organizations to design effective CRM systems, it is people who must implement those systems and customers who must appreciate them, use them with ease, and feel safe in the process. Organizations must appreciate "the dance of change," the inevitable interplay between growth and limits/benefits and costs if positive outcomes are to accrue.[22] CRM systems hold the promise of growth and benefits but the implementation of such systems carries with it limits, costs, and other risks.

POTENTIAL BENEFITS OF CRM SYSTEMS FOR CUSTOMERS

Customers may also profit from CRM approaches and relationship marketing efforts. First, the **continuity** derived from a relationship with the same seller simplifies the buying process. Continuity implies a stable connection or linkage. A Honda advertisement says, "Life is full of complicated decisions. Simplify." This advertisement reflects an understanding that people want their buying decisions to be easier. Many buyers do not to want to evaluate too many factors when choosing among alternatives. If a firm can consistently meet a customer's needs over time, the continuity of the exchanges serves to simplify the process and reduce the risk of dealing with a new supplier.

Buyers become regular customers because they want to do business with organizations that will provide a consistent level of product or service quality. For example, most people are loyal to their hairdressers or barbers. They do not want to risk service quality that is below their expectations or risk disappointing the provider of this personal service. Being a regular can reduce customers' perceived risk. Many CRM systems enable customers to have a similar on-going dialog or conversation with larger organizations as well. Effective CRM systems provide a number of contact points, or touch points, where customers can communicate and explain their needs, thus enabling the organization to learn more about each customer's requirements. A **contact point** is a method of interaction such as the telephone, e-mail, point-of-purchase, customer service desk, or mail, to name a few.

Sales personnel at boutique clothing stores ask regular customers about their jobs, families, and lifestyles. They keep an eye out for clothes to suit their customers' tastes and put aside possible selections. In the past, sales personnel noted such information in notebooks. The jewelry store salesperson would often send a note to a male customer just before his wife's birthday. Unfortunately, if the salesperson left the company, so did the client information. CRM systems are designed to offer the salesperson's notebook to the entire firm.

In an age when personalization is rare, CRM information technology is bringing it back. **Personalization** implies that the organization knows the customer by name, knows the customer's normal purchasing routine, and can forecast the customer's need for variety as well. With the appropriate information technology, customers can increasingly benefit from personalized service. Relationship marketing has been called "*one-to-one marketing*" because it allows marketers to tailor offerings to individuals.[23] A major benefit that customers gain from CRM is increased customization of goods and personalization of services.

Neiman Marcus stores now track customers' buying habits, preferences, and special dates through their computerized cash registers. Sales associates can notify a client when new merchandise comes in or send a reminder about buying a gift for a personal event like an anniversary. For the customer, over time, the CRM system should increase the value of the relationship, increase satisfaction, reduce the risk associated with interactions, and thereby increase the safety and comfort of having needs met. Customers may benefit from feeling special and enjoy being recognized as an important entity to the organization. Such benefits do not arrive without the requisite costs associated with them.

POTENTIAL COSTS OF CRM SYSTEMS FOR CUSTOMERS

Perhaps the most obvious cost of the widespread adoption of CRM systems by organizations is the inevitable loss of privacy for customers. Privacy means confidentiality or a feeling that you can have some space to yourself where other people cannot intrude. Organizations want to know which people purchase which products in which colors on which days of the week with which credit card. Customers want to feel that no one knows that much about their personal choices. The ability of organizations to track related purchases is extensive and potentially tied to the customer's phone number, bank account, or credit card number.

Microsoft marketed a product, Passport, which was described as offering superior security for providing credit card information online. However, "Microsoft admitted that it had not properly protected the privacy and security of people who provided personal information through Passport as it settled a complaint with the Federal Trade Commission (FTC)."[24] Further, the company admitted that its technical support staff tied personal information and purchase histories to the user's sign-in history and retained that data for months at a time. Microsoft is not alone in its collection, use, and analysis of individual customer data, a topic for discussion throughout this text.

Another intangible cost to the customer of developing a sole-source relationship with an organization is the **opportunity cost** associated with ignoring other offers from competitive sources. If customers take the time to search, they may find a better price for the same features or find options that better meet the original need. Yet, once a habit is formed, most customers will refrain from exerting the effort to assess other options. And, as firms "reward" loyal customers by sending them prizes, extra frequent flyer miles, or discounts on other products, customers become less inclined to search for alternatives—a goal of CRM systems.

LIFETIME VALUE OF THE RELATIONSHIP

Whether the final customer is a business or a household, CRM systems are formed to facilitate exchanges and interactions over time. It may be helpful to recall at this early stage of the text that a customer can be an organization, another supplier, or a household, as shown in Exhibit 1.3. To improve profits, organizations have traditionally focused on reducing costs within the **supply chain**—the firms that coordinate processes to move supplies and products from conception or raw material stage to final consumption. Since the heart of effective supply chain processes is the development of communication networks,[25] CRM systems represent the logical next step in improving lifetime value for organizations and customers within the system.

Exhibit 1.3 shows a simple supply chain for vacuum cleaners. Both households and businesses need a system for removing dust and dirt. Delivering a vacuum cleaner requires many interactions between suppliers, manufacturers, distributors, sales representatives, agents, and final customers. While the easiest example and the most often used application for CRM systems may be customers, CRM approaches can be used to benefit each member within the supply chain.

The **lifetime value of the relationship** can be simply defined as the net benefit to each party in an exchange over the length of time that interactions occur. When a customer purchases a new car, the dealership should work to ensure that the customer experiences great service, friendly repairs on maintenance, and reasonable prices. The customer, hopefully, will then return to the same dealership when the time arrives to purchase another new car. When a large firm, such as DaimlerChrysler, purchases notebook computers for all of its dealerships, the selling organization should work to ensure that DaimlerChrysler is so pleased with the value of the product and service that repeat sales are assured.

A focus on lifetime value does not ignore the fact that costs accrue, but rather it emphasizes the need to view the long-term potential in the exchange. CRM systems have

EXHIBIT 1.3   CUSTOMERS OCCUR IN ALL PHASES OF THE SUPPLY CHAIN

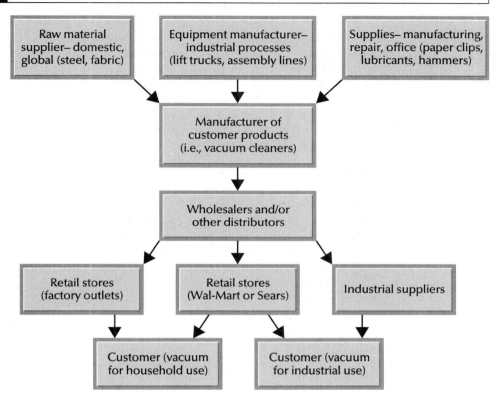

the potential to increase revenue for organizations, through cross-selling or up-selling, for example, as well as to reduce costs. CRM systems may offer customers better service at more reasonable prices as well. The basic idea is to have disparate organizations and people function with the same ultimate goal—to satisfy each other as they maximize the value of exchanges over a lifetime.

Throughout this book, we will explore methods for implementing effective CRM systems as well as the costs and benefits of such approaches. The first half of the text focuses on the information technology associated with CRM systems as well as the marketing information necessary to effectively plot strategies. The second half of the text then emphasizes effective usage and implementation of these concepts.

SUMMARY

Customer relationship management (CRM) is a business strategy that uses information technology to provide the enterprise with a comprehensive, reliable, and integrated view of its customer base so that all business processes and customer interactions help maintain and expand mutually beneficial relationships. CRM systems help organizations improve the profitability of their interactions with current and potential customers while at the same time making those interactions safer and friendlier through individualization and personalization. The system's goals are to enhance customer service, improve customer satisfaction, and ensure customer retention.

Information technology enables CRM. In recent years, advances in information technology have led to vast improvements in CRM systems. While CRM approaches rely heavily on information technology, it is a mistake to think about CRM *exclusively* in technological terms.

Customer retention and customer loyalty are major benefits of CRM systems to the organization. Working to retain existing customers by managing relationships with them will generally increase revenues and, in most cases, reduce costs. Positive outcomes can include a larger share of a customer's business as a result of activities such as cross-selling and up-selling. There are also real costs to the organization from implementing CRM systems, including investment in information technologies and the reactions of people to process changes.

Customers benefit from CRM systems and relationship marketing in a number of ways, including simpler buying processes, ongoing dialogs with the firm, and personalized attention. Costs to customers of CRM systems include a loss of privacy and, perhaps, missed opportunities to learn about or to purchase offerings from other organizations.

The lifetime value of a relationship focuses on the net gain to each party in an exchange over the period of time when interactions occur. A quick view of the supply chain serves as a reminder that customers can be members of a household or other organization (i.e., suppliers, retail stores, wholesalers). While CRM systems can be expensive to implement, the long-term benefits should become apparent as time progresses, repeat purchases occur, and customer loyalty deepens.

KEY TERMS

best customers	customer relationship	privacy
bundling	management	process change
concept of marketing	customer retention	relationship management
contact points (touch	information technology	(relationship marketing)
points)	infrastructure	share of customer
continuity	lifetime value of the	(share of wallet)
cross-selling	relationship	supply chain
customer focus	opportunity cost	up-selling
	personalization	

QUESTIONS FOR REVIEW AND CRITICAL THINKING

1. What is the definition and purpose of a CRM system?
2. What benefits does a CRM system offer to an organization? What are the potential costs of a CRM system for an organization?
3. What benefits does a CRM approach offer to a customer? What are the potential costs of a CRM system for customers?
4. Give an example of an experience that you have had with a company that uses a CRM system.

5. Provide an example of an organization with a CRM system that appears to increase comfort or satisfaction. Provide an example of an organization using a CRM system that may cause customer concerns over the loss of privacy.

NOTES

1. Excerpt reprinted with permission from Meridith Levinson, "Harrah's Knows What You Did Last Night," *Darwin Magazine,* May 2001, <http://www.darwinmag .com/read/050101/harrahs.html>.
2. Theodore Levitt, "Marketing Intangible Products and Product Intangibles," *Harvard Business Review* (May–June 1981): 94–102.
3. Christian Gronroos, "Relationship Marketing: The Strategy Continuum," *Journal of the Academy of Marketing Science* (fall 1995): 252.
4. Patricia M. Doney and Joseph P. Cannon, "An Examination of the Nature of Trust in Buyer-Seller Relationships," *Journal of Marketing* (April 1997): 35–51.
5. Mary J. Bitner, "Building Service Relationships: It's All about Promises," *Journal of Academy of Marketing Science* (fall 1995): 246.
6. See Regis McKenna, "Marketing Is Everything," *Harvard Business Review* (January–February 1991): 65–79.
7. Adrian J. Palmer, "Relationship Marketing: A Universal Paradigm or Management Fad?" *The Learning Organization* 3:3 (1996):18–25.
8. Tony Cram, *Customers that Count* (London: Financial Times-Prentice Hall, 2001): 12.
9. Herb Edelstein, "How CRM Differs from OLAP: What You Need to Understand When Implementing Mining Techniques for Analytic CRM," *Planet IT,* 13 June 2000, <http://www.planetit.com/techcenters/docs/database/opinion/PIT20000612S0001>.
10. Stewart Deck , "What Is CRM?" *Darwin Online,* 16 May 2001, <http://www.darwinmag.com/learn/curve/column.html?ArticleID=104>.11. Adapted from Louise Fickel, "Know Your Customers," CIO Magazine, 15 August 1999, <http://www.cio.com/archive/081599/customer.html>.
12. whatis.com, <http://whatis.techtarget.com/definition/0,289893,sid9_gci213567,00.html>.
13. James R. Rosenfield, "Manager's Journal: Avoid Dark Side of Database Marketing," *The Wall Street Journal* as reprinted in *Insights: Readings in Marketing* (New York: West Publishing Co., 1995): 45–47.
14. Christian Gronroos, "Relationship Approach to Marketing in Service Contexts: The Marketing and Organizational Behavior Interface," *Journal of Business Research* 20 (January 1990): 3–11.
15. Debabroto Chatterjee, Rajdeep Grewal, and V. Sambamurthy, "Shaping Up for E-Commerce: Institutional Enablers of the Organizational Assimilation of Web Technologies," *MIS Quarterly* 26:2 (June 2002): 65–89.
16. Peppers/Rogers Group, "CRM in a Down Economy" (white paper), 8 February 2001.
17. Attributed to Peter Drucker.
18. John Foley, "Market of One: Ready, Aim, Sell!" InformationWeek, 17 February 1997.
19. The term "share of wallet" is sometimes used.
20. Warren Karlenzig, "Tap into the Power of Knowledge Collaboration," *Customer Interaction Solutions* 20:11 (May 2002) 22–26.
21. Adrian J. Palmer, "Relationship Marketing: A Universal Paradigm or Management Fad?" *The Learning Organization* 3:3 (1996) 18–25.
22. Peter Senge, *The Dance of Change: A Fifth Discipline Resource* (New York: Doubleday, 1999).
23. Don Peppers and Martha Rogers, *The One to One Future: Building Relationships One Customer at a Time* (New York: Doubleday, 1993).
24. "Microsoft Admits to Privacy Errors with Passport," <www.crm-forum.com>, 9 August 2002.
25. Mehmet C. Kocakulah, Abbas Foroughi, and Mitchell Lannert, "Streamlining Supply Chain Management with E-Business," *The Review of Business Information Systems* 6:2 (spring 2002): 1–7.

CHAPTER 2

Understanding Customer Differences

In the world of direct marketing, getting prospects to open their mail is half the battle.[1] Surprisingly, the odds are quite good that consumers will open their mail if it's packaged in an appealing way and the timing is right. In fact, three out of four adults (77 percent) regularly read their direct mail, and 59 percent of adults have read theirs in the past week, according to a recent survey.

Even the 23 percent of adults who never read their direct mail may not necessarily be rejecting the letters out of disdain. "Half of those [people] just don't have the time," says the director of strategic marketing at Webcraft, a direct marketing service firm, which conducted a telephone survey of 2,000 adults. Understanding which consumers are most receptive to mailings is key to increasing the efficiency of such efforts. Start with the 9 percent of America that reads every piece of mail they receive. This group is composed primarily of women (59 percent) and people with household incomes under $30,000 (46 percent). Then there are the people who read only mail that is related to products that they've already been eyeing to buy (16 percent). For instance, the majority of readers of finance-related direct mail (61 percent) say that timing, personalization, and appearance are the top factors that influence their decision to tear open an envelope.

Because so many people want to transfer credit card balances at any one time, finance-related direct mail actually has one of the highest response rates of all direct marketing efforts. In fact, four out of ten multiple credit card users say they read their finance-related direct mail. These folks are also prime targets for other marketers using the medium: 82 percent of multiple credit card users say they read direct mail from all marketers at least some of the time.

Credit card companies hoping to increase their customer base should also look at which demographic groups are most likely to be receptive to specific types of offers. For instance, 39 percent of seniors (which the study defined as age 72 and older) and 38 percent of those between 56 and 71 say that "no annual fee" is the language that most appeals to them when selecting a credit card, compared with 32 percent of Gen Xers (ages 25 to 36) and 28 percent of Gen Yers (ages 18 to 24). On the other hand, 39 percent of Gen Xers, 37 percent of Baby Boomers, and 33 percent of Gen Yers care slightly more about getting a low annual percentage rate on purchases.

As for insurance companies that use direct mail as a medium, consumers with changing needs make the best prospects. Two-thirds of all adults surveyed—including 75 percent each of Gen Xers and of adults with incomes between $30,000 and $50,000—say they would find it helpful if insurance companies mailed them information about insurance following major life changes, such as marriage, the birth of a new child or grandchild, a home purchase, or retirement.

Then there are those who automatically toss direct mail into the trash. Mail chuckers are most likely to be men (56 percent) between the ages of 56 and 71 (21 percent) with household incomes below $30,000 (42 percent). Chuckers tend to want to be entertained, unlike direct mail readers who want less flash and more substance.[2]

VIEWS OF CUSTOMERS

A potential payoff to the organization for investing in an effective CRM system is in differentiating segments, such as the mail chuckers, from others so that strategic initiatives can be implemented with precision. Organizations with sophisticated CRM systems often have databases that record a customer's **RFM** (recency, frequency, and monetary) **scores.** Recency of purchase, frequency of purchase, and a customer's average purchase size (monetary) are important behaviors to track if organizations are to increase the efficiency of their operations. Buyers of many products and services vary in their consumption patterns. Some customers have had only a single experience with the organization, others are repeat customers, while still others are so firmly loyal they will accept no substitutes.

Concentrating on the heavy user market segment is an attractive strategy because a small percentage of all users of a product—the best customers—account for a large portion of an organization's sales. The **80/20 principle** is the name given to this phenomenon because typically, 20 percent of the customers buy 80 percent of the product sold. This 20 percent (which may really be 25 percent or some similar percentage) are "heavy users" or "major customers." Both the New York Mets and the New York Metropolitan Opera offer season tickets to heavy users of their services. Similarly, airlines, such as Delta and American, use product (service) usage and brand loyalty as the basis for their frequent flyer programs.

> When Southwest Airlines identified Rich Marcott as its top frequent flier out of Chicago a few years ago, the company did more than just give him elite status. It got to know him personally. First, Southwest gave him tickets to

Chicago sporting events. Then it arranged for him to throw out a pitch at a Cubs game. Finally, learning that he was a big fan of Southwest's former CEO Herb Kelleher, Southwest set up a meeting between the two while Kelleher was in Chicago.[3]

Organizations must be focused on the biggest spenders for many reasons. Since it's very difficult to gain new business right now, losing the biggest clients is simply not an option. But concentrating on the largest or heaviest user segment may not always be the best course of action. Some organizations mistakenly aim at such a segment just because it is so obviously attractive. These organizations have fallen hook, line, and sinker for the majority fallacy. The **majority fallacy** is the name given to the blind pursuit of the largest, most easily identified, or most accessible market segment. Why is it a fallacy? Simply because that segment is the one that everybody knows is the biggest or "best" segment. Therefore, it is the segment that probably attracts the most intense competition and may actually prove to be the least profitable. Clearly, the organization's strategic view of customers is a critical component of selecting appropriate segments to target with market offers.

When segmentation is applied with skill, the organization has a picture of the customer to use in developing products, communicating messages, selecting distribution options, and deciding on an appropriate price. CRM systems can aid the organization in obtaining the "pictures" of various segment options.

> The assumed classification stereotypes of the image-conscious Baby Boomer, the cynical Generation Xer, independent Generation Yer, and the diverse and influential Senior are now enhanced with greater emphasis on digital databases to further refine these groups and more narrowly target intended messages through generational bias in advertising and one-to-one marketing.[4]

As this concept illustrates, the most effective CRM systems may well be those that can blend traditional approaches in marketing with the capabilities provided through information technology—the goal of this text.

STRATEGIC OPTIONS FOR APPROACHING CUSTOMERS

While economics textbooks may give the impression that all consumers are alike, they are ignoring variances in the way different groups treat a product, such as direct mail solicitations. Economists draw few distinctions among different types of buyers as long as they have the financial ability to buy. Men and women, young and old, people who drink a bottle of wine a day, those who drink one glass of wine on New Year's Eve, and those who do not drink at all are lumped together from that perspective. Exhibit 2.1 uses the term **unsegmented, mass marketing** to describe this approach. An organization selling paper clips may engage in unsegmented, mass marketing because there is little diversity among customer needs or because it is more cost effective to target the aggregate market. The product is standardized, one model for the entire market, which may result in economies of scale in production, distribution, and/or promotion.

The danger with the unsegmented, mass marketing approach is that trying to appeal to everyone may result in the organization appealing to no one or missing key opportunities to attract an important segment of the market. Salt, for example, is a product that may seem logical for a mass marketing approach and indeed, Morton salt is available in every

EXHIBIT 2.1	STRATEGIES FOR DEALING WITH CUSTOMERS

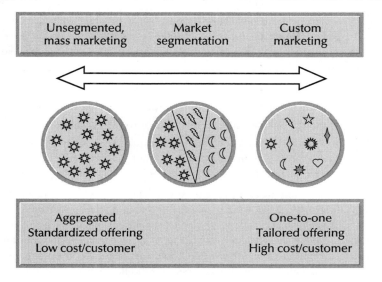

grocery store. Yet some customers prefer light salt or no-salt seasoning options such as Mrs. Dash, while other customers pay less for the generic version. Even with salt, a **market segmentation** approach is evident where organizations provide product options that meet the needs of a defined group. For example, most automobile manufacturers provide models for budget-conscious customers, families, and those who desire luxury options. Each car or truck is designed to meet the needs of a specific group. When organizations attempt to meet the needs of individuals, customization occurs.

Traditionally, most services, such as those provided by architects, tailors, doctors, or lawyers, require that each customer be treated in a unique way. With **custom** or **one-to-one marketing,** each individual customer receives personalized treatment, thus, each customer gets exactly what he or she wants. While the effectiveness of reaching the hearts of customers with this strategy is assumed to be high, marketing costs must be considered as well.

Managers of CRM systems typically collect data about items purchased, size of orders, payment method, purchase frequency, service requirements, and any of a number of other customer attributes. Information about how, when, where, and why customers contact the organization, make purchases, or complain fosters an understanding of each customer's interaction history. While interaction histories do not tell the entire story of future choice, the information is helpful in forecasting subsequent preferences. Then organizations can customize marketing efforts, manage the supply chain, create highly targeted offers, and personalize messages.

It has been observed that for many organizations, focusing too closely at the individual level can be a mistake. The crucial process, which not many enterprises have yet mastered, is to find the **right level of aggregation**—to categorize customers in groups that are neither too big nor too small. The promise of CRM technology is to define segments that are large enough to approach with a unique marketing mix. To understand this assertion we must continually attempt to understand market segmentation and the choices available to firms for differentiating customer preferences.

MARKET SEGMENTATION

Dividing a heterogeneous market into a number of smaller, more homogeneous subgroups is called **market segmentation** (or **customer segmentation**). While there is a great diversity in the number of ways a market can be divided, the basic logic behind a segmentation strategy is the same.

- Not all buyers are alike.
- Subgroups of people with similar behaviors or values may be identified.
- Subgroups will be smaller and more homogeneous than the market as a whole.
- A marketing effort targeted at the unique needs of smaller groups of similar customers should be more effective than a marketing effort to satisfy the diverse needs of a large group of heterogeneous customers.

Usually marketers are able to cluster similar customers into specific market segments with different, and sometimes unique, demands. As one example, consider Exhibit 2.2 and how the computer market can be divided into potential segments. First, domestic and foreign markets may vary in preferences for features, pricing, or delivery options as well as in the size of their business and home user segments. The home user segment can be further subdivided into sophisticated personal computer users, people who hate personal computers but have one so their children can use it for schoolwork, people who use computers only for e-mail, and so on. Each of these markets can be further segmented by preferences for a desktop or laptop and whether this is the first, second, or third computer purchased. The number of market segments within the total market depends largely on the strategist's ingenuity and creativity in identifying those segments.

Perhaps the most fundamental way of distinguishing markets is on the basis of the buyer's use of the good or service being purchased. When the buyer is an individual consumer

| EXHIBIT 2.2 | AN EXAMPLE OF POTENTIAL SEGMENTS WITHIN THE COMPUTER MARKET |

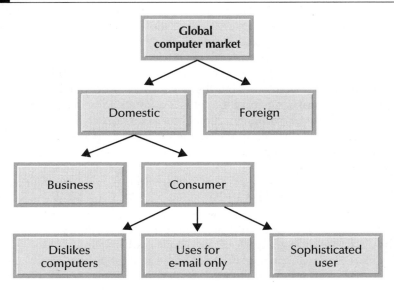

who will use the product to satisfy personal or household needs, the good or service is a consumer product sold in the **business-to-consumer market (B2C).** When the buyer is a firm or organization that will use a product to help operate its business, or when the product is a component part for the product the firm produces, or when a firm will buy and resell a product to another customer, the good or service is within the **business-to-business market (B2B).** Defining and choosing a **target market**—that is, the specific group toward which the firm aims its marketing plan—allows the organization to tailor a marketing mix to the specific needs or characteristics of that group.

IDENTIFYING CUSTOMER DIFFERENCES

The essence of a market segmentation strategy is to look at total markets and find meaningful differences across defined groups that affect the success of long-term relationships. The traditional bases for differentiating market segments are virtually unlimited. Although the possible segmenting variables are numerous, a far smaller number of variables are, in fact, the ones most commonly used, and these are shown in Exhibit 2.3.

Geographic Variables

Geographic market segmentation often begins with the broad distinction between domestic and foreign markets. International marketers recognize that people in different nations may have different tastes, needs, and behaviors. In Argentina, for example, most Coca-Cola is consumed with food, but in many Asian countries it is rarely served with meals.

Another basis for segmentation is political boundaries, such as state and city lines and the like. However, populations are not always adequately described by political boundaries. Marketers are most often concerned with the population map—where the people are—rather than with such matters as the imaginary line that separates Billings Heights, Montana, from Billings, Montana. Various expressions are used to reflect this fact: "Greater New York," "the Dallas-Fort Worth Metroplex," "the Bay Area," "the Twin Cities." These phrases and others like them indicate that for certain market segments there is no distinct political boundary line that differentiates purchasing patterns. The decision as to how to input geographic information into the CRM system varies by its intended use.

Direct marketers, especially those that sell through catalogs sent by mail, often use zip codes as a basis for market segmentation. The phrase "birds of a feather flock together" is quite appropriate here. People and households in the same zip code area are often demographically similar. Claritas's PRIZM system has analyzed each of the 36,000 zip codes in the United States and, based on demographic and lifestyle similarities, classified them into 40 market segments. Each has a colorful name, like Shotguns and Pickups (large rural families with modest means) or Gray Power (active retirees).

Geographic information systems (GIS) use software to tie demographic information to specific locations, such as street addresses, codes, and census tracts.[5] The resulting maps of a location can pinpoint the characteristics of customers and potential customers that are tied to product or service purchasing patterns. For example, a department store in Texas analyzed credit card receipts by code to determine that the majority of its customers travel along a particular freeway. This enabled the store to advertise on the billboards along that route. Software products such as ArcView can overlap demographic characteristics and geographic locations to create a clear picture of market segments.

EXHIBIT 2.3	TYPICAL WAYS TO SEGMENT MARKETS

Segmenting variables	Examples of typical options or levels	
Geographic variables	domestic/foreign/global, regions, zip codes, climate, population density, terrain	
Demographic variables	Gender	female, male
	Income	<$25,000; $25,000-$64,999; >$65,000
	Age	infant, child, preteen, teen, young adult, adult, elderly
	Education	high school, vocational school, college, grad school
	Marital status	married, single, divorced, widowed
	Family life cycle	single no children, married with children, empty nest
	Ethnicity	national identity, sub-cultural identity
Lifestyles/Psychographics	activities (golf, fishing), interests (shopping), opinions values (patriotism, religion)	
Behavioral patterns	RFM	recency, frequency, monetary value of purchases
	Channel	catalog, mail, television, Internet, store, specialty shop
	Benefits sought	lowest price, best technology, greatest value
	Service required	telephone support, in-person, e-mail
	Loyalty	none, some, emotionally bonded, committed
	Permission granted	ask to send e-mails, mail, or further phone calls
Analytically derived	Data mining	deal seekers, stockpilers, regularly priced, premium

Demographic Segmentation Variables

Demographic segmentation variables are those characteristics, such as gender, income, age, marital status, family life cycle, race, and ethnicity, that are easily understood, easily found (www.census.gov for starters), and often related to customer purchasing behavior. For these reasons, demographic characteristics are among the most commonly used segmentation variables.

Income is a factor that may influence willingness and ability to purchase. The annual income for the owner of a Porsche or Rolls-Royce automobile may be expected to differ from the annual income of the owner of a Saturn or Hyundai, but the incomes of subscribers to the local cable service may not serve to differentiate segments as well.

Variations in preferences for clothing, scents, or jewelry may occur simply because of **gender** differences. More men than women may be expected to buy the Gillette MACH3 razor, but more women than men may buy the Gillette Venus.

Infants and toddlers, young children, teenagers, adults, and senior citizens are typical **age-based** segments—a useful distinction when people of different ages have different purchasing behaviors. The heaviest consumption of soft drinks, for example, occurs among teenagers. Changing age distributions may affect a firm as well. At the beginning of this century, only one person in 25 was over 65. Today, one American in five is over 65. With the growth in the number of older consumers, more firms will be targeting this segment with products—such as appliances with large letters and big knobs—that reflect their needs.

Family life cycle defines segments whose purchasing patterns differ with marital status, age, and the presence/absence of children. Exhibit 2.4 shows a few typical stages of life that may affect purchasing behaviors and thus may be of interest to firms.

Lifestyles and Psychographics

Lifestyles and psychographics are often used to segment markets. A lifestyle is a pattern in an individual's pursuit of life goals—in how the person spends his or her time and money. An individual's activities, interests, opinions, and values represent the aspects of life that seem tied to purchasing behaviors. You probably know someone who has an "outdoor" lifestyle, for example, who owns canoes, tents, backpacks, and a Coleman stove. Quantitative measures of lifestyles are known as psychographics.

Similar to adding geographic information to demographic data, psychographic market segmentation provides a richer portrait of customer groups than simple demographic information can yield. Stanford Research Institute's VALS 2 system combines psychographic measures with resource (income) data to yield categories of customers described by such labels as Achievers, Believers, or Strugglers. Firms can subscribe to this information source and combine it within a GIS to paint a picture of trading areas within each city or town.

EXHIBIT 2.4	EXAMPLES OF STAGES OF THE FAMILY LIFE CYCLE

FLC Stage	Typical Items/Expenditures
Young single	Entertainment, housing, cars
Young married DINKS–Dual Income, No Kids	Furniture, nesting
Married with kids	
Children under 6	Child care, car seats, diapers
Children over 6	Schools, lessons, bicycles
Younger and older singles/divorced	
With children	Child care, health care
Without children	Travel, entertainment
Empty nest	Redefine life together, travel, cruises, college courses
Widow/Widower	Activities, meals-on-wheels
Nontraditional families	Non-related blends, roommates, same gender

Behavioral Patterns

Individual consumers exhibit different shopping **behavioral patterns** that may be worthy of attention. Some individuals purchase apparel only at specialty shops for premium prices, for example, while others will drive for miles on the rumor of a sale, and still others will search the Web for the very best price and delivery options. Such **consumption channel** preferences are a basic information need for a firm in order to meet the needs of varying markets. The **RFM** data can differentiate the need for complementary products. For example, someone who owns a Harley-Davidson motorcycle may be more likely to purchase a black leather jacket or a Harley-Davidson T-shirt than someone who does not own a motorcycle.

To define **benefit segments,** organizations must collect information about the features most desired by customers. In any given group of people (i.e., the other students in a class or co-workers on the job), some customers will always buy the lowest priced option while others want the highest prestige. In car buying, some segments focus on fuel efficiency while others want the benefit of a sporty look.

Dell Computer and Gateway represent two very different approaches to satisfying service requirements for segments. Gateway has a retail store presence that is particularly suited for novice consumers who need high levels of technical support, training, and assistance. Dell, in contrast, appears to target the more sophisticated computer owners who are delighted to have e-mail and telephone support. The costs of these behavioral patterns for service requirements are very different. The cost of conducting business with some customer segments may be so great that it will never be profitable. Different customers represent different levels of profit for the company.[6]

Most CRM strategists believe that the loyal customers are the most profitable and should be given special treatment. So it makes sense to investigate how customers may be segmented based on the **degree of loyalty** they have to an organization, brand, or store. Marketing managers using a CRM system think of loyalty in terms other than the tendency to repurchase the same brand from a current supplier. Inertia or indifference may be the reason for repeat purchase behavior.[7] True loyalty involves an emotional bonding, trust, and a commitment to maintain a relationship.[8] Customers range from those who show absolutely no loyalty to those who have a high repeat patronage and a mindset that reflects an emotional attachment to the brand or supplier. Customer loyalty is such an important concept that we devote Chapter 5 to the topic.

Many customers do not want to be called on the telephone or be sent unsolicited e-mail messages. Because organizations do not want to offend these customers, it is a common CRM strategy to ask customers for **permission** to send e-mail with product updates or other messages. Permission segments suggest that records indicate which customers have agreed to learn more about a company and its products and thus, is a relevant data input for CRM-based segmentation efforts. Customers can also be segmented based on their preferences for the method and frequency of contacts from different firms.

Analytically Derived Segments

Information technology can be used to analyze data and create segments that are unique to an enterprise's specific business needs. **Analytically derived** segments are said to be data-driven because they are created by the analysis of customer data. A comprehensive CRM system may identify a firm's most profitable customers and the behaviors and characteristics held in common by the group. **On-line analytical processing (OLAP),** data mining, and advanced statistical techniques are used to analyze data and to describe customer segments. We define and discuss these techniques in Chapter 9. A key to designing and using OLAP systems effectively is an awareness on the part of the marketing manager of the options for defining segments.

As an example, consider Boots, the largest pharmacy and retail chain in the United Kingdom. The firm used data from its almost 13 million "Advantage Card" members to describe customer segments within the health and beauty product category.[9] Deal seekers used coupons, stockpilers only shopped at the store to make bulk purchases when items were on sale, store loyals purchased a larger amount of the sale items than they regularly purchased and continued to patronize the store, and new market customers purchased a sale item and then continued to buy it at the regular price after the sale had ended.[10] Imagine the difference in the value of each of these groups to the organization. The intelligent goal may be to engage in activities that attract store loyals and new market customers rather than to attract deal seekers or stockpilers.

In fact, it is much less costly to retain a current customer than it is to attract a new one, and some estimate that the gap is growing wider. A classic study by a major management consulting firm investigated the real cost and long-term returns associated with customer acquisition and customer retention.[11] It found that acquisition costs were understated by most organizations and that the high cost of acquiring new customers caused many customer relationships to be unprofitable during their early years. Determining which customer segments and which individual customers are their best customers is crucial to the success of most firms.

Customer lifetime value can be defined, in a quantitative sense, as the net present value (NPV) of the future profits (margin contribution) to be received from a *given* number of newly acquired or existing customers during a specified period of years.[12] As shown in Exhibit 2.5, calculation of a customer segment's lifetime value requires information

---

EXHIBIT 2.5   ENVISIONING CALCULATIONS FOR A CUSTOMER'S LIFETIME VALUE

Per unit expectations

Price	$100
Cost of goods	20
Contribution margin	$ 80
Direct expenses	10
Allocated costs	20
Per unit net profit, expected	$ 50
Times the number of units purchased per time frame	× 6
Times the number of time frames expected	× 100
Unadjusted lifetime profit expectations	$30,000

	Time$_1$	Time$_2$	Time$_3$
Profit expectations	$10,000	$10,000	$10,000
Divided by the discount rate	1	1.08	1.17
Net present value of lifetime	$10,000 +	$9,259.26 +	$8,547.01 = $27,806.27

about four factors:[13] (1) *Profit margin,* the annual revenue that customers generate minus the costs a company incurs in serving them, (2) *Retention rate,* the percentage of total customers expected to repeat purchase, (3) *Discount rate,* the current cost of capital, and (4) *Time,* the expected duration of the relationship. You can review these concepts in a basic accounting or financial management text, but remember that your goal is not to specify a number for lifetime value, but, rather, to estimate relative values for different segments over time.

The basic equation for net profit is to subtract costs from sales revenues. Calculating the lifetime value of a customer or segment of the market begins by estimating the sales revenues as reduced by the total costs of acquiring and maintaining a relationship over a customer's lifetime. (In CRM terms, "lifetime" means the number of years the company retains a customer's business and not the number of years the customer lives.)

A simple formula to calculate the *lifetime revenue of a customer* is to multiply the average value of a customer transaction by the number of transactions per year times the number of years the company expects to retain the customer. Thus, if a subscriber to a satellite television service pays \$30 per month for 12 months in a year and is expected to remain a customer for 5 years, the calculated lifetime revenue is: \$30 $\times$ 12 $\times$ 5 or \$1,800. (If there are 20,000 potential customers who live down one rural road, the calculated lifetime revenue for the entire segment can be estimated).

Many estimates of customer value take **intangible benefits,** such as customer referrals, suggestions for product improvements, or ideas for new products, into account. Intangible benefits are positive contributions that do not lend themselves to quantification. As such, firms view some customers as more valuable assets than their calculated lifetime revenue alone would suggest.

The *lifetime cost of a relationship with a customer* includes the direct costs of providing the product or service as well as the indirect costs, or overhead, that may be allocated. The marketing manager would argue that the lifetime costs estimated for a customer should only include the direct costs associated with the relationship. The financial manager might argue that the lifetime costs should include both the direct costs and a proportion of the overhead or fixed costs.

Because money has a time value, future profits must be adjusted by dividing by a discount rate. This discounting is necessary because money to be received in the future is not as valuable as money in hand right now. The formula for the discount rate is $D = (1 + i)^n$, where i equals the market rate of interest and n equals the number of years that you must wait to receive payment.[14] As an example, suppose that the market rate of interest to borrow money is 8 percent. The discount rate in the third year is $D = (1 + 0.08)^2 = 1.664$. Dividing the gross profits in each year by the discount rate produces the net present value (NPV) of expected profits. When each year's profits have been adjusted, they are summed to get the cumulative total.

The example above is quite simplistic. For example, a proportion of customers will not renew and new ones may be obtained; thus, the profit expectation should change over time. In addition to retention, the market rate of interest will change as will the types and levels of costs. The benefit of the concept to the decision maker is in the ability to consider varying lifetime values for different segments.

PERSONALIZE B2C MESSAGES AT THE RIGHT LEVEL OF AGGREGATION

At the beginning of this chapter, you learned that it is important to find the right level of aggregation—to categorize customers in segments that are neither too big nor too small. Consider the marketer of computers from the beginning of this chapter who selects computer-haters and those who use computers only for e-mails as two viable segments. The marketer's organization sends different messages to each of these groups, and the CRM system simplifies the process of personalizing the greeting portion of e-mails, letters, or catalogs. With the right information in a data set, a personalized salutation, such as Dear Mr. Corley, may be used to suggest the purchase of a phone that would have e-mail capabilities; while a different salutation, such as Dear Mr. Watson, may match the needs of the individual who hates computers but needs to provide one for his child. Some of the content for the two segments may be the same (i.e., company information) while other parts of the content must be tailored (financial payment offers to those with lower incomes or discount coupons for repeat purchases). Another difference may be the timing of the e-mails because of production differences or some other factor. In this simple example, market segmentation has been combined with personal information so that the marketer goes one-on-one with each customer. Thus, the messages are tailored to groups of adequate size, but customers perceive that the offer fits their individual needs. Although it is a literal contradiction, this CRM approach uses **mass-personalization,** or the ability to tailor a message to large numbers of people.

USING CRM SYSTEMS IN B2B MARKETING

To a great extent, business markets may be segmented by use of variables similar to the ones just discussed. The difference, of course, is that instead of using characteristics and behavior of the individual consumer, CRM approaches use characteristics and behaviors of people within organizations. For example, marketers of electrical resistors decided to investigate their market on the basis of benefit segmentation. A study of the benefits sought from electrical resistors uncovered two major benefit segments. Military engineers purchasing for the government were concerned with failure rate and promptness in review of specifications, but engineers purchasing for consumer electronic companies wanted the lowest price.

If we think of business customers as key assets, it seems logical to ask what the business customer is worth today and in the future. Due to the smaller numbers, typically, of business customers in comparison to consumers, selling firms can be much more accurate in calculating the expected lifetime value of a relationship. As shown in Exhibit 2.6, the results of cross-classifying the past and future value of customers creates a simple matrix.[15] Obviously, firms should not target or spend money on **undesirable customers** because these segments have a poor purchase history and low expectations of any purchases in the

| **EXHIBIT 2.6** | **CUSTOMER TYPES BY EXPECTED VALUE** |

		Expected Future Value to the Firm	
		High	Low
Historical Value to the Firm	High	Premium	Uneconomical
	Low	Prospect	Undesirable

future. In contrast, **premium customers** exhibit a good purchase history and a high probability of continued loyalty to the firm. **Prospect customers** may have little or no past purchase history with the firm but exhibit a high potential for value in the future and should be cultivated even if the firm loses money in the short run. Potentially **uneconomical customers** express a low likelihood of purchasing from the firm in the future making them a judgment call as to the level of funds to be spent in their pursuit.

Within B2B exchanges, the momentum is focused on understanding the needs of proactive buyers who are seeking joint efforts with different parties in the supply chain.[16] While there are many benefits to be gained from using information technology to track needs and facilitate exchanges, the BSB market is characterized by smaller numbers and more personalized interactions.

Value-added partnerships, VAPs, are not necessarily dependent upon technology. VAPs comprise a set of independent companies that work closely together to manage the flow of goods and services along the entire supply chain from raw material to final consumer. While they may emerge as the result of computerized links between companies, they depend largely on the attitudes and practices of the participating managers.[17]

Business markets may be segmented on the basis of geography, organizational characteristics, purchase behavior and usage patterns, among other variables. The process is complicated by the fact that organizations assess both the elements of the marketing mix as well as the relationships between people that occur as one organization interacts with people from another firm.[18]

While the focus of this text is on individual customers or households, most of the principles can also be applied in the B2B context, with some modifications. Thus, B2B examples are embedded throughout the text.

SUMMARY

A fundamental principle of CRM is that all customers are not the same. Marketing strategy becomes effective and efficient when managers realize that CRM is based on the idea of treating different customers differently.

There are three strategies for dealing with customers: unsegmented, mass marketing, market segmentation, and custom marketing. Unsegmented, mass marketing treats all customers the same. With custom marketing, each individual customer receives personalized treatment. Effectiveness of marketing one-on-one is high, but so are marketing costs. The crucial process, which not many enterprises have yet mastered, is to find the right level of aggregation—to categorize customers in groups that are neither too big nor too small. Market segmentation (or customer segmentation) consists of dividing a heterogeneous market into a number of smaller, more homogeneous subgroups.

The most fundamental way of distinguishing among markets is on the basis of the buyer's use of the good or service being purchased. When the buyer is an individual consumer who will use the product to satisfy personal or household needs, the good or service is a consumer product sold in the consumer market. When the buyer is an organization that will use a product to help its business operation, the good or service is an organizational or business product sold in the business-to-business market.

Almost any variable may be used as a segmenting variable. Some typical ways to segment consumer markets are by geographical variables, demographic variables, gender, income, age, education, marital status, family life cycle, ethnicity, lifestyle and psychographic variables, behavior patterns and expectations, ownership, recency of purchase, purchase frequency, consumption habits, benefits sought, customer service requirements, customer loyalty, permission granted, and lifetime customer value. CRM sometimes analytically derives segments.

CRM systems stress profitability as well as a relationship orientation. All customers are not of equal value to a company. An effective CRM strategy determines the lifetime value of each of its customers. It assigns its customers into segments with labels that may be as elementary as high lifetime value, medium lifetime value, and low lifetime value. Sometimes companies add intangible benefits, such as customer referrals, into their calculations of customer value.

KEY TERMS

80/20 principle
analytically derived
   segments
behavioral patterns
benefit segments
business-to-consumer
   market (B2C)
business-to-business
   market (B2B)
custom marketing
customer lifetime value
degree of loyalty
demographic segmentation
   variables

geographic information
   systems (GIS)
geographic segmentation
   variables
intangible benefits
lifestyles
majority fallacy
market segmentation (or
   customer segmentation)
mass-personalization
one-to-one marketing
on-line analytical
   processing (OLAP)
permission segments

premium customers
prospect customers
psychographics
RFM Score
right level of aggregation
target market
undesirable customers
uneconomical customers
unsegmented,
   mass marketing
value-added
   partnerships (VAPs)

QUESTIONS FOR REVIEW AND CRITICAL THINKING

1. What are the advantages and disadvantages of each of the following?
   a. unsegmented mass marketing
   b. custom or one-on-one marketing
   c. market segmentation
2. Describe two different ways that each of the following companies might segment the market.
   a. a gambling casino
   b. an automobile rental company
   c. a bank
   d. an airline
3. Define lifetime customer value. How would you calculate it?
4. What is an analytically derived segment?
5. What variable do you think is best for segmenting a market?
6. What variables might a business-to-business marketer use to segment a market?
7. What type of intangible benefits might add to a customer's value?

8. Pick a business in your town, city, or urban area and describe the segment of customers that seem to provide the majority of business for the firm or organization. Based on your assumptions of the amount spent by the number of customers in that segment, what would be the lifetime customer value?

9. Describe two or three different types of benefit segments that would differentiate preferences for golf courses.

NOTES

1. Adapted with permission from "Mail Openers; Converting Direct Mail Prospects into Customers,"American Demographics, (1 October 2001): 20.

2. "Making Customer Relationship Management Work," 3 July 2001, available from Knowledge@Wharton.

3. Mark McMaster, "Build Loyalty with Targeted Perks," *Sales & Marketing Management* 154:8 (August 2002): 16.

4. Michael K. Rich, "Are We Losing Trust through Technology?" *Journal of Business and Industrial Marketing* 17: 2/3 (2002): 215–222.

5. Christian Harder, *ArcView GIS Means Business* (Redlands, California: Environmental Systems Research Institute, Inc., 1997).

6. Peppers/Rogers Group, "CRM in a Down Economy" (white paper), 8 February 2001: 3.

7. Jill Griffin, "Learn the Loyalty Levels to Build Customer Base," *Austin Business Journal,* print edition (1 December 2000): available at <http://austin.bizjournals.com/austin/stories/2000 /12/04/smallb3.html> and Alan S. Dick and Kunal Basu, "Customer Loyalty: Toward an Integrated Conceptual Framework," *Journal of the Academy of Marketing Science* (spring 1994): 99–113.

8. Tony Cram, *Customers that Count* (London: Financial Times-Prentice Hall, 2001): 18.

9. http://www.bized.ac.uk/compfact/boots/boots2.htm, (downloaded April 16, 2002)

10. Jill Dyche, *The CRM Handbook* (Boston: Addison-Wesley, 2002): 23.

11. Frederick F. Reichheld, "E-Loyalty," *Harvard Business Review* (July–August 2000) 106; and Michael R. Czinkota and Masaaki Kotabe, *Marketing Management* (Cincinnati: South-Western College Publishing, 2001): 453.

12. Arthur Hughes, "How Lifetime Value Is Used to Evaluate Customer Relationship Management," *DBMarketing.com,* <http://www.dbmarketing.com/articles/Art194.htm>.

13. Lauren Keller Johnson. "The Real Value of Customer Loyalty: Customer-Lifetime Value Is More Than a Metric; It's a Way of Thinking and of Doing Business," *MIT Sloan Management Review* 43:2 (winter 2002): 14.

14. More advanced calculations include a risk factor. A risk factor of 1 equates to no risk.

15. Henrick Ekstam, Daniel Karrlson, and Terttu Orci, *Customer Relationship Management: A Maturity Model,* <http://www.crm-forum.com/library/aca/aca-017/aca-017.pdf>.16. Bill Donaldson, "Industrial Marketing Relationships and Open-to-Tender Contracts," *Journal of Marketing Practice: Applied Marketing Science* 2:2 (1996): 23–34.

17. Russell Johnston and Raul R. Lawrence, "Beyond Vertical Integration—The Rise of the Value Adding Partnership," *Harvard Business Review* (July–August 1988): 94–100.

18. Kenneth H. Wathne, Harald Biong, and Jan B. Heide, "Choice of Supplier in Embedded Markets: Relationship and Marketing Program Effects," *Journal of Marketing* 65:2 (April 2001): 54–66.

CHAPTER 3

Information Technology and Collecting Customer Data

The Tyrolit Group is Europe's largest manufacturer of grinding, cutting, sawing, and drilling tools. Founded in 1917 as the in-house tooling supplier for the prestigious Swarovski Crystal Works, Tyrolit now generates $416 million in annual revenue from more than 70,000 unique products manufactured in 19 plants for customers in 60 different countries. The current structure uses a trade division to market all of the products manufactured in the five other divisions: metal fabrication, precision machining, natural stone, glass, and construction.

In order to integrate its products and processes, Tyrolit needed to address supply chain management and e-commerce presence, a diverse array of application specific expertise, the machines of end-users, and after sales service issues. The original equipment manufacturers (OEMs), the firm's customers, began to streamline supply chains to reduce the number of suppliers, products, and contact points, which forced Tyrolit to adopt a system for CRM.

The potential benefits to Tyrolit from its implementation of a SAP CRM system included all of the following: an 80 percent reduction in customer account personnel, reduced costs associated with data entry errors and wrong shipments, improved cash flow from matching delivery cycle times to customer needs, increased customer satisfaction from an integrated set of brands and products that provided a complete solution, increased revenue from cross-selling and up-selling opportunities, and reduced paper product catalog and shipping costs.

The costs of implementing the SAP CRM system included software, hardware, external consulting, and internal IT staff. The projected internal rate of return on the investment of over 1 million Euro into CRM by Tyrolit is expected to provide a return on investment (ROI) of at least 83 percent.[1]

One CRM application that is receiving increased interest is price optimization, a method in which the organization tailors prices to each customer with the objective of optimizing overall revenue. Innovations in information technology (IT) and data warehousing make this possible.

To collect relevant customer data, information technology must appreciate the needs of customer contact personnel. For example, the system previously used by DHL Worldwide Express to provide approval to its 500 U.S. salespeople to quote prices for high-volume shipments took ten days. Now, using Metreo's Supplier Response and Supplier Insight software to analyze data in its customer master file, data warehouse, and billing system, the salespeople's quotes can be approved "on the spot."[2] The software combines business rules with historical data to enable the salespersons to answer such questions as these:

- At what price level am I winning and losing business?
- What quotes did the customer previously accept or reject?
- Which competitors has the customer used?
- What is the cost of providing the shipment, based on such factors as shipment density?

Innovations in information technology (IT) and data warehousing make it possible for firms to succeed in using such tactics as tailoring price to each customer with the objective of optimizing overall revenue. The heart of the CRM system is the data warehouse, and the data warehouse would be impossible without fast, relatively low-cost computer storage. Use of a data warehouse is essentially a three-step process: (1) data input, (2) data storage, and (3) data analysis and information delivery. In this chapter, we first provide an overview of how IT is used in CRM and conclude with a discussion of data input. We devote Chapter 4 to data storage and Chapter 9 to issues of data analysis and delivery.

INFORMATION TECHNOLOGY AND CRM

Marketers have always recognized the importance of customer information. In even the earliest computer systems, data entry operators keyed in data that identified the details of each sales transaction—which customers bought how many of which products. The availability of this detailed data enabled the preparation of such sales analysis reports as sales by customer, sales by product, and sales by salesperson. When computers entered the picture, the same detailed recording was continued, using magnetic tape and disks. Organizations have thus long recognized the importance of gathering detailed data for the purpose of producing information that enables them to develop marketing strategies.

Today, marketing managers make use of information technology that goes beyond that of files of recent sales transaction data. Both hardware and software technology enable the retention of massive files of in-depth data for long periods of time in a data warehouse. A **data warehouse** is a large reservoir of detailed and summary data that describes the firm and its activities, organized by the various business units in a way to facilitate easy retrieval of information that describes the firm's activities.[3]

CRM ARCHITECTURE

The data warehouse is the central element in the CRM system, which is pictured in Exhibit 3.1. Data sources, both inside and outside the firm, provide data that describes relationships with customers. A data gathering system converts this incoming data to an electronic medium if it is not already in that format. The data warehouse system prepares the data for storage, stores the data, describes the data so that it might later be retrieved, and performs a management and control function. An information delivery system makes the contents of the data warehouse available to the information users in the form of electronic or printed information reports and displays.

The CRM architecture facilitates gathering data, storing it, transforming it into information, and presenting the information to users. The system therefore transforms data into information. *Data* consists of facts and figures that are difficult to use because of their volume. *Information* consists of meaningful compilations and summaries of data that tell the user something that he or she did not already know.

Data Sources

The two main categories of data sources are internal and external. Internal sources exist within the firm in the form of the various business units. For example, the manufacturing unit can provide data concerning product quality, and the finance unit can provide data concerning customers' payment habits. The sales representatives can offer insight into customer responses to features and pricing as well as to competitive options. External data sources consist of organizations and individuals outside the firm. These external sources consist of customers, suppliers, the government, and even competitors. As competitors advertise sales, special features, or discounts, organizations can track these issues over time.

Data Acquisition

The data that is gathered from internal sources is most likely already in a computer-readable format and is entered into the data warehouse as activities in the business units are performed. Much of the data gathered from external sources is converted to a computer format as transactions are performed, however, much data must also be keyed into the firm's computer system by data entry operators. Customers and other external sources can also provide data in a computer format by interfacing with the firm's Web site.

EXHIBIT 3.1   **A BASIC CRM MODEL**

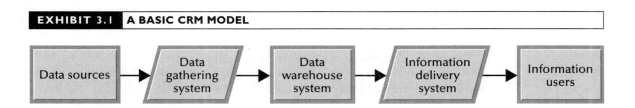

Data Storage

The data warehouse system consists of the stored data, software that maintains the data in an up-to-date condition, and software that manages and controls the warehouse.

Business data has traditionally been stored in the form of records and files. The record includes all of the data relating to a particular subject, and the file consists of all of the records. For example, a customer file contains a record for each transaction with a customer.

As managers sought to use the stored data in problem solving and decision making, difficulties in integrating the contents of several files triggered innovations in how the data was stored. Technicians found that files could be designed as tables, and the contents of the tables could be integrated with logical linkages. The term database was coined to reflect this view of data as a usable resource. A **database** is an accumulation of computer-based data that is arranged in a format to facilitate retrieval. A database is a corporate resource, and a firm can have more than one. For example, the marketing department can have its own customer and salesperson databases.

An extension of the database concept is the data warehouse. The task of the database is to provide detailed data on those entities that are important to the firm's meeting its objectives—entities such as products, customers, employees, and money—and not to provide a detailed audit trail of everything the firm has done. That audit trail is the focus of the data warehouse.

The data warehouse supports the entire firm, but subsets can exist in the form of data marts. A **data mart** is a subset of the data warehouse that contains data relating to a portion of the firm's transactions. As an example, there can be a marketing data mart, a human resources data mart, and so on.

Data Management

The first firms that sought to create databases of their activities encountered two road-blocks. First was the tremendous workload of entering the vast quantities of data. The second was keeping the data current—adding, deleting, and changing records as needed. Little relief was provided for the data entry, but hardware and software vendors developed special database software to manage the data once it was in storage. The software that maintains the data and makes it available for use is called a **database management system (DBMS).** Currently popular DBMS examples are DB2, Sybase, and Oracle for larger computers and Microsoft Access for smaller ones. Some data warehouses are managed by a DBMS and some are managed by specially developed warehouse management systems.

Exhibit 3.2 shows the main elements of a DBMS. A data description language processor enables you to describe the data to be stored. This description is called the schema. Once the data is in the database, the database manager portion of the DBMS is software that performs all of the functions in managing it—responding to user queries for information, retrieving the needed data, and providing the information in displayed or printed outputs.

Most of the organization's information systems make use of the database. Therefore, it is important that system developers understand the schema, which is documented in the form of a data dictionary. Exhibit 3.3 is an entry from a *data dictionary,*

EXHIBIT 3.2 A DATABASE MANAGEMENT SYSTEM MODEL

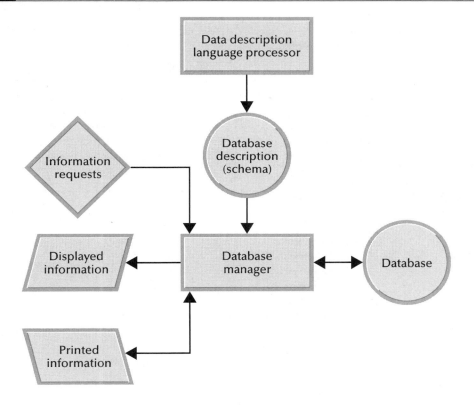

a detailed description of each data element in the database. This example is of the customer identification number.

Management and Control

Since the database or data warehouse represents a valuable resource, steps should be taken to ensure that it is not misused and that it is always available for use by authorized users. Data security can be achieved by use of passwords and supplemented with directories that specify the operations that particular users can perform. Knowing that hardware, software, and human failure can inadvertently damage or destroy the database, the management and control component can create backup files and perform recovery operations. These abilities are usually a part of the DBMS for large-scale systems.

Information Delivery

CRM users typically obtain information by querying the data warehouse. The query responses are displayed on the users' workstations. The users make one query after another, refining the queries each time until they are satisfied with the responses.

EXHIBIT 3.3   **A DATA DICTIONARY ENTRY**

C:Documents and Settings\CRMDW.mdb   Thursday, May 15, 2002
Table: tblCustomer   Page 1

PROPERTIES

Date Created:	5/15/02 10:10:10 AM	GUID:	Long binary data
Last Updated:	5/15/02 2:25:30 PM	NameMap:	Long binary data
OrderByOn:	False	Orientation:	0
RecordCount:	0	Updatable:	True

Columns

Name	Type	Size
Customer ID	Text	8

AllowZeroLength:	False
Attributes:	Variable Length
Collating Order:	General
ColumnHidden:	False
ColumnOrder:	Default
ColumnWidth:	Default
Data Updatable:	False
Description:	Unique identification number for each customer
DisplayControl:	Text Box
GUID:	Long binary data
Ordinal Position:	1
Required:	True
Source Field:	Customer ID
Source Table:	tblCustomer
UnicodeCompression:	True

GROUP PERMISSIONS

Admins   Delete, Read Permissions, Set Permissions, Change Owner, Read Definition, Write Definition, Read Data, Insert Data, Update Data, Delete Data

Users   Delete, Read Permissions, Set Permissions, Change Owner, Read Definition, Write Definition, Read Data, Insert Data, Update Data, Delete Data

Information Users

Interest in customer relationship management spans the entire organization, and CRM system users can be found at all organizational levels, from the president to sales clerks. Executives can use the system in formulating corporate strategies involving the organization's customers. Sales clerks can use the system in working with their customers. The Neiman Marcus CRM system, for example, provides sales clerks with profiles of their customers. The profiles help the clerks tailor products and services to the customers' needs.

The CRM user interface is designed to facilitate navigation through the data and to enable the users to make queries easily. Web interfaces enable users to communicate with the CRM system by means of the Internet.

COMPUTER ARCHITECTURES

The concepts of the data warehouse and CRM have emerged during the time when the most popular form of computer architecture is called client/server. In **client/server,** the stored data and the functions that are performed on the data are allocated to the central server and to the user, called the client. The layers of technology are called tiers, with the clients being on the lower tier and one or more servers being on the upper tiers. The first diagram in Exhibit 3.4 illustrates a two-tiered arrangement consisting of the warehouse server and clients, and the second shows a four-tiered architecture. Separate servers can be used to interface with the clients, to perform the clients' applications, and to monitor the warehouse.

There is not just a single pattern for distributing the network data and functions among the clients and the servers. The distribution can vary from one organization to another. Essentially, there are three commodities that are distributed: (1) control over the user interface (how the information is displayed on the user's screen), (2) the location of the software that performs the user's functions, and (3) the location of the data. When all, or most, of these commodities reside at the client level, the architecture is called a *fat client.* When all, or most, reside in the server, it is called a *thin client.* Although all of the user interface control and functions can be downloaded to the client, all of the data is never downloaded. Some data is always maintained in the server.

Data Input

If the CRM system is to meet the users' needs, all of the data that will be used in delivering the information must be stored in the data warehouse. The problem is that users often cannot

EXHIBIT 3.4 **CLIENT/SERVER ARCHITECTURES**

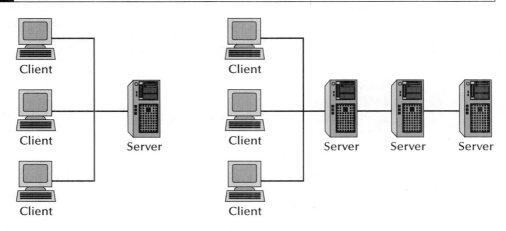

A. Two-tiered architecture   B. Multi-tiered architecture

anticipate their needs when the system is being developed. In this setting, the strategy for warehouse design is to gather every piece of data that describes the firm's operations that affect the customer both directly and indirectly, and supplement it with additional data as needed to meet new, unanticipated user needs. Most of the data will come from the systems that interact with customers.

Contact Points

A customer **contact point,** or **touch point,** is any transaction or customer interaction with the organization. A purchase transaction is a contact point. A telephone call to get in touch with a technical support person is a contact point. Filling out and returning a warranty card, sending an e-mail, or standing at the customer desk are all contact points.

Planning the outcome of each customer contact is essential to CRM. Organizations should constantly ask themselves how they can collect information that will help them to better know the customer.

One desirable outcome of a customer contact is the input of additional data. A contact provides the opportunity to learn more about the customer's behavior, background, and needs. A clerk at a cash register can ask for a phone number. A technical support person can ask about the type of operating system the customer is using. A warranty card can ask for demographic information.

CRM developers must determine how much information the customer is willing to provide at each contact point. When is asking for information inappropriate? When is the speed of customer service more important than data?

In any case, because new data can be entered during each contact point, this activity is an ongoing process and must be managed.

Point of Sale Input

The best way to collect customer contact data is by using point of sale (POS) terminals or electronic data interchange (EDI). POS terminals can scan product data from the bar codes and customer data from credit cards and identification cards. This is the approach taken by the Randall's food store chain in Texas that issues its customers an encoded identification card that entitles them to discounts. The identification card associates the customer's address, phone number, and e-mail address with the purchases made in the store. Consider one example of the benefit of such information. The manufacturer of Little Cesar's dog food purchased a mailing list of all customers who buy dog food in small cans (Pedigree, Mighty Dog) and mailed each one a free sample of Little Cesar's. The organization could then track, specifically, the customers who switched to its product, and complete a cost/benefit analysis of the free sample promotion.

Organizations engaged in business-to-business activity can transmit customer sales order data using electronic data interchange (EDI). The buying firm transmits purchase order data from its computer system to that of the selling firm.

Keyed and Scanned Data Input

When POS terminals and EDI cannot be used, the data most likely will have to be keyed into workstations by data entry operators. Some systems are designed so that data can be optically scanned from such source documents as credit card invoices and airline tickets.

Internet Input

As Web-based systems become more prevalent and sophisticated, more and more customer data can be gathered using the Internet. When customers make purchases, they can be asked to provide all of the data that the firm wants to enter into the data warehouse.

Data Storage

Computer storage that is built into the processor is called **main memory**. Storage in other units is called **secondary storage**. Secondary storage can employ various technologies such as magnetic disk and integrated chip. The term **direct access storage (DAS)** is used to describe these devices since the access mechanism can go directly to a location without having to search for it—a requirement for fast access.

Such enterprise-wide applications as CRM are putting severe demands on firms' storage. It has been estimated that worldwide storage capacity will swell from 283,000 terabytes (a trillion bytes or characters) in 2000 to more than 5 million terabytes in 2005.[4] As a result, organizations are rethinking how they allocate their storage resources. Rather than assigning DAS units to specific servers, organizations are creating storage networks. A *storage area network (SAN)* allows business units throughout the organization to store data on different servers. Another storage strategy that is currently evolving is the use of *storage resource management (SRM)* software to overlook the firm's storage network and allocate the storage in the most efficient way—locating unused storage and allocating it where it can best be used. Soon after implementing SRM software, Computer Associates was able to identify three terabytes of unused storage among the 50-odd terabytes on the network.[5]

As CRM applications increase in popularity, organizations will devise storage strategies to ensure that sufficient storage is available for this and other mission-critical enterprise applications.

DATABASE STRUCTURES

The main objective in database design is to arrange the data so that it can easily be retrieved. A number of database structures have been used. The first, called hierarchical and network structures, required that special physical links be built into the records to integrate data from multiple files. This requirement imposed unrealistic demands on users at the time of design and led to the emergence of the structure that is currently popular—the relational structure. The beauty of this structure is that it makes use of data elements already in the data tables to integrate the contents of multiple tables. Users are not expected to anticipate at the time of design which tables must be linked.

Exhibit 3.5 illustrates how two tables are linked using the salesperson number that is included in both the salesperson table and the customer table. Assume that a sales manager wants to prepare a salesperson report showing the year-to-date sales for each customer in a salesperson's territory. The salesperson number and name for inclusion in the report heading can be obtained from the salesperson table. The salesperson number can also be used to identify the salesperson's customers in the customer table. The customer data can be printed in the body of the report as columns containing customer

EXHIBIT 3.5	DATA ATTRIBUTES ENABLE RELATIONS

Salesperson Number	Sales Region Number	Salesperson Name
123	1	Carolyn Wright
150	1	Ronald Hudson
188	1	Wally Collins
198	1	Sandy Lee
205	2	Richard Glenn
220	2	Vincent Garza
235	2	Ray Cox

A. Salesperson table

Customer Number	Customer Name	Salesperson Number	Year-to-Date Sales
30788	Austin Auto	123	2,500
30801	Jitney Jungle	235	16,283
30885	Central Repair	123	432,850
31246	Ace Body Shop	198	325
31980	Armadillo Imports	123	37,098
32659	Southern Motors	123	2,375
32776	Bonham Bearings	150	16,201
32829	Wrecking Bar	188	88,567
35294	Continental Cars	150	14,219
36291	Cowboy Trailers	220	59,263
41283	Nomad Motors	205	12,504

B. Customer table

number, customer name, and year-to-date sales. In the example, boldface is used to show where Carolyn Wright's customers are located in the customer table.

In this example, the salesperson number element is a logical entry in the salesperson table (it serves as the **primary key,** identifying the table) and is also a logical entry in the customer table (it is a **secondary key,** providing the linkage).

Multidimensional Databases

Relational database structures are the current standard for the storage of business data, and they are used on computer systems of all sizes and types. They function well for certain data warehouses and data marts, but they were not specifically designed to handle data views that involve a large number of dimensions. A **data dimension** is an array of data in a particular order. For example, if sales records are viewed in terms of the customer dimension, the records are arrayed in customer number sequence. The same records viewed in the salesperson dimension are arrayed in salesperson number sequence.

Typical analyses of business data involve only one, two, or three dimensions. For example, a graph that shows the monthly fluctuation of sales is a one-dimension analysis. The sales amounts are displayed by month, with time being the dimension. A report that shows customer sales by month is a two-dimension analysis (customer and time), and a customer sales report that shows sales of each product for each year is an example of a three-dimensional analysis (customer, product, time).

CRM users often engage in analysis of only a few data dimensions. But they also perform analysis involving many dimensions—**multidimensional analysis.** As the number of dimensions increases, the relational database structures become less effective. To overcome this limitation, software vendors have developed database management systems for **multidimensional databases (MDDBs).**

As the number of dimensions increases, it becomes difficult to perceive the view. One- and two-dimensions can be perceived as tables or graphs, and three dimensions can be viewed as cubes. The term *hypercube* has been coined to describe data arrayed by three or more dimensions.

Exhibit 3.6 shows the three-dimensional analysis of customer, product, and time. The star identifies the location in the cube where a quantitative measure (such as sales amount) for customer 5, product F, and the year 2001 is stored.

More than three dimensions can be viewed with the use of vertical scales—one for each dimension. Exhibit 3.7 shows how data could be arranged in terms of sales region, customer territory, product, and month.

Data Analysis and Information Delivery

Users of the CRM system can analyze data in the data warehouse using the same analysis tools and delivery methods that business computer system users have used for years. These

EXHIBIT 3.6 **DATA STORED IN HYPERCUBES**

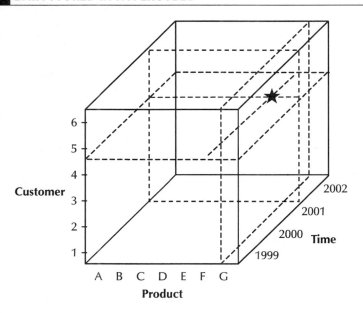

EXHIBIT 3.7	VISUALIZING MORE THAN THREE DATA DIMENSIONS

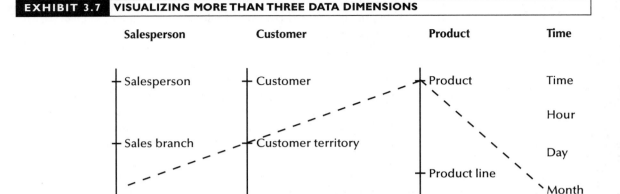

tools include reports, database queries, and mathematical modeling. With the data resource residing in a data warehouse or data mart, CRM users can also use a special tool called online analytical processing (OLAP) that was developed especially for data mining.

Reports and Database Queries

Reports are the traditional way to obtain information from a computer system, and they can be repetitive or special. A **repetitive report** (or **periodic report**) is prepared according to a schedule, such as monthly. Users do not have to request periodic reports—the reports are received automatically. A **special report** is prepared when a special information need arises. A response to a database or data warehouse query is a special report.

Information specialists and users use report writer software to prepare programs to produce the needed reports. Electronic spreadsheets and database management systems incorporate a report writing capability. Some software is especially well-suited to prepare CRM reports from data warehouses. For example, Boots The Chemists, a UK health and beauty retailer with 1,400 stores, uses Microstrategy's business intelligence software to prepare reports used in demographic profiling, basket analysis, shopper profiling, and direct marketing response.[6]

Both reports and query responses can be displayed on the user's workstation monitor or printed in hardcopy form. Exhibit 3.8 is an example of a report or query response showing two dimensions of data.[7]

In making repetitive queries, the CRM users often start with the big picture, viewing the data at a summary level, and then getting more and more detailed with each query. This is called *drill down*—successively increasing the degree of detail, or *granularity,* of the data. Exhibit 3.9 illustrates how a marketing manager might execute drill down. In Exhibit 3.9 Table A, the manager brings up a display showing actual sales compared to quota for three product types and sees that the CD/Tape/Radio type is below quota by 8.8 percent. Seeking to learn more about the poor performance, the user issues a query for a display showing

EXHIBIT 3.8	A REPORT OR QUERY RESPONSE SHOWING TWO DIMENSIONS OF DATA

Customer Sales by Salesperson Report

Sales Region Number	Salesperson Number	Salesperson Name	Y-T-D Sales
1	123	Dixie Williamson	474,823
1	150	Ronald Hudson	30,420
1	188	Wally Collins	88,567
1	198	Sandy Lee	325
		Region 1 Total	594,135
2	205	Richard Glenn	12,504
2	220	Vincent Garza	59,263
2	235	Ray Cox	16,283
		Region 2 Total	88,050
		Company Total	682,185

sales of the three products in the CD/Tape/Radio product type and receives the display in Exhibit 3.9 Table B. The manager sees that the Patriot product is the cause of the poor showing. The manager wants to know if there is any variation in Patriot sales by retail store and requests the display in Exhibit 3.9 Table C. For some reason, the Phoenix and Santa Fe stores are experiencing poor sales whereas Rapid City and Boise are not. Perhaps store visits to learn the causes of the varying sales performances are in order.

Mathematical Modeling

Reports and query response typically provide views of what has happened in the past or what is currently happening. Users of information systems often want to look into the future, and this look can be provided by mathematical modeling. A mathematical model is constructed in a software form and uses data and users' instructions to project what might happen in the future. An example is a model used by a marketing manager to simulate the effect of changes in promotion budget and price on product demand. CRM users can use data in the data warehouse to model possible effects of customer relationship strategies.

Data Mining

We have recognized that when a firm creates a data warehouse, the size can be enormous—measured in gigabytes or terabytes. The term **data mining** describes how the user extracts previously unknown information from the large reservoir of the data warehouse. The process is not unlike the way miners extract gold, coal, diamonds, and so on from the earth.

There are two basic techniques for conducting data mining. One, called the **verification mode,** is when the user has reason to believe that the warehouse contains data in certain forms

| EXHIBIT 3.9 | DRILLING DOWN TO FINER GRANULARITY |

Product Sales in Dollars May 2003

Product Line	Quota	Actual	Variance %
CD/tape/radio	200,000	182,305	-8.8
TV	750,000	831,200	+10.8
Computer	375,000	402,117	+7.2
Total	1,325,000	1,415,622	+6.8

A. Product sales by product line

CD/Tape/Radio Sales in Dollars May 2003

Product	Quota	Actual	Variance %
Patriot	150,000	104,900	-30.1
Series 30	30,000	31,200	+4.0
Series 50	20,000	46,205	+231.0
Total	200,000	182,305	-8.8

B. CD/Tape/Radio sales

Patriot Model CD/Tape/Radio Sales by Retail Store May 2003

Retail Store	Quota	Actual	Variance %
Phoenix	45,000	20,010	-55.5
Santa Fe	50,000	25,877	-48.2
Rapid City	32,500	33,338	+2.6
Boise	22,500	25,675	+14.1
Total	150,000	104,900	-30.1

C. Patriot model CD/Tape/Radio sales by retail store

or patterns and conducts repetitive queries to support this hypothesis. For example, the CRM user might believe that retail shoppers purchase certain groups of products at the same time. Osco Drugs used their CRM system to learn that a man buying diapers between 6 and 8 P.M. sometimes purchases a six-pack of beer as well.[8]

The second data mining technique is called **knowledge discovery,** a method in which the user lets the system determine the path to follow in conducting the analysis. Whereas the verification mode confirms or rejects something that the user believes to exist, knowledge discovery reveals something completely new to the user.

EXHIBIT 3.10	HYPOTHESIS VERIFICATION AND KNOWLEDGE DISCOVERY BY SUCCESSIVE QUERIES

Sale Date	Customer	Product
02-12-03	Ed Flynn	TV
02-15-03	Adele Rice	Computer
02-18-03	Ric Knowles	TV
03-01-03	Ed Flynn	Computer
03-19-03	Angela Forest	TV
03-30-03	Robin Lin	Computer
04-05-03	Robin Lin	CD/Tape/Radio
04-11-03	Ed Flynn	CD/Tape/Radio
04-21-03	Adele Rice	TV
05-16-03	Richard Rodriguez	TV
05-17-03	Robin Lin	TV
05-26-03	Joe Wardlaw	Computer
05-29-03	Angela Forest	CD/Tape/Radio
05-29-03	Richard Rodriguez	CD/Tape/Radio
05-30-03	Cynthia Garfield	Computer

A. Query 1 for transaction data for the Rapid City store February through May

Product Sales Sequence	Customers
TV, Computer, CD/Tape/Radio	Ed Flynn
Computer, CD/Tape/Radio, TV	Robin Lin
Computer, TV	Adele Rice
TV, CD/Tape/Radio	Angela Forest
TV, CD/Tape/Radio	Richard Rodriguez
Computer	Joe Wardlaw, Cynthia Garfield
TV	Ric Knowles

B. Query 2 for product sales sequences

Product Sales Sequence	Customers	Support Factor
TV, Computer	Flynn	.125
TV, CD/Tape/Radio	Flynn, Forest, Rodriguez	.375
Computer, CD/Tape/Radio	Flynn, Lin	.250
Computer, TV	Lin, Rice,	.250
TV, Computer, CD/Tape/Radio	Flynn	.125
Computer, CD/Tape/Radio, TV	Lin	.125

C. Query 3 for support factors for product sales sequences

Exhibit 3.10 illustrates hypothesis verification. In seeking additional information about CD/Tape/Radio sales in the Rapid City store, the user can ask for a display of all product sales in a time sequence (a one-dimension analysis) and receive the display shown in Exhibit 3.10 Table A. The user can then request a display showing all possible sales sequences and receive the display in Exhibit 3.10 Table B. If the user is wondering how often certain sequences occur, the user can request that the CRM system compute a mathematical measure of sequence frequency, called a support factor, and receive the display in Exhibit 3.10 Table C. The sequence of first purchasing a TV and then a CD/tape/radio product occurs most frequently—in 37.5 percent of the sequences. The same findings could be obtained by the user supplying certain parameters and instructing the CRM system to engage in knowledge discovery.

Online Analytical Processing

An approach for quickly and easily conducting multidimensional analysis of data in a data warehouse is called **online analytical processing (OLAP)**. As the name implies, the user is online with the system, using the client workstation to enter instructions and receive query responses.

OLAP was conceived by E. F. Codd, who, along with C. J. Date, is credited with originating the idea of the relational database. In 1993, Dr. Codd wrote a white paper that identified 12 requirements for mining multidimensional data.[9] One of the requirements was that users could perform the processing by using the mouse to point and click rather than by searching through menus. Another stated that the system should not degrade in terms of performance level as the number of dimensions increases. Codd felt that a system should be able to handle 20 or so dimensions.

CLOSED-LOOP MARKETING

At this point, we have completed the overview of information technology use in CRM. We have recognized that the technology is used in a three-step process—data gathering, data storage, and information delivery. The primary focus of the data gathering is the firm's customers, and the primary users of the delivered information are the firm's managers. The main purpose of this data gathering and storage and information delivery is to enable the organization's managers to develop marketing strategies that enable the firm to better meet the product and service needs of the customers. Exhibit 3.11 shows how the strategies close the CRM system loop. **Feedback loops** are characteristics of systems that can control their own operations. The CRM system enables managers to tailor the firm's operations to customer needs. The loop is composed of three ingredients—first is data, next is information, and finally is strategy. The CRM system transforms the data into information, and managers transform the information into strategy. For example, the CRM gathers data that indicates that customers are changing certain buying behavior. These changes are reported to managers who formulate new marketing strategies that are directed at the customers.

EXHIBIT 3.11   CRM-BASED MARKETING STRATEGIES CLOSE THE LOOP

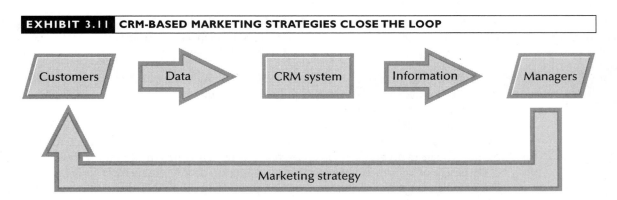

COLLECTING CUSTOMER DATA

There are few, if any, constraints on the amount of data that is stored in the data warehouse. Any data that might have value in understanding and guiding the firm's operations is included. This encompassing view encourages the collection of data from all possible sources—organizations and individuals within the firm as well as outside.

The data that is collected from some of these sources describes activities that involve the firm, such as sales, shipments, payments, and receipts. Some of the data does not describe the firm's activities. An example is marketing intelligence gathered by monitoring a competitor's activities.

The firm's computer-based systems represent a rich source of warehouse data. The data is in a computer-readable form and can easily be migrated to the warehouse after its intended use. The firm's systems are internal data sources. Additional data can be brought into the firm from external data sources—elements in the firm's environment such as customers, government, suppliers, and competitors.

INTERNAL DATA SOURCES

Organizations use multiple systems to process their various transactions with customers, suppliers, employees, and so on. Together, these systems are called **transaction processing systems.** Exhibit 3.12 is a data flow diagram that shows four of these systems

EXHIBIT 3.12   **GATHERING DATA FROM ORDER-PROCESSING SYSTEMS**

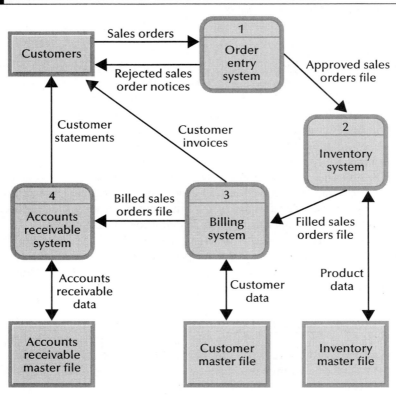

(the numbered symbols, connected by flows of data) that are used to process customer sales orders. Another set of similarly integrated systems is used to order replenishment inventory from suppliers, and there are additional systems such as those that project materials requirements for the production process and compensate the employees.

Most of the marketing data comes from the order-processing systems in Exhibit 3.12. This diagram best suits business-to-business sales in which customers are other organizations, and orders are placed with order forms. Starting in the upper-left-hand corner, the customers' sales orders are input to the order entry system, which logs in all orders, edits the orders for completeness, conducts credit checks, and notifies the customers when orders are rejected for any reason. Approved order data is passed to the inventory system, which checks the inventory master file to determine whether sufficient quantities exist to fill the orders. Orders that can be filled are described in the filled sales orders file, which is provided to the billing system. The billing system uses the customer master file to prepare invoices that are mailed or transmitted electronically to the customers. The billing system also notifies the accounts receivable system of the billed transactions so that the receivable's system can send statements to collect unpaid bills. The accounts receivable master file contains records for all unpaid bills.

These systems provide a wealth of information on the firm's relationships with its customers. The files provide answers to such questions as these:

- Which customers are ordering and which are not? (Sales orders file compared to the customer master file)

- What products do our customers order? (Sales orders file)

- What percent of our customers are bad credit risks? (Rejected sales order notices compared to the sales orders file)

- What percent of the sales orders are filled? (Approved sales orders file compared to the filled sales orders file)

- What are the paying habits of our customers? (Accounts receivable master file)

The diagram also includes two entities that typically provide dimensions for multidimensional analysis. These entities are customer and product. In the next chapter we will see how such dimensions are described with hierarchies of data, and in Chapter 9 we will see how dimensions are used in data mining.

More and more of the CRM interface with the customer is being handled by the Internet. Customers can learn about the firm and its products and place sales orders by logging on to the firm's Web site. As customers click on links to navigate the site, they generate **web data,** and their actions can be logged as **clickstream data** and later analyzed. The analysis reveals what features of the firm's site are of most interest to the customers and how the Web site might be redesigned to improve the navigation.

When customers elect to make purchases using the firm's Web site, they not only reveal product preferences but also provide personal information. Web-based purchases have the potential to provide the firm with more information about its customers than when the customers visit the firm's stores.

EXTERNAL DATA SOURCES

Customers provide data as described above when placing sales orders. Three other elements in the firm's environment are also good providers of warehouse data. These elements are the government, suppliers, and competitors.

Governments on all levels, especially at the state and local level, maintain public records that contain data describing certain activities of firms' customers. These records are open to the public, and examples of such public data include license registrations, voter registrations, and real estate purchases.

The term **suppliers** normally creates thoughts about the supply chain and those organizations that provide such physical products as raw materials for use in manufacturing, finished goods for resale, and machines. However, there is a sizeable network of firms that engage in supplying information for a fee. Examples of such firms include compilers of telephone directories, credit bureaus, and such sellers of syndicated data as A.C. Nielsen, Dun & Bradstreet, and Reuters. This data has long been used to provide marketers with more depth in understanding their customers. Today, this data is being entered into the data warehouse and is mined using OLAP.

Competitors do not usually provide information to the organization on a voluntary basis. The organization must use marketing intelligence to acquire it. **Marketing intelligence** is an ethical business activity that uses inputs available to the general public to learn about competitiors' activities, products, and services. The organization can attend competitors' new product announcements and store openings, scan competitors' ads, shop at competitors' stores, and so on.

SUMMARY

A CRM system consists of three subsystems—data gathering, data warehouse, and information delivery. A data warehouse is a large-scale reservoir of detailed and summary data that describes the firm's activities over time, and it is intended for use in decision making. A data warehouse can be subdivided into data marts to meet the specialized needs of business areas such as marketing. The data warehouse system prepares input data for storage, stores the data, describes the data so that it may be retrieved, and performs a management and control function.

The most popular computer architecture for the CRM system is client/server in which one or more servers perform central functions and the users are the clients that interface with the system by means of their workstations. The control over the user interface, the location of the software, and the location of the hardware can be distributed to varying degrees at either the client or server tier.

Input data describes the details of each contact point with the customer, and it can be entered using point-of-sale terminals, data entry workstations, electronic scanning, or the Internet.

Data is stored in the data warehouse in tables. The data element that identifies the table is the primary key, and a data element that links the table with another table is called the secondary key. Each table can represent a dimension of data. It is common to integrate multiple tables for multidimensional analysis—the tables forming a multidimensional cube, called a hypercube.

CRM system users obtain information by means of repetitive reports, queries, mathematical models, and data mining. Data mining tells the user something that he or she did not previously know. It can either verify hypotheses or discover knowledge. Online analytical processing (OLAP) is a data mining method tailored especially to data warehousing for performing multidimensional analysis.

The CRM system facilitates closed-loop marketing in which customer data is transformed into information by the system, the information is transformed into marketing strategy by managers, and the strategy is directed at the customers.

Most of the input data is generated by the organization's transaction processing systems, but some comes from other internal systems. Additional data is provided by such environmental entities as customers, the government, suppliers, and even competitors' activities.

KEY TERMS

client/server
clickstream data
competitors
data dictionary
data dimension
data mart
data mining
data warehouse
database
database management
   system (DBMS)
direct access storage (DAS)
drill dow
feedback loops

granularity
hypercube
knowledge discovery
main memory
marketing intelligence
multidimensional analysis
multidimensional
   databases (MDDBs)
online analytical
   processing (OLAP)
primary key
repetitive report
   (periodic report)
secondary key

secondary storage
special report
storage area
   network (SAN)
storage resource
   management (SRM)
suppliers
transaction processing
   systems
verification mode
Web data

QUESTIONS FOR REVIEW AND CRITICAL THINKING

1. What is the difference between a data warehouse and a database?
2. What is the reason for storing detailed data in the data warehouse? Why should organizations store summary data?
3. What would be an example of multidimensional analysis involving four dimensions?
4. What distinguishes data mining in the data warehouse from querying the database of a transaction processing system?
5. Why is the Internet especially well-suited to gathering data about customers?

NOTES

1. Ali Pirnar, Linda Plazonja, and Robert Scalea, "CRM Impacts Sales Margins and Focuses Profitability at Tyrolit, with an Estimated 83% ROI," *The ROI Report* (Boston: Hill Holliday): Material number 50 056 101 <www.SAP.COM>.
2. David L. Margulius, "Priced to Sell…to You," 18 February 2002, <WWW.INFOWORLD.COM>.
3. We use the term *firm* to describe any kind of organization—public or private, profit-seeking or non-profit, and so on. *Organization* would probably be better, but it requires much more ink.
4. Carol Hildebrand, "Storage Is Already As Big As An Elephant and Getting Bigger," *CIO Magazine*, 15 May 2002.
5. Ibid.
6. "Boots The Chemists Gets a Business Intelligence Makeover with Microstrategy," 10 July 2002, <www.microstrategy.com/Customers/Successes/boots.asp>.
7. You cannot determine whether an output is a report or a query response simply based on appearance. The determining factor is whether the output was requested (a query response) or is received automatically (a report).
8. Todd Wasserman, Gerry Khermouch, and Jeff Green, "Mining Everyone's Business," *Brandweek*, 28 February 2000, 34.
9. E. F. Codd and Associates, "Providing Online Analytical Processing to User Analysts," (white paper), 1993.

4

The CRM Data Warehouse

The gambling industry is among the leaders in using IT for CRM. Casinos such as MGM Mirage, Harrah's, and Foxwoods have created huge data warehouses of customer data that enable them to know not only who their customers are, but also their likes and dislikes. In its annual report, Harrah's claims that it has the data to know that "Tom likes NASCAR, Clint Holmes, thick steaks. Joyce and Ted like oceanfront views, barbershop quartets, Elvis slots...."[1]

The feature that enables the casinos to learn so much is the loyalty card— a magnetically encoded card that customers swipe when they gamble at a table or use a slot machine. This action provides the casino with details about the wagers being made. In return for this information, the casino awards points that can be cashed in for such prizes as free hotel rooms and show tickets. In 2000, MGM Mirage awarded $286.3 million in prizes, using information mined from its data warehouse of six terabytes. The Foxwood's data warehouse contains 200 gigabytes, and Harrah's has not deleted any of the data that it has gathered on 23 million of its customers since 1995. All this would be impossible without IT.

What Is a Data Warehouse?

Although computers have been used in business applications for almost a half-century, the concept of a data warehouse is relatively recent. A main reason why the concept was slow in evolving is because it is a substantial extension beyond a database in terms of the quantity of data stored. Whereas a database is intended to support the organization's day-to-day transaction processing systems—such as customer sales order processing, materials requirements planning, and payroll—and also support problem solving and decision making, a data warehouse is a separate resource that has only a decision making focus. The data warehouse stores data that comes from the transaction processing systems and from other sources as well. The decision-making support of the data warehouse improves upon that of the transaction processing systems.

We can define a **data warehouse** as a large reservoir of detailed and summary data that describes the organization and its activities, organized by the various business dimensions in a way that facilitates easy retrieval of information that describes the organization's activities. Three components of this definition are important.

- The component of a *large reservoir* imposes a demand that the data warehouse have enough storage capacity to store any and all data that might be needed for decision support. This requires that the computer storage have a much greater capacity than has normally been associated with supporting the operational, transaction processing, systems.

- The use of *business dimensions* recognizes that the data warehouse is a conceptual representation of the organization as a physical system. Just as the organization's physical resources (personnel, materials, machines, etc.) are organized by such business areas as marketing, finance, and human resources, the data warehouse maintains its data in the same fashion. Think of the data warehouse as a mirror image of the organization, capable of reflecting the most minute details of the organization's operations on demand.

- The requirement of *easy retrieval* is made more difficult by the large storage capacity. Generally, the larger the storage, the more difficult the retrieval. The requirement of easy retrieval demanded that innovations in storage hardware be matched by innovations in storage and retrieval software.

The data warehouse is a normal progression beyond the database. Organizations that have established effective databases are now augmenting them with data warehouses to meet demands for the type of decision-making information that the databases cannot provide.

Data Warehouses and Data Marts

When organizations develop information systems, they can take either a top-down or bottom-up approach. With a top-down approach, the overall system is mapped out and then the detail is gradually introduced into successively lower subsystem levels. With a bottom-up approach, the subsystems are individually developed and then integrated.

Organizations can take similar approaches in developing a data warehouse. With a top-down approach, a data warehouse to support the entire organization is first developed, and then it is subdivided into smaller warehouses to support the various business areas. The name **data mart** has been coined to represent a subset of the data warehouse that is tailored to meet the specialized needs of a particular group of users. A bottom-up approach to data warehouse development consists of the data marts being created first and then integrated.

Since our interest is in CRM, we might be inclined to focus on a marketing data mart, recognizing that marketing has the primary responsibility in the organization to interface with the organization's customers. However, this view is too narrow. The data needs of CRM require data not only from marketing but also from other business areas. CRM is a responsibility of the entire organization, not just of marketing. So, our focus should be on the data warehouse, recognizing that it can include data marts not only for marketing but also for other business areas.

DATA WAREHOUSING OBJECTIVES

Although a data warehouse consists of sophisticated computer hardware and software, its main task is very simple—it stores data to be used in decision making. In performing this task, a data warehouse must meet these five objectives:

- Keep the warehouse data current. Data is copied to the data warehouse from operational databases according to a certain schedule, such as daily or weekly.
- Ensure that the warehouse data is accurate. This is accomplished by thoroughly screening and cleaning the data upon entry. Unlike data in the database, where changes are made to keep the contents current, once data is loaded into the data warehouse, it is not updated. The warehouse data is nonvolatile, eliminating a common cause of inadvertent data damage or destruction.
- Keep the warehouse data secure. Since the data is a valuable corporate resource, it should be made available only to authorized users.
- Make the warehouse data easily available to authorized users. Ideally, the warehouse should be usable by both experienced and inexperienced computer users with no special training.
- Maintain descriptions of the warehouse data so that users and systems developers can understand the meaning of each element.

Each of these objectives is achieved by components of the data warehouse architecture.

DATA WAREHOUSE ARCHITECTURE

In the previous chapter, we positioned the data warehouse system between the data gathering system and the information delivery system (Exhibit 3.1). In this chapter, we expand on that central system, explaining each of the data warehouse subsystems. Exhibit 4.1 is a model of the data warehouse system.

The data warehouse system consists of four main components—two providing a processing capability and two providing data to be used in processing. Processing is performed by the staging area and by management and control; data is provided by the warehouse data repository and the metadata repository. In exhibit 4.1, data flows are shown with solid lines and control flows with dashed lines.

Essentially, the **staging area** is where data is prepared to be moved into the warehouse data repository and the metadata repository. **Metadata** is "data about data," or descriptions of the data in the data warehouse. Metadata is used by **information delivery,** which transforms the warehouse repository data into information, and by the *management and control* component, which controls the overall warehouse operation.

It is important for both users and systems developers to understand each data element. Designers of executive information systems recognize this need by including in screen displays the names and addresses of persons in the organization who are experts on the data being displayed. This allows users to contact experts when additional explanations are required. To meet the same type of need, data warehouse users can inquire into the metadata storage to gain explanations of the contents of the data warehouse, with the explanations being made available by the information delivery system.

Exhibit 4.1 shows each of the components of the data warehouse system.

MANAGEMENT AND CONTROL

The data warehouse management and control component interacts with all of the other components to cause the data to flow as it should. The management and control component is, therefore, like a traffic officer standing in the middle of a street intersection, controlling the flow of traffic through the intersection. The management and control component causes the following data flows:

EXHIBIT 4.1 **A DATA WAREHOUSE SYSTEM MODEL**

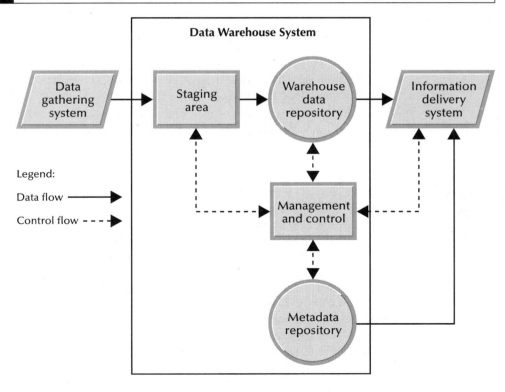

- into the staging area
- through the staging area as the various screening processes are performed
- from the staging area to the warehouse data repository
- from the warehouse data repository to information delivery
- from the metadata repository to information delivery

The management and control component does not perform the staging processes, the warehouse data manipulations, or the metadata manipulations. However, it facilitates those processes by providing the input and output data connections.

STAGING AREA

Providers of warehouse data for the CRM system include internal transaction processing systems, marketing research, and marketing intelligence, and also such external sources as customers, suppliers, and the government. The task is to get this data, existing in a variety of formats and conditions, into the data warehouse. This is a big task, not unlike assembling all of the floats and bands for a Rose Bowl parade. Just like the floats and bands organize in a staging area before the parade begins, the warehouse data is processed through a staging area that prepares the data for warehouse entry. The activities of this staging area are often called **ETL**—for **extraction, transformation,** and **loading.**

When warehouse data originates in the organization's internal operational systems, the data must be **extracted** from the databases and files of those systems. This extraction is accomplished according to a schedule. The extracted data is combined with data from the other sources. This data must be **transformed** into a format for loading into the warehouse—a process that includes cleaning, standardizing, reformatting, and summarizing.

- Cleaning is a big job because some of the data sources fail to remove inaccuracies and inconsistencies. Organizations typically concentrate their attention on those systems that handle money, and this means that data from non-money-handling systems can contain errors—from 2 percent (the error rate of data entry operators) to as high as 15 percent when data is being entered by visitors to the organization's Web site.[2]

- Standardizing involves converting the cleansed data to a uniform format for data element names, codes, and units of measure. The data dictionary is a good example of standard data element names. Information systems make liberal use of codes—customer codes, product codes, geographic codes, and so on—and these codes should be uniform throughout the organization. Units of measure— such as *dozens, pounds,* and *each*—should be common for all like items.

- Reformatting is required when the gathered data is in a different format than that of the warehouse data repository. This is most often necessary when the data is gathered from sources and systems outside the organization.

- Summarizing is performed so that requested summary information can be presented without the need for processing, thus speeding up the delivery.

Data cleaning is an area in which special data warehouse software is available that can make a potentially difficult job much easier. For example, a package from Evoke Software of San Francisco can detect such errors as a driver's license number entered where a social security number should be, and a customer's address appearing twice in the same file. [3]

When data is written into the data warehouse, the data is **loaded.** Initial loading is accomplished when the organization first builds its warehouse, and the data is kept current by either adding new data on a periodic basis or by performing a complete refresh process. The adding of new data is more complicated than a complete refresh since changes to the operational data must ripple through the entire warehouse, but refreshing takes longer since the entire warehouse must be reloaded.

Once the ETL processes are completed, the data resides in the warehouse data repository, waiting to be used.

WAREHOUSE DATA REPOSITORY

The warehouse data repository is where the warehouse data is stored within the computer system or systems. The data warehouse to support the entire enterprise, and also the data marts to support the specialized user areas, are stored in the secondary storage units of central computers, servers, or a storage area network (SAN).

DATA CONTENT

When used in the CRM system, the main task of the data warehouse is to support decision-making, and the purpose of the decision making is to formulate strategies related to customers. In making these decisions, managers need a picture of the customer that is as complete and accurate as possible. This picture is a compilation of geographic, demographic, activity, psychographic, and behavioral data as described in Chapter 2.

One type of **geographic data** describes where the customer is physically located or where the customer-related transaction or activity occurs. An organization's industrial customers, involved in business-to-business transactions, are assigned sales territories based on their geographic location. The territories, as are all other geographic identifiers, are represented by numeric codes. The territory data element is a part of the customer master record or table. These records and tables are maintained in an up-to-date condition by the transaction processing systems and loaded into the data warehouse on a scheduled basis.

Organizations that market through distribution channels also assign codes to manufacturing locations, distribution center locations, and retail store locations. These codes provide a record of the trail that products follow in reaching the customers.

Marketers also want to gather geographic data on individual customers or consumers. This data can be obtained as customers fill out sales order forms when ordering from catalogs, and when sales clerks ask customers for data such as home address or zip code as transaction data is being entered into point-of-sale terminals.

Demographic data consists of those customer characteristics that are either permanent or slow to change. Examples are gender, birth date, ethnic origin, religion, number of years of education or education level, occupation, family income, and number of people in the household. As with the geographic data, demographic data usually consists of codes that are maintained in the customer record or table.

Activity data traces the activities of customers as they interact with the organization by making purchases, returning items, making inquiries, seeking service, and so on. This data is generated in high volumes each day by the transaction processing systems. The data specifies which customers have purchased what quantities of which products on which days. This data can be used to calculate each customer's RFM score and support such marketing strategies as cross selling and up-selling. Other activity data is generated by telemarketing systems and help desk systems as telephone contacts are made with customers. This data can reveal shopping behavior patterns and be used to project each customer's lifetime value.

Activity data explains *what* customer behavior has occurred, and psychographic data seeks to explain *why* it occurred. **Psychographic data** consists of psychological and sociological characteristics that influence customer behavior. **Behavioral data** captures the unique shopping behavior patterns and consumption habits of individual consumers. Psychographic and behavioral data is the most difficult of the four types of data to obtain. An excellent starting point as a source is the warranty card that purchasers are encouraged to complete after they make a purchase.

Some examples of psychographic data that can be gathered by checking boxes on the warranty card are

- The main reasons for purchasing the product
- How the customer learned about the product
- A special occasion (such as a birthday or anniversary) for which the purchase was made
- Recent activity in making purchases by mail or over the Internet
- Activities (hobbies and interests) of persons in the household

The warranty card can also provide such behavioral data as

- Other brands of the product that the customer owns
- Credit cards used

Other psychographic and behavioral data can be inferred from activity data. For example, sales of groups of items and the sequential pattern of making purchases can be calculated. This is the type of analysis frequently performed by online analytical processing (OLAP) to gain an understanding of customer buying behavior.

Data Characteristics

Computer systems essentially transform data into information. To do this, the first system developers had to communicate to the hardware a specification of the types of data to be processed—a requirement that continues to this day. In addition to the data types, developers of modern data warehouses must consider data granularity, data hierarchies, and data dimensions.

Data Types

Much of the warehouse data is structured in that the data element is specified in terms of its format. A customer number element, for example, may be specified as a field that is always eight digits. Some data is difficult to fit in a fixed-length format and, therefore, is defined as variable-length. An example is customer name. The name field might vary from 20 positions to 50 depending on name length. Some textual data, such as comments that a customer might enter in a questionnaire, can be stored in variable-length locations and can be alphanumeric—any combination of letters, numbers, or special characters. Modern multimedia systems also have the capability of handling data in a graphic, audio, or video form by representing the data digitally.

Data Granularity

Information systems can process data at different levels of detail. Users on upper-management levels are assumed to prefer information in a highly summarized form, whereas employees on lower levels require details. **Data granularity** addresses the degree of detail that is represented by the data. The greater the detail, the finer the granularity.

Data Hierarchies

The term **data hierarchy** recognizes that multiple attributes can describe a single entity. An **attribute** is a data element that identifies or describes an occurrence of a data entity. For example, a particular customer is identified by a customer number attribute.

Exhibit 4.2 shows how multiple attributes describe the customer entity. In this example, a simple list, all of the attributes are demographic data. The first entry is the customer number. It identifies the entity.

Some of the attributes in a data hierarchy can also reflect a type of leveled relationship. For example, four attributes may represent geographic sales areas that exist on four levels (from highest to lowest):

- sales region
- sales district
- sales branch
- sales territory

The user can obtain a display of sales by region and then drill down to the district level, seeing sales for each district within the region. The drill down can continue to the branch and territory levels.

| EXHIBIT 4.2 | AN EXAMPLE OF A DATA HIERARCHY |

Customer

Customer number
Customer age
Customer gender
Customer marital status
Customer number of dependents
Customer education
Customer dwelling type
Customer state
Customer city
Customer zip code

Data Dimensions

The data attributes enable a view of the data from various perspectives. The data can be structured in terms of various dimensions. For example, a manager can query the data warehouse for a display of data according to salesperson, customer, product, and time. Refer back to Exhibit 3.7 in Chapter 3 for an illustration of how these hierarchies can provide the dimensions of a multi-dimensional analysis. When the query is processed by OLAP, the returned information will show some measure such as sales dollars by (1) sales region, (2) customer territory, (3) product, and (4) month.

In Exhibit 4.2, a different attribute is selected from each hierarchy. It is also possible to combine multiple attributes from a single dimension. Referring again to Exhibit 3.7, a sales manager could request a display of sales amount by (1) salesperson within, (2) sales branch within, (3) sales region within, and (4) subsidiary.

As we conclude this discussion of data dimensions, we should recognize that the time attribute is contained within each record generated by the transaction processing systems. It is important to know when a particular transaction occurs. Having the time attribute in the records enables users to analyze the data in any time increment—year, quarter, month, day, and, in some cases, hour and minute. Exhibit 4.3 illustrates how the time element is incorporated in the records generated by a sales processing system.

METADATA REPOSITORY

In addition to the warehouse data repository, the other element in the data warehouse system that provides data is the metadata repository. We established earlier that the term **metadata** means "data about data." When applied to the data warehouse, metadata describes the data in the warehouse. For example, customer numbers of all of the organization's customers reside in the warehouse. Metadata in the metadata repository describes the customer number attribute—its format, editing rules, and so on. This same type of description exists in the data dictionary of a DBMS. The data dictionary of a transaction processing system database is a form of metadata, but the metadata repository of a data warehouse is more complete. The metadata repository describes the flow of data from the time that the data is captured until it is archived.

EXHIBIT 4.3   **EVERY DATA RECORD CONTAINS THE TIME ELEMENT**

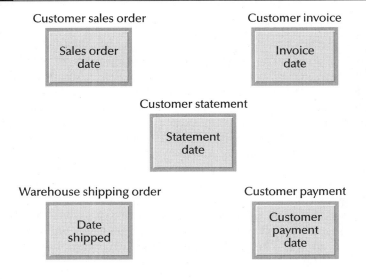

TYPES OF METADATA

Some metadata is maintained for use by data warehouse users; some is maintained for use by systems developers.

Metadata for Users

Users want to understand the data that they are using in their analysis, and they want to know how to perform the various analyses. Examples of this type of metadata are an identification of the source systems, the time of the last update, the different report formats that are available, and the process for finding data in the data warehouse.

Metadata for Systems Developers

Systems developers want to understand the data so that they can maintain, revise, and reengineer the data warehouse system. The developers need to know the various rules that were employed in creating the warehouse data repository. They need to know rules for extraction, cleansing, transforming, purging, and archiving.

As changes are made to the metadata, the effects of the changes ripple through the warehouse data repository. For example, when a transaction processing system revises a record, the time of the last update is revised, and when a rule for purging records in the warehouse data repository is changed, records are purged in accordance with the new rule.

Sources of Metadata

In most cases, special effort does not have to be made to create metadata; it exists as a byproduct of the organization's previous and ongoing systems development efforts. The metadata can come from data and process models, CASE tools, and database management systems.

DATA AND PROCESS MODELS

As such operational systems as transaction processing systems are developed, the information specialists prepare data and process models that guide their development efforts. Examples of data models are object diagrams and entity-relationship diagrams. Examples of process models are use cases, use case diagrams, and data flow diagrams. These documentation tools document the systems and the data used by the systems. We illustrated the sales order transaction processing system in Exhibit 3.12 with a data flow diagram. Each data flow and data file can be documented with a dictionary.[4]

CASE TOOLS

CASE stands for computer-aided system engineering. It is a way to use the computer to develop systems. When a CASE tool is used, the system design begins with data and process models in an electronic form, which the CASE software transforms into functioning databases and software.

DBMS SYSTEMS

Database management systems include a data dictionary component that contains excellent descriptions of the data in the database or data warehouse. We illustrated a data dictionary entry in Chapter 3 in Exhibit 3.3.

Data descriptions from the data dictionary that exist in the proper format need only be copied to the metadata repository. Otherwise, the descriptions must be formulated and keyed into the repository.

How Data Is Stored in the Data Warehouse

Data is stored in both a transaction processing database and in the data warehouse repository in tables. However, in a relational database, all of the data for a particular entity is maintained in a single table. For example, the customer table contains all of the attributes that describe a customer and the customer's activities. The table includes such descriptive attributes as customer name and address, sales territory, and credit rating, as well as quantitative measures of activity such as current month sales and current year sales. The data in the data warehouse is segregated into two types of tables—dimension and fact.

A dimension table consists of a list of all of the attributes that identify and describe a particular entity. Exhibit 4.4 is an example of a customer dimension table. A data warehouse user can analyze customer data in terms of all of these dimensions either separately or in combination.

A **fact table** is a list of all the facts that relate to some type of the organization's activity. The example in Exhibit 4.5 is a list of facts relating to the organization's commercial sales (sales to other organizations). Facts are quantitative measures of activity. Commercial sales can be analyzed in terms of such measures as actual units, budgeted units, actual amounts, and budgeted amounts.

At this point you are probably saying "That's nice that we can analyze the data in so many dimensions and can report on so many facts, but it would be nice if we could combine the two." That's a good observation and is exactly what the designers of the data warehouse repository have done. They've created a structure that brings the dimensions and facts together. The structure is called an information package.

Information Packages

A table that is maintained in the data warehouse repository that identifies both the dimensions and the facts that relate to a business activity is called an **information package.** Exhibit 4.6 illustrates the format. The dimensions that can be used in analyzing the activity are identified in the upper portion. Each dimension is identified by its key, followed by the hierarchy of attributes

EXHIBIT 4.4   A SAMPLE DIMENSION TABLE

Customer

Customer number
Customer name
Customer phone number
Customer e-mail address
Customer territory
Customer credit code
Customer standard industry code
Customer city
Customer state
Customer zip code

EXHIBIT 4.5   A SAMPLE FACT TABLE

Commercial Sales Facts

Actual sales units
Budgeted sales units
Actual sales amount
Budgeted sales amount
Sales discount amount
Net sales amount
Sales commission amount
Sales bonus amount
Sales tax amount

EXHIBIT 4.6	INFORMATION PACKAGE FORMAT

Subject: Name of business activity being measured

Dimension Name	Dimension Name	Dimension Name	Dimension Name
Dimension key	Dimension key	Dimension key	Dimension key
Dimension 1	Dimension 1	Dimension 1	Dimension 1
Dimension 2	Dimension 2	Dimension 2	Dimension 2
Dimension 3	Dimension 3	Dimension n	Dimension 3
Dimension 4	Dimension n		Dimension 4
Dimension n			Dimension n

Facts: Numeric measures of the business activity

that describe that dimension. A **key** is a number that identifies a particular occurrence of the dimension. The customer dimension, for example, is identified by customer number. Customer number is the key. The facts that measure the business activity in a quantitative way are identified in the lower portion.

For an example of an information package, refer to Exhibit 4.7. This package is for commercial sales, and it identifies (1) the dimensions that can be used in analyzing commercial sales, and (2) the various quantitative measures of commercial sales. With data in the data warehouse repository organized in terms of this information package, a user can analyze any of the facts in terms of any of the dimensions. A user can, for example, analyze sales commission amounts by time, salesperson, customer, product, or any combination of these categories.

Star Schemas

An information package usually identifies multiple dimension tables for a single fact table. The arrangement, called a star schema, has the appearance of a star, with the fact table in the center and the dimension tables forming the points. The format is illustrated in Exhibit 4.8.

EXHIBIT 4.7	A SAMPLE INFORMATION PACKAGE

Subject: Commercial sales

Time	Salesperson	Customer	Product
Time key	Salesperson key	Customer key	Product key
Hour	Salesperson name	Customer name	Product name
Day	Sales branch	Customer territory	Product model
Month	Sales region	Customer credit code	Product brand
Quarter	Subsidiary		Product line
Year			

Facts: Actual sales units, budgeted sales units, actual sales amount, budgeted sales amount, sales discount amount, net sales amount, sales commission amount, sales bonus amount, sales tax amount

The fact table is linked to the dimension tables by means of the keys identified at the top of the fact table. These keys are called **foreign keys** because they do not serve to identify the fact table but to identify keys of other, "foreign" tables.

This linkage is illustrated in Exhibit 4.9 for an activity called product sales facts. The keys of the product, customer, salesperson, and time dimensions are identified at the top of the fact table. These keys make it possible to analyze the different measures of sales facts by any of the dimensions in the dimension tables.

EXHIBIT 4.8   STAR SCHEMA FORMAT

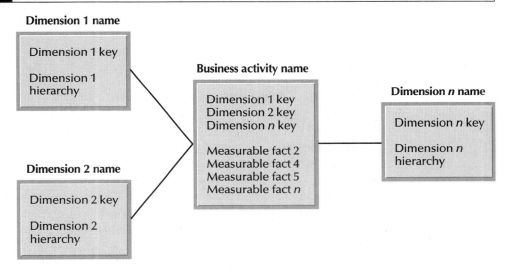

EXHIBIT 4.9   A SAMPLE STAR SCHEMA

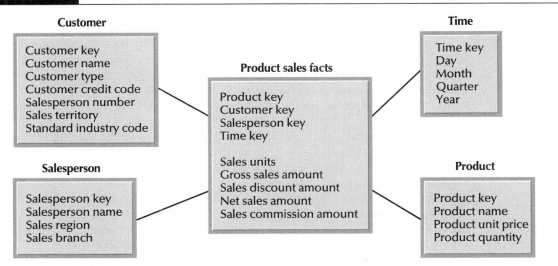

Most data warehouses consist of multiple star schemas, with each one representing some aspect of the organization's business. The Exhibit 4.9 example represents product sales. Other star schemas would represent purchasing, manufacturing, logistics, human resources, financial performance, and so on.

The star schemas unfold in a top-down manner, beginning with the organization's strategic objectives. These objectives are restated in the form of performance measures that guide the organization's managers in meeting the objectives. The managers specify what information the data warehouse must provide to help them meet the objectives, and the systems developers develop the star schema.

Data Warehouse Navigation

The data warehouse user engages in hypothesis verification or knowledge discovery by making repeated queries, modifying them each time to obtain the information needed for decision-making. The warehouse interface is designed to enable the user to easily perform the querying.

In Dr. Codd's 1993 white paper, four of his twelve guidelines for online analytical processing addressed ease of use.[5] These guidelines, reworded from the original, are:

- The data model provided by the data warehouse should provide the user with the same logical and intuitive view of the enterprise that matches how the user perceives the enterprise.

- The warehouse should provide only the information that the user requests—nothing more or nothing less.

- The processing software should enable the user to analyze the data by navigating up, down, and across the hierarchical levels of data with ease.

- The interface should feature a graphical view using the mouse to point and click rather than to navigate up and down levels of menus.

Exhibit 4.10 illustrates navigation paths through the warehouse data as the user formulates queries. At the top of the diagram, *summary information* consists of preprocessed data that provides the user with exactly the content that is needed. For example, the sales manager might want to know the net sales for the Western sales region. The user is able to **drill down** through levels of data from the upper summary levels to lower detailed levels. Continuing the Western region example, the sales manager might want to know the net sales for a particular salesperson (number 3742) in that region. The sales manager then might want to know the sales units for salesperson 3742, and **drill through** the hierarchical levels of summary data to the finest level of data granularity.

The most common pattern is a top-down navigation in which the user seeks more detail in an effort to understand the summary information. However, the user can also **roll up,** summarizing data to "see the forest rather than the trees." Perhaps the user can request that summary graphs be prepared to provide a clearer picture of the details. The user can also easily **drill across** from one data hierarchy to another. As an example, the sales manager can request information on customer sales, then request information on salesperson sales, and then information on product sales. In this manner, the warehouse user is able to "slice and dice" the data in the manner that is needed.

Data Warehouse Security

An organization's information resources include not only hardware, software, and data, but also the people who develop and use the systems, and the procedures that govern system use. These resources must be protected. **Information systems security** consists of those measures that are instituted to reduce or eliminate the risks that information systems face. The information systems risks include such acts as damage, destruction, theft, and misuse. Unintentional damage is much more common than damage from hackers or other wrongdoers. Data warehouse security is therefore concerned with protecting the data warehouse resources from these risks, and it is achieved within a corporate security environment.

The Corporate Security Environment

The corporate environment that facilitates information system security consists of four actions that are taken in sequence.[6] These actions, illustrated in Exhibit 4.11, are called the **security action cycle,** and they include a feedback loop.

- *Deterrence.* The organization first puts into place security policies and procedures that are intended to deter security violations. Examples of these measures are guidelines for proper system use and the requirement that users change their passwords periodically. The organization communicates this information to persons both inside and outside the organization who can influence security. The communications can take the form of security training programs that identify potential security threats and spell out punishments for offenders.

EXHIBIT 4.10 NAVIGATION PATHS

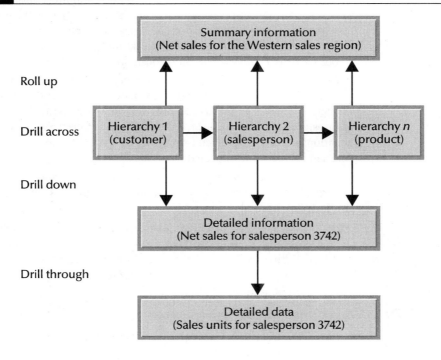

EXHIBIT 4.11	THE SECURITY ACTION CYCLE

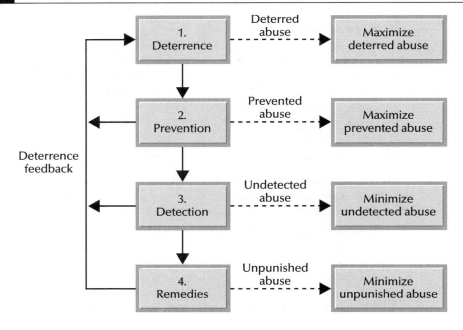

- *Prevention.* Preventative measures are aimed at those persons who ignore the deterrence, and include such things as locks on computer rooms, user passwords, and file permissions that spell out the actions that users are authorized to take on stored data once access has been granted. Prevention may also include hiring outside consultants to try to "break into" the system so that security flaws can be corrected before a real threat occurs.
- *Detection.* The organization wants to be alert to breaches or (more ideally) potential breaches in security. Proactive actions include system audits, reports of suspicious activity, and virus scanning software. Reactive actions take the form of investigations. The purpose of these actions is to learn the details of security violations that have occurred or may occur. A security violation that is not detected is likely to be repeated.
- *Remedies.* Knowing that a security breach has occurred and who committed it, the organization can respond with warnings, reprimands, termination of employment, or legal action.

As the four actions are taken, potential violators, especially those within the organization, become convinced of the seriousness with which management is establishing and enforcing security measures, and they will show less of a tendency to breach the system security in the future. This reinforcing action is seen in the deterrence feedback loop in the exhibit.

Data Warehouse Security Measures

Within this corporate security environment, specific measures can be taken to protect the data warehouse. Someone likened data security to the layers of an onion. To access the data, you have to go through the various security layers, which consist of measures designed to protect the network, files, and the database or data warehouse.

- *Network Security.* Persons both inside and outside the organization must be granted access to the network that houses the servers and data files, databases, data warehouses, and data marts. Some organizations permit their customers to access the CRM data warehouse by means of the Internet. A security mechanism that restricts access to the organization's internal network from the Internet is the firewall, one or more filtering devices that allow only authorized users to gain access. The firewall software can check the user's password and also verify that the user's physical location (as identified by an address) is one that is authorized to gain access.

- *Data Security.* Once access to the network has been achieved, the data warehouse user must gain access to the data. The data files may be located on multiple servers on the network, and the user must provide a second password and also be screened in terms of which files may be made available and which operations can be performed on the file data.

- *Database or Data Warehouse Security.* With approval to access certain files and perform certain operations on the file data, the user must finally satisfy the security checks of the database management system (DBMS). These checks may include a third password, verification of user name, and also verification of access to particular data tables, records, and even record fields.

The responsibility for establishing data warehouse security within the corporate environment falls to the organization's network administrator and database administrator. These persons, who are usually a part of the IT unit, put the above layers into place and then monitor system performance to ensure that the security measures are effective.

SUMMARY

A data warehouse is a large reservoir of data that represents the physical resources and activities of the organization and is designed to facilitate easy retrieval. A data mart is a subset of the data warehouse containing data that is tailored to the needs of an organizational unit such as a business area.

A data warehouse has five objectives. A data warehouse should keep data current, ensure its accuracy, keep it secure, make it easily available to authorized users, and maintain descriptions of the data for users and systems developers.

The management and control component keeps the data flowing between the other components—through the staging area to the warehouse data repository, and from the warehouse data repository and the metadata repository to information delivery. The staging area is where ETL occurs—extraction, transformation, and loading. Transformation consists of cleaning, standardizing, reformatting, and summarizing.

The warehouse data repository contains geographic data, demographic data, activity data, and psychographic and behavioral data. The data types can be numeric, alphanumeric, and even graphic, audio, and video. The data can also have varying granularity—from high-level summaries to the most detailed—and can describe entities at different hierarchical levels. The multiple attributes that describe an entity can be used for multidimensional analysis—looking at the data from various perspectives.

Metadata plays an important role in the data warehouse by providing users with descriptions of the data so that the users can make full use of the system. Metadata also provides systems developers with descriptions that are necessary for maintaining, revising, and re-engineering the data warehouse system as needed. Much of the metadata can come from data and process models, CASE and DBMSs.

Data is stored in the data warehouse in tables. Descriptions of an entity are stored in dimension tables, and quantitative measures of business activity are stored in fact tables. Information packages relate the dimension tables to the fact tables. When the tables are viewed graphically, with the fact table in the center and the dimension tables around the periphery, the pattern is like a star, hence the name star schema. When Dr. Codd envisioned how the data warehouse could be used, he recognized the importance of ease of navigation. Users can drill down, drill through, roll up, and drill across.

Data warehouse security is achieved within a corporate security environment, and consists of four steps—deterrence, prevention, detection, and remedies. Access to the data warehouse contents requires that users gain access to the network housing the data, gain approval to access certain data files, and satisfy the screens provided by the DBMS.

You should now understand the basics of how data is stored in the warehouse data repository. In Chapter 9 we will focus on online analytical processing—how the users obtain information from the warehouse data.

KEY TERMS

activity data	drill down	information package
attributes	drill through	key
behavioral data	ETL (extraction,	loaded
CASE	transformation,	metadata
data granularity	loading)	psychographic data
data hierarchy	extracted	roll up
data mart	fact table	security action cycle
data warehouse	firewall	star schema
demographic data	foreign keys	transformed
dimension table	information systems	
drill across	security	

QUESTIONS FOR REVIEW AND CRITICAL THINKING

1. How have casinos come to the forefront in implementing CRM systems?
2. How does a data warehouse differ from a database?
3. The chapter suggests that data marts can be developed for such business areas as marketing and human resources. What are some other possible subsets of the data warehouse?
4. Match the data warehousing objectives with the system components pictured in the model in Exhibit 4.1.
5. What happens in the staging area that contributes to the currency, accuracy, and security of the warehouse data?

6. Which type of customer data would be the most volatile—geographic, demographic, activity, or psychographic and behavioral? Which would be least volatile?

7. What role do data hierarchies play in viewing data from multiple dimensions?

8. What distinguishes the contents of the dimension and fact tables?

9. What kind of table relates the dimensions to the facts?

10. What forms the connections between the fact table and the multiple dimension tables in a star schema?

11. Why did Dr. Codd insist that online analytical processing should be easy to use?

12. Using the data in Exhibit 4.9, give an example of drill down performed by a sales manager.

NOTES

1. Kim S. Nash, "Casinos Hit Jackpot with Customer Data," *Computerworld*, 2 July 2001, 16.

2. Paul Krill, "CRM Plagued by Data Quality Issues," *InfoWorld*, 5 October 2001, 1:01 PT, Internet display.

3. Dylan Tweney, "Cleaning Up Dirty Data," *Business*, 30 August 2001, Internet display.

4. For examples of data dictionary entry forms to support DFDs, see Raymond McLeod, Jr., and George Schell, *Management Information Systems, Eighth Edition* (Englewood Cliffs, N.J.: Prentice-Hall, 2001): 397—399.

5. E. F. Codd and Associates, "Providing On-Line Analytical Processing to User Analysts," (white paper), 1993.

6. Information in this section is derived from D. W. Straub and R. J. Welke, "Coping with Systems Risk: Security Planning Models for Management Decision-Making," *MIS Quarterly 22*, no. 4 (December 1998): 441–469.

5

Customer Loyalty

A quick perusal of the van parked in the driveway provides a more than subtle hint that the homeowner is a Chicago Cubs fan: the Georgia license plate reads "CUBVAN."[1] Once inside the home, a visitor is inundated with further evidence of the owner's devotion to her favorite major league baseball team. Indeed, to walk into Eileen's home is to walk into a veritable shrine to the Chicago Cubs. On one wall, a Harry Carey poster resides next to a framed official Cubs program signed by Ernie Banks. An adjacent wall is dominated by a Chicago Cubs pennant, beneath which hangs a replica of the Wrigley Field masthead proclaiming the Cubs as the 1984 National League East Champs. A Wrigley Field sign tucked above a doorway invites guests into a lower level restroom bedecked with Chicago Cubs wallpaper, pinstripes, framed pictures of Wrigley Field, and towels and wash-cloths bearing the Chicago Cubs logo. Perhaps Eileen's allegiance to the team is best summed up by a placard that recognizes her as "a certified member in good standing, since 1967, in the Die-Hard Cub Fan Club."

Most marketing organizations would love to be able to develop and maintain customer loyalty on a par with the team allegiance and devotion demonstrated by Eileen.

This chapter investigates the meaning of brand loyalty and customer loyalty. It attempts to explain the factors that lead customers to be loyal to certain brands, stores, manufactures, and service providers, and it explores factors that affect loyalty in an e-commerce landscape.

PERSPECTIVES OF BRAND LOYALTY

The term **customer loyalty** refers to a customer's commitment or attachment to a brand, store, manufacturer, service provider, or other entity based on favorable attitudes and behavioral responses, such as repeat purchases. Two basic perspectives of loyalty describe brand loyalty as a behavior toward the product and customer loyalty as an attitude, or predisposition to behave. The unwavering positive attitude towards the Cubs baseball team in the opening example reflects a high degree of customer loyalty.

There is considerable variation in the terms used to describe loyal customers. Some companies call their most loyal buyers—the 20 percent of the customers that supply 80 percent of the sales, profits, or visits to the organization's contact points (store, catalog, mail box, or Web site)—*premium customers, key accounts,* or *elites.* Airlines and credit card companies often refer to key accounts as precious metals such as gold, silver, or platinum.

BRAND LOYALTY AS BEHAVIOR

Early academic research investigated the purchase behavior of customers to identify and measure brand loyalty. This **behavioral brand loyalty** approach explored how consistent customers were in repurchasing brands. If the customer bought Heinz brand ketchup every time he or she went to the store, the customer was said to be brand loyal.

Behavioral brand loyalty is measured by the *proportion of purchases*—the number of times the most frequently purchased brand is purchased, divided by the total number of times the product category is purchased. While it is possible for a customer to demonstrate undivided loyalty by purchasing a brand of a product 100 percent of the time, the behavioral view recognizes that this is not always the case. Researchers view a brand loyalty continuum and classify customers from complete undivided loyalty to complete brand **indifference.**[2] Customers can also be classified into different categories based on the *sequence* of their brand switching. Exhibit 5.1 shows five types of behavior toward the purchase of brands.

As shown in Exhibit 5.1, **undivided loyalty** describes the behavior of a customer who always selects the same brand. An **occasional switcher** usually selects the same brand over time but may want a change of pace now and then, or may face an out-of stock situation. If the soft drink machine is out of your favorite choice but you are quite thirsty, you may select another flavor or brand. **Switched loyalty** describes a customer who has experienced a change of heart, or a change of brand, while **divided loyalty** shows a customer who is loyal to more than one brand. For example, many customers use more than one shampoo on a regular basis and switch back and forth between two or three favorites. The behavioral pattern of **indifference** represents

EXHIBIT 5.1	VARIATIONS IN BEHAVIORAL BRAND LOYALTY
Undivided loyalty	A A A A A A A A A A
Occasional switcher	A A A B A A A C A A
Switched loyalty	A A A A A B B B B
Divided loyalty	A A A B B B A A B B
Indifference	A B C D C A D E A C
	Purchases over time →

the customer who sees no distinctions between brands or who could not care less which brand is purchased.

The term **churn rate** indicates the rate at which new customers try a product or service and then stop using it.[3] Often it refers to a given time rate such as the yearly churn rate. CRM systems may allow mathematical model builders with databases containing extensive purchase histories to use proportion of purchases, sequence of purchase, and most recent purchase to predict the *probability* of a consumer purchasing one brand over alternative choices. Point of sale (POS) systems are designed to provide such inputs for the data warehouse.

You may recall from Chapter 2 that a customer's RFM (recency, frequency, and monetary) score reflects the recency of purchase, frequency of purchases, and a customer's average purchase size (monetary). These basic behavioral variables can be key components in segmenting the overall market and key starting points in developing an understanding of loyal customers. However, a strict behavioral definition of loyalty does not attempt to understand why the behavior is occurring, nor does it distinguish between loyal behavior and behavioral inertia. As shown in Exhibit 5.2, **inertia** suggests a low sensitivity to the brand since purchases are made without a real motive for the choice.[4] Thus, to supplement behavioral data, organizations also need to explore methods of collecting information about customer attitudes.

BRAND LOYALTY AS ATTITUDE

Measuring proportion of purchases, sequence of purchase, or most recent purchase has a major shortcoming: It does not tell the marketer why a brand was selected. A customer may be making a repeat purchase not because of any true loyalty or commitment but because of convenience, price, availability, or inertia due to habit.

The *attitudinal brand loyalty* approach takes the view that loyalty involves much more than repeat purchase behavior. This view holds that brand loyalty must also include a favorable attitude that reflects a preference or commitment expressed over time. In other words, brand loyalty is a behavioral response to an attitude toward a brand.

An attitude serves an object appraisal function. Is the brand favorable or unfavorable, liked or disliked, desirable or undesirable? An attitude involves an evaluation. More specifically, an attitude comprises an individual's general affective, cognitive, and behavioral responses to a given object, issue, or person.[5] To understand attitudes, organizations would describe what people know or believe to be true about the brand, how people feel about

---

EXHIBIT 5.2 | **LOYALTY VERSUS INERTIA**

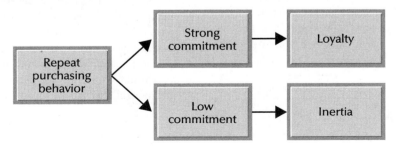

the brand or their level of emotional attachment, and what people intend to do about those beliefs and feelings.

People learn attitudes. For true brand loyalty—that is, attitudinal-loyalty—to develop, there must be a psychological process that involves evaluation, decision-making, and awareness of a strong predisposition toward purchase as well as an overall liking of a brand.[6] An attitude implies a predisposition to purchase suggesting that an emotional attachment exists. The emotional component of loyalty may be most difficult to capture within the data warehouse of the organization. When used together, attitude, loyalty, and behavior provide a framework for thinking about customer loyalty that would differentiate no loyalty from latent loyalty and inertia.[7]

Customers who fall in the no loyalty category have a weak attitude, exhibit indifferent behavioral response to the brand, and have low repeat patronage behavior. It may be that the non-loyal customers view all companies or all brands in a product category to be similar. Often, price consciousness is associated with the lack of loyalty where people will purchase whichever brand is on sale. Marketing efforts directed at these customers may cost more than they are worth.

Inertial loyalty has also been called **spurious loyalty** to indicate that behavior appears to be "bogus" because there is no strong attitudinal influence. These customers may exhibit inertia because they have low-involvement with what they perceive to be undifferentiated companies, stores, or brands. The behavior of these customers can be driven by habit.—"My mother used Tide and I've always used it." With **latent loyalty,** customers have strong attitudes, but repeat purchase is low. Situational factors, such as preferences of joint-decision makers, have a stronger influence than attitudinal factors. When a teenage girl uses her parent's credit card to buy a high priced, prestigious perfume, she may be very satisfied and hold strong positive attitudes. However, when her parents learn of her behavior, they may voice their disapproval. Thus, the social norm about "obeying one's parents" creates a latent loyalty.

The implied goal is to define loyalty by describing behavioral patterns that result from attitudinal predispositions that are modified by situations over time. Customers who exhibit inertia may be more costly to encourage to switch to a new provider than are those with no loyalty or behavioral pattern.

RELATIONSHIP COMMITMENT

Loyal customers, high in repeat purchase behavior and strong in attitude, are, theoretically, the most desirable customers. Not only do they purchase a large amount of the product, but they may also advocate the product to others. They may enjoy sharing their knowledge and experiences with friends and family. Customers of Miracle Grow may faithfully tell fellow gardeners and neighbors how the plant food has made their flowers fast growing and beautiful.

Loyalty indicates a commitment to and support of a relationship. *Relationship commitment* is defined as an enduring desire to maintain a valued relationship.[8] Commitment implies an attitude or affective response, a willingness to invest, and the idea that the interactions or relationship will exist over time.[9] A strong commitment to a relationship develops if the relationship is *mutually beneficial* to the parties. A committed partner believes the relationship has value and is willing to work at preserving it. This is especially true of business-to-business relationships among suppliers and intermediaries.

EXHIBIT 5.3	TRANSACTIONAL/RELATIONAL CONTINUUM

	Transactions ◄——► Relationships	
Objective	Make a sale	Create a customer
Characteristic	Anonymity	Interdependence
Criteria of success	Volume, price, new customers	Value enhancements, Repeat exchanges
Interaction tone	Sale as a conquest Discreet event	Sale as an agreement Continuing process

The transactional/relational continuum, shown in Exhibit 5.3, portrays a view of options within a range of relationship choices. **Transactions** are discrete events that result in no feeling of relationship and no anticipation of future interactions. Customers oriented to the transaction seek to maximize their own benefit in the current exchange, while those who are committed to the relationship may be more willing to negotiate or compromise to maintain interactions over time. In contrast, **relationalism** suggests an approach characterized by cooperative actions, compromises, sharing of benefits and costs, as well as plans for future interactions.[10] The overall objective of relationalism is to build trust and loyalty, which leads to an altered focus for the marketing management process.[11]

Another way of considering relationalism is based on the richness of interactions that are necessary to initiate, maintain, and grow a relationship over time. The more transactional or discrete interactions may exhibit an arms-length attitude and low trust while committing a limited number of resources to maintaining the relationship. Switching costs are perceived as low and there are few personal relationships between the organization and its customers. High relational richness, in contrast, is characterized more by high levels of trust, personal friendships, similar goals, and a synergy in learning and knowledge capabilities.[12]

FACTORS THAT AFFECT CUSTOMER LOYALTY

Since every marketer wants loyal customers, a logical question to ask is "what affects customer loyalty?"[13] Exhibit 5.4 depicts some fundamental components that are expected to affect customer loyalty.

CUSTOMER SATISFACTION

As Exhibit 5.5 shows, people develop beliefs about what they expect to happen before they make a choice. Customer satisfaction is a post-purchase or post-choice evaluation that results from a comparison between those pre-purchase expectations and actual performance. Fulfillment of an expectation is confirmation. If there is a disconfirmation, expectations are not met. Dissatisfied customers may complain, choose never to purchase the transactional experience is thus seen to result in confirmation or disconfirmation, yet for

EXHIBIT 5.4 | **WHAT AFFECTS CUSTOMER LOYALTY?**

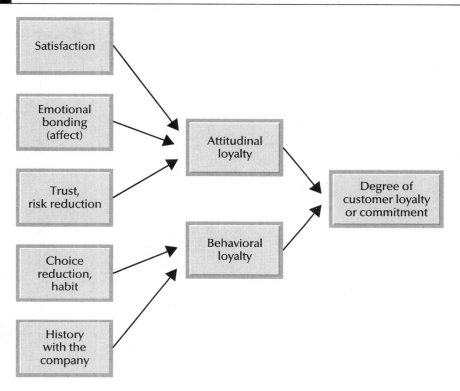

most organizations, the goal is to measure and manage customer satisfaction with the cumulative experiences customers have with the brand, product, organization, or location.[14]

Effective marketers try to understand if the discrepancy between expectations and performance is large or small. The term **delightful surprises** has been use to describe situations in which customers receive fulfillment that exceeds the satisfaction of unexpected needs or wants. A delightful surprise may be a defining moment in which a regular customer becomes a loyal advocate. Effective marketers likewise try to understand the degree of discrepancy when marketers fail to meet expectations and the causes of consumer dissatisfaction.

Satisfied customers may not be loyal customers. One explanation is that expectations, which shape satisfaction, are complex and exist at different levels.[15] People may formulate expectations in terms of a *desired level*—what should be done—and in terms of an a*dequate level*—what will be done. Many marketers believe customers have a **zone of tolerance** where expectations (and satisfaction) range from what they hope to receive to what is minimally acceptable to unacceptable performance. Xerox revealed an interesting finding in a study of satisfaction. The company ranked satisfaction on a 5-point scale ranging from 1 for completely dissatisfied to 5 for completely satisfied. It found that customers who rated their satisfaction as 4 were six times more likely to switch to a competitive offering than those who marked 5 were.[16] So, while satisfaction is important in knowing what shapes loyalty, we have to go deeper to fully understand loyalty.

EXHIBIT 5.5	CONFIRMATION/DISCONFIRMATION OF EXPECTATIONS DETERMINES DISSATISFACTION/SATISFACTION/DELIGHT

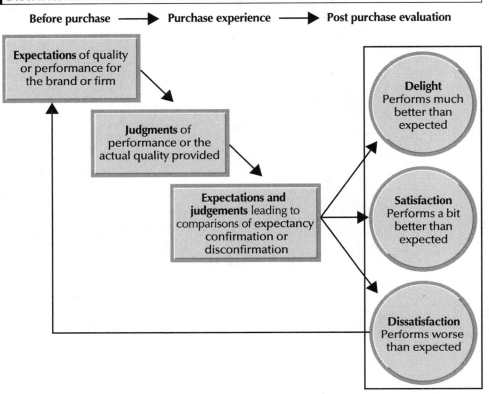

Why do satisfied customers often switch brands or buy from other companies? There are several explanations. The first is that a company's satisfied customer might also have had a positive experience with and be equally satisfied with a competitor's offering. Thus, *relative* satisfaction should be considered in the role that customer satisfaction plays in shaping customer loyalty. Another has to do with familiarity and a need for variety. People may simply opt for a new experience because they get less and less satisfaction from the old one. A third explanation is that new information changes customer expectations about a previously untried offering.

EMOTIONAL BONDING

The second component of the model shown in Exhibit 5.2 builds on the idea that, over time, customer loyalty requires *emotional bonding*. Customers have a positive *brand affect*, which is an affinity with the brand, or they have a *company attachment*, which means they like the company.17 In many circumstances, consumers may identify with and become emotionally attached to mental images that a company or a brand develops or acquires. For example, many customers identify with Polo Ralph Lauren. They identify with the brand because the brand identifies them and their friends. From a consumer's perspective, the *brand equity*[18] associated with Polo leads to customer loyalty. Brand equity is the value of the brand name associated with a product or service that goes beyond the functional aspects alone. For example, many customers feel a closeness with other people who also use the good or service.

Some companies know how to connect emotionally with their customers while others have more difficulty in accomplishing this level of commitment. CRM must reach beyond the idea of the rational consumer and strive to establish feelings of closeness, affection, and trust as true emotional bonding is often based on trust and respect.[19]

Though CRM systems attempt to build emotional bonds with customers, IT linkages within CRM systems may actually limit emotional bonds between organizations and their customers. Personal contacts are very powerful within a relationship-building process and can reveal many subtle issues that affect a customer's willingness to buy. Non-verbal signals, friendships, and personal interactions are critical actions that build trust and that may be short-changed as efforts increase to reduce labor costs by developing strong IT linkages.[20]

TRUST

Trust, the third component of the model, is interrelated with emotional bonding. Trust exists when one party has confidence that he or she can rely on the other exchange partner.[21] **Trust** can be defined as the willingness of the customer to rely on the organization or brand to perform its stated function. Trust reduces uncertainty/risk and is viewed as a carefully thought out process, whereas brand affect may be an instantaneous response.[22] In many situations, trust means a customer believes that the marketer is reliable and has integrity. In many personal selling situations, trust means that a customer has confidence that the sales representative is honest, fair, and responsible and that his or her word can be relied on. If a delivery date is given, the buyer has confidence that the product will be shipped on time. When there is trust in a relationship, all partners believe that none will act opportunistically. Marketers, especially the marketers of services, establish trust by maintaining open and honest communication and by keeping the promises they make.

CHOICE REDUCTION AND HABIT

The fourth component of customer loyalty is **choice reduction and habit.** Contrary to traditional economic theory, consumer research shows that people have a natural tendency to reduce choices. In fact, consumers like to reduce their choices to a manageable set, usually not more than three.[23] People feel comfortable with familiar brands and well-known situations that have been rewarding. Part of customer loyalty, such as the absence of brand switching behavior, is based on an accumulation of experiences over time. With simple repetition, we become familiar with a brand, store, company, Web site, or search engine. We develop habits that result in continuity. For example, it has been estimated that consumers go to the same supermarket up to 90 percent of the time.[24]

There can be a switching cost associated with change to the unfamiliar, the untried, or the new. There may be a cost in time, money, or personal risk. In other words, as the adage "If it ain't broke, don't fix it" suggests, there may be a perceived risk in change. Perceived risk means the customer may be uncertain about the consequences of making a purchase. There may be perceived performance risk or social risk. The customer may think the new brand will not perform as well as the current brand. The customer may believe his or her friends will not like the new brand as well.

HISTORY WITH THE COMPANY

A final component of customer loyalty involves the customer's **history with the company.** One's history with the company influences one's habits. But we should draw a distinction between repeat behavior and contact history with the company and its image. A positive **corporate image**—the perception of the organization as a whole—can have a favorable impact on customer loyalty, creating habitual responses to the company name itself.[25] Wal-Mart, for example is known for everyday low prices while another department store, such as Nordstrom, may be known for excellent customer service. Thus, perceptions of the company's historical image can impact customer intentions, loyalty, and likelihood of buying. The CRM system, however, is usually more focused on a customer's actual purchasing history.

In many situations, people have a long history with a company. There may even be **intergenerational influences,** that is, within-family transmission of information, beliefs, and resources from one generation to the next.[26] For example, a customer who, as a child, saw his or her parents consistently purchase Ford cars might be expected to accept the parents' history of using the brand and remain loyal to Ford vehicles.

A customer's initial or regular experience with a product may be quite positive. Consider a long-time customer of Northwestern Mutual Life Insurance. The customer receives a letter that explains the company is now giving a superior underwriting price to non-smokers. The company is not limiting the better pricing to new customers but will provide it, retroactively, to all policyholders. The price of the customer's policy, therefore, is decreasing with no effort on the customer's part.[27] This positive customer experience, or unexpected delight, is bound to contribute to customer loyalty.

Service experiences are an important part of a customer's history with a company. A customer who calls the Butterball Turkey hotline on Thanksgiving Day with a problem and talks to a customer service representative who patiently listens to the problem may be eternally grateful to the company. Companies that create a mutually beneficial dialog to learn what the customer really wants engender loyalty.

Alternatively, consider the customer who telephones a catalog retailer with a complaint. After listening to a menu of options and pushing several buttons, the customer is put on hold. The music plays and periodically there is a recording that says, "All our service representatives are busy, but please stay on the line because your call is important to us." When the call is answered, the person seeking redress finds an unsympathetic and rude clerk on the other end of the line. In this situation, unsatisfactory complaint resolution will not create customer loyalty.

ATTITUDINAL AND BEHAVIORAL COMPONENTS OF LOYALTY

The five components that we have just discussed influence customer loyalty in different ways. Satisfaction, emotional bonding, and trust contribute to attitudinal loyalty. Choice reduction and habit, including perceptions of risk and the history with the organization, contribute to behavioral loyalty. Attitudinal and behavioral loyalty combine to then affect the degree of customer commitment and loyalty to products and organizations.

LOYALTY AS ONE-TO-ONE RELATIONSHIPS

To provide a customer relationship system that generates emotional commitment, organizations may benefit from understanding the bases of customer loyalty in online environments,[28] as well as toward different facets of the organization or its product. Loyalty is multi-faceted and more than a repetition of a behavior. As shown in Exhibit 5.6, customers can exhibit loyalty to price, brand, company, other customers, a place, or any number of other potential options.

Consider the cell phone. Some customers are loyal to the product itself. Such people know about different brands, plans, and the relative costs of each. Others who are not loyal to cell phones seem to be bewildered by the many plan options and ambivalent to alternative providers. But when people do express loyalty toward a certain brand of cell phone, then the company should reinforce its complementary, or flanker, products such as cell phone covers or hands-off connectors.

If customers feel loyalty toward the company, then institutional advertising, tours, and public relations might reinforce that attachment. Many purchasers of Saturn automobiles gather for reunions each year, thus exhibiting a type of loyalty toward the other purchasers of this car as well as toward the brand image of the car itself. Similar to Saturn, many organizations can benefit from carefully reinforcing the image of the target market.

While these examples are simple, it is clear that loyalty is a complex issue. The company's goal may be to develop a one-to-one, or customized, approach to building loyalty as shown in Exhibit 5.7. Frequently, organizations attempt to recognize individuals, cultivate relationships through interactions that delight customers, and develop feelings of trust within the community over time.

As discussed in Chapter 2, a one-to-one, or customization, strategy is tailored to the needs of the individual customer. When people walk into a bank in a small town, the employees typically recognize loyal customers and call them by name. The promise of effective CRM systems is the ability for organizations to acknowledge each customer—to mass personalize the offering. **Recognition** implies a personal greeting that is based on knowledge of the past history of interactions. Using data about past purchases in conjunction with other segmentation variables (demographics, lifestyles, geography), the organization may

---

EXHIBIT 5.6 | **LOYALTY AND ORGANIZATIONAL OPTIONS**

Customer loyalty to:	Organizational options
Brand	Brand image/positioning/extensions/flankers…promotion
Product	Accessories, complementary items, reliability…production
Company	Personal connections/reinforcement/trust…public relations
Customers	Interpersonal meetings, chats, reunions…target markets
Price	Discounts, coupons, everyday low pricing…efficiencies
Place	Outlets, aromas, sounds, excitement…atmospherics
Variety	New options, variations, flankers…production

EXHIBIT 5.7	LOYALTY AND CRM SYSTEM GUIDELINES

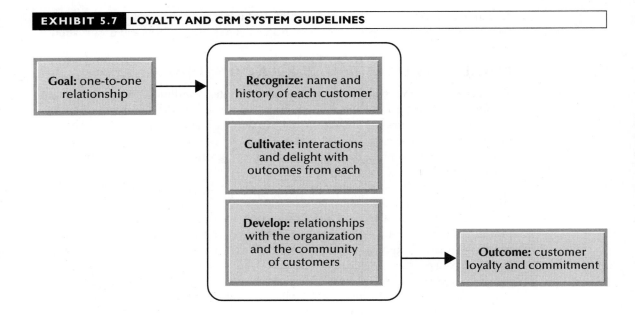

have a positive impact on attitudinal and behavioral commitment. In effect, the organization is interacting as if each customer were a platinum choice.

Cultivation implies meaningful interactions between the organization and the customer, similar to the courtship phase prior to marriage. The organization attempts to satisfy customer expectations with each interaction and/or to provide reasons for customers to revisit the Web site, catalog, or store, again and again. When we converse with other people, we exchange information, but when we talk with friends we avidly approach the interaction and are engaged in the joy of sharing feelings as well as ideas. Cultivation within CRM systems involves the need to gather information over time and to continually reinforce the type of loyalty that is important to the customer. When it works well, CRM systems allow the firm to create delightful interactions.

Development of the relationship with customers requires a clear image for the organization and all of its services or brands. When customers think of Disney, Dell, or Hershey's, a clear picture of quality in entertainment, computers, or chocolate comes to mind. Likewise, a particular image comes to the mind of a woman who buys a Coach purse and to the minds of the Saturn owners who gather for their reunions. As customers identify with the brand and with the people who use that brand, loyalty and commitment are reinforced.

FACTORS THAT MAY LESSEN CUSTOMER LOYALTY

If customers perceive that a company has a deficiency in any of the factors that positively contribute to customer loyalty, they may be less loyal. There are other factors that tend to lessen loyalty as well.

Competitive Parity

When the offerings of different organizations are not differentiated, **competitive parity** exists. If customers perceive that brands are identical, perceived risk is low and there is a greater tendency for brand switching as the likelihood of loyalty toward the product declines.

Variety-Seeking Behavior

As we have already mentioned, people who become bored and have a need for variety may engage in variety-seeking behavior. People may simply want a new experience because of the declining benefits associated with repeat patronage or because they feel energized by the prospect of having a new experience. Organizations can benefit from variety seeking behavior by satisfying the need and creating flanker brands, new flavors, or other extensions of the basic product.

Low Involvement

A low level of personal relevance or perceived importance of a product or service to the individual is referred to simply as **low involvement.** Low involvement consumers often engage in "satisfying" behavior in which they make decisions that are "good enough" and not necessarily optimal.[29] If a person has a low interest in a product category, he or she is less likely to be loyal to a particular company or brand.

Customers who are low in involvement tend to be **price sensitive,** another factor which lessens loyalty toward the brand or organization. Conversely, customers who are involved with the product tend to be less price sensitive. *Deal proneness*, or receptivity to sales promotion incentives, can also be used by organizations if they can provide the low cost option.

If a brand or company has a low **share of voice,** that is, if a brand's, store's, or company's relative promotional expenditures are low, customer loyalty may decline.[30] Customers may not know how to interact with the organization and may not get a clear picture of the community of customers, or the target base.

SUMMARY

There are two basic perspectives on brand loyalty—the behavioral approach and the attitudinal approach. The behavioral approach to brand loyalty investigates how consistent consumers are in their repurchase of a brand. The attitudinal approach to brand loyalty considers beliefs, emotional responses, and intentions that form a predisposition toward the brand that is expressed over time.

The term *customer loyalty* refers to a customer's commitment or attachment to a brand, store, manufacturer, service provider, or other entity based on favorable attitudes and behavioral responses, such as repeat purchases. Using attitude loyalty and behavior to provide a framework for thinking about customer loyalty yields four categories of customers: No Loyalty—customers have a weak attitude and low repeat patronage behavior; Inertia Loyalty—customers are strong on repeat behavior but weak on attitude; Latent Loyalty—customers have strong attitudes but repeat purchase is low; and Loyalty, customers are high in repeat purchase behavior and strong in attitude. Loyal customers are the most desirable customers because they purchase a large amount of the product and/or may advocate the product to others. Relationship commitment is defined as an enduring desire to maintain valued interactions.

The fundamental components that are expected to affect customer loyalty are customer satisfaction, emotional bonding, trust, choice reduction/habit, and company history. People can develop loyalty toward many facets of an organization—its product, its image, other customers, price, or brand image. To implement the promise of a one-to-one segmentation plan, organizations work to recognize each customer, cultivate the information and understanding of expectations and preferences, and develop a sense of community. Factors that may lessen loyalty include competitive parity, variety-seeking behavior, low involvement, price sensitivity, deal proneness, and a low share of voice or presence in the informational landscape.

KEY TERMS

attitudinal brand loyalty	development	relationalism
behavioral brand loyalty	divided loyalty	relationship commitment
brand affect	emotional bonding	share of voice
brand equity	history with the company	spurious loyalty
choice reduction/habit	indifference	switched loyalty
churn rate	inertia	switching cost
competitive parity	intergenerational	transactions
corporate image	latent loyalty	trust
cultivation	low involvement	undivided loyalty
customer loyalty	occasional switcher	variety-seeking behavior
customer satisfaction	perceived risk	zone of tolerance
deal proneness	price sensitive	
delightful surprises	recognition	

QUESTIONS FOR REVIEW AND CRITICAL THINKING

1. Define brand loyalty. What are its components?
2. What are the four types of customer loyalty?
3. What factors seem to affect customer loyalty?
4. Define customer satisfaction. What accounts for the difference between satisfaction and dissatisfaction?
5. How does a company develop customer trust?
6. Use Exhibit 5.7 to describe variations in your own loyalties to brands, organizations, prices, or places.
7. What factors tend to lessen customer loyalty?
8. Use the information from this chapter to suggest specific actions that your school, college, or university could take to increase student and alumni loyalty toward the institution, its services, and its image.
9. Select one of your favorite restaurants. What specific actions could the owners of the restaurant take to ensure that you are "delighted" with your next visit?

NOTES

1. Excerpt reprinted with permission from Dennis N. Bristow and Richard J. Sebastian, "Holy Cow! Wait 'til Next Year! A Closer Look at the Brand Loyalty of Chicago Cubs Baseball Fans," *Journal of Consumer Marketing* 18 (2001).

2. John C. Mowen and Michael Minor, *Consumer Behavior* (Englewood Cliffs, N.J.: Prentice-Hall, 1998): 436.

3. "Churn rate," at Investorwords.com at <http://www.investorwords.com/cgi-bin/getword.cgi?857>.

4. Yorick Odin, Nathalie Odin, and Pierre Valette-Florence, "Conceptual and Operational Aspects of Brand Loyalty: An Empirical Investigation," *Journal of Business Research* 53:2 (August 2001): 75–84.

5. Many psychologists believe in a three-component theory of attitudes. The ABC model is the traditional way to view attitudes. In this view, an attitude has three parts. The *A* component is the affective, or emotional, component. It reflects a person's feelings toward an object. Is the brand good or bad? Is it desirable? Likable? The *B* component is the behavioral component, which reflects the action the person wants to take toward the object. This component includes a predisposition to action. The *C* component is the cognitive component. It involves all the consumer's beliefs, knowledge, and thoughts about the object—the consumer's perception of the product's attributes or characteristics. Is it durable? Expensive?

6. Jagdish N. Sheth, Banwaari Mittal, and Bruce I. Newman, *Consumer Behavior* (Ft. Worth, Tex.: Dryden Press, 1999): 700.

7. Jill Griffin, "Learn the Loyalty Levels to Build Customer Base," *Austin Business Journal,* print edition (1 December 2000): available at <http://austin.bizjournals.com/austin/stories/2000/12/04/smallb3.html> and Alan S. Dick and Kunal Basu, "Customer Loyalty: Toward an Integrated Conceptual Framework," *Journal of the Academy of Marketing Science* (spring 1994): 99–113.

8. Robert Morgan and Shelby D. Hunt, "The Commitment-Trust Theory of Relationship Marketing," *Journal of Marketing* (July 1994), and Christine Moorman, Rohit Deshpande, and Gerald Zaltman, "Factors Affecting Trust in Market Research Relationships," *Journal of Marketing* (January 1993)

9. Ellen Garbarino and Mark S. Johnson, "The Different Roles of Satisfaction, Trust, and Commitment in Customer Relationships," *Journal of Marketing* 63:2 (April 1999): 70–87.

10. Ibid.

11. Uta Juttner and Hans Peter Wehrli, "Relationship Marketing from a Value System Perspective," *International Journal of Service Industry Management* 5:5 (1995): 54–73.

12. Michael Harvey and Cheri Speier, "Developing an Inter-Organization Relational Management Perspective," *Journal of Marketing Channels* 7:4 (2000): 23–44.

13. For alternative views of this concept see Jagdish N. Sheth, Banwaari Mittal, and Bruce I. Newman, *Consumer Behavior* (Ft. Worth, Tex.: Dryden Press, 1999): 702–706 and Arjun Chaudhuri and Morris B. Holbrook, "The Chain of Effects from Brand Trust and Brand Affect to Brand Performance," *Journal of Marketing* (April 2001): 81–93.

14. Richard L. Oliver, "Cognitive, Affective, and Attribute Bases of the Satisfaction Response," *Journal of Consumer Research* 20 (December 1993): 418–430.

15. Hans Kasper, Piet van Helsdingen, and Wouter de Vries, Jr., *Service Marketing Management: An International Perspective* (West Sussex, England: John Wiley and Sons, 1999): 196.

16. Frank R. Kardes, *Consumer Behavior* (Reading, Mass.: Addison-Wessley, 1999): 110.

17. Arjun Chaudhuri and Morris B. Holbrook, "The Chain of Effects from Brand Trust and Brand Affect to Brand Performance," *Journal of Marketing* (April 2001): 81–93.

18. The liabilities and negative associations linked to a brand are also part of brand equity, but they do not apply in this example.

19. Tony Cram, *Customers that Count* (London: Financial Times-Prentice Hall, 2001):18.

20. Michael K. Rich, "Are We Losing Trust through Technology?" *Journal of Business & Industrial Marketing* 17:2/3 (2002): 215–222.

21. Robert Morgan and Shelby D. Hunt, "The Commitment-Trust Theory of Relationship Marketing," *Journal of Marketing* (July 1994), and Christine Moorman, Rohit Deshpande, and Gerald Zaltman, "Factors Affecting Trust in Market Research Relationships," *Journal of Marketing* (January 1993).

22. Arjun Chaudhuri and Morris B. Holbrook, "The Chain of Effects from Brand Trust and Brand Affect to Brand Performance: The Role of Brand Loyalty," *Journal of Marketing* 65:2 (April 2001): 81–93.

23. Jagdish N. Sheth and Atul Pavatiyar, "Relationship Marketing in Consumer Markets, Antecedents and Consequences," *Journal of the Academy of Marketing Science* (fall 1995): 263.

24. Jagdish N. Sheth and Atul Pavatiyar, "Relationship Marketing in Consumer Markets, Antecedents and Consequences," *Journal of the Academy of Marketing Science* (fall 1995): 256.

25. T. W. Andreassen, " What Drives Customer Loyalty with Complaint Resolution?" *Journal of Service Research* (May 1999): 324–332.

26. Elizabeth S. Moore, William L. Wilkie, and Richard J. Lutz, "Passing the Torch: Intergenerational Influences as a Source of Brand Equity," *Journal of Marketing* (April 2002): 17.

27. Exclusive interview with Fred Reichheld for *Relationship Management Report* May (June 1999) 1:2;] <http://www3.ncr.com/product/publications/crm2/fred-s.html>.

28. Srini S. Srinivasan, Rolph Anderson, and Kishore Ponnabolu, "Customer Loyalty in E-Commerce: An Exploration of Its Antecedents and Consequences," *Journal of Retailing* 78 (2002): 41–50.

29. John C. Mowen and Michael Minor, *Consumer Behavior* (Englewood Cliffs, N.J.: Prentice-Hall, 1998): 395.

30. Arjun Chaudhuri and Morris B. Holbrook, "The Chain of Effects from Brand Trust and Brand Affect to Brand Performance," *Journal of Marketing* (April 2001): 81–93.

6

Customer Retention Strategies

One way to retain customers is to give them better service than they expected. Avis's rental car business, for example, trains its frontline employees to provide first-rate service. Employees enjoy the freedom to adjust their services to exceed customer expectations. Consider the experience of Ernesto Martinez, a U.S. government employee from El Paso, Texas.

Martinez, accompanied by his boss and a coworker, was standing at an Avis car rental counter in Monterey, California. He couldn't understand why the Avis sales agents were fussing over his license.

"Uh-oh," the agent, Suzy Caston, exclaimed after Martinez passed his license across the counter.

"Something is going to have to be done about that," said another.

"Do something," a third agent told Caston.

That day was Martinez's 57th birthday, and Caston did something about it. First, she gave Martinez a free upgrade to the biggest Cadillac on the Avis lot. Then she tipped off his hotel—a Hyatt Regency—which assigned him to a deluxe room with a king-size bed and a window facing the golf course.

"It's nice to be able to spoil people," says Caston, an Avis employee for eight years. "He was coming out of his skin, he was so excited."

Martinez still hasn't gotten over it. "I've been working for the government for 30 years and I've traveled on my birthday before. But nobody has ever treated me like that," he said. "Thanks to Suzy, it turned out to be a great day. Her gracious act impressed the heck out of a lot of seasoned travelers who thought they'd experienced about everything."[1]

This chapter's focus is on using just such effective CRM techniques to retain existing customers and to convert high-value customers into loyal advocates.

THE EVOLUTION OF RELATIONSHIP MARKETING PROGRAMS

Strategies of organization-customer relationships have been evolving in the past 25 years. It is useful to begin our discussion of retention by discussing three aspects of relationship programs: financial, social, and structural-interactive. The categories and a few implications of each for the organization are shown in Exhibit 6.1.

FINANCIAL RELATIONSHIPS: FREQUENT BUYER PROGRAMS

Frequent buyer programs have been called rewards programs, loyalty programs, and other names. They are among the earliest efforts to retain an organization's best customers, and most are based on financial incentives. **Financial incentives** are discounts, product upgrades, or prizes that serve as rewards for customers who exhibit loyalty or who frequently purchase from the organization. Season ticket holders for professional hockey games or the opera receive discounts for establishing a relationship with the organization.

EXHIBIT 6.1	ASPECTS OF RELATIONSHIP PROGRAMS
Relational facet	**Organizational implications**
Financial incentives	Frequent flyer/reader/buyer/visitor...rewards
	Discounts, product upgrades, awards, prizes
	Related products or providers expand the net
	Increased customer loyalty to price, incentives
Social bonding	Friendly companionship, trust...connections
	Personal insights, recognition, mutual affection
	Interpersonal interactions expand the link
	Increased customer loyalty to the organization
Structural-interactions	Systemic mass personalization...management
	Mass personalization, cultivation, simulation
	Artificial intelligence continues the connections
	Increased customer loyalty to the experiences

Banks often offer higher interest rates for deposits that will be kept in an account for a longer duration. Frequent flyer programs offer a free trip or upgrades in seating after a customer flies a certain number of segments or miles.

America West's FlightFund is a typical frequent buyer program. It offers travelers a chance to enjoy awards once they have accumulated a minimum of 20,000 FlightFund miles. Certificates are redeemable for award travel on America West, America West Express, and select domestic and international carriers. Awards can also be redeemed with participating FlightFund hotel and car rental partners, which include many different hotel chains and rental car agencies. In addition to being able to earn miles by patronizing car, hotel, and airline partners, FlightFund members can earn miles by using MCI long distance service, H&R Block, and the America West FlightFund Visa card. Thus, a financial benefit—in the form of travel, a hotel room, a rental car, or some other benefit—is the reward for increased patronage of America West and its partners.

As another example, consider the Waldenbooks Preferred Reader program through which members pay an annual membership fee, receive a percentage discount on purchases, and receive a gift certificate on every $100 of purchasing volume. Early in the process of implementing this program, Waldenbooks was successful, with over 4.5 million enrolled members and 20 million new dollars worth of customer-volunteered funds. Customers want to be treated as "special" and are quite willing to pay for it.[2]

Relationships that concentrate *exclusively* on incentives tend to be weak. The average American consumer participates in 3.2 incentive programs, and some consumers belong to 10 or more.[3] A major disadvantage of a frequent buyer reward program is that competitors can easily duplicate financial incentive programs and offer higher rewards. The novelty of reward programs wears off and many customers do not want to load their wallets with frequent buyer cards just to get a slight discount. Additionally, reward programs may increase customer loyalty to price or to the incentive as opposed to loyalty to the organization or its brand.

SOCIAL BONDING

The formation of a social bond between the organization and its customers may create a stronger relationship. A **social bond** refers to a friendly companionship or an affective tie. Many people know about the thousands of Saturn owners who converge annually on the car company's headquarters in Spring Hill, Tennessee, for a barbecue, a plant tour, and a chance to talk with other Saturn owners about how much they love their cars.

Similarly, Chrysler attempts to bond with its Jeep owners. One weekend each year, dozens of owners driving their Jeeps meet in the mountains of the western United States for Chrysler's "Jeep Jamboree." For two days and nights, they get to test their vehicles on narrow roads in nature's roughest terrain. The Jeep Jamboree adventure offers a rare chance for customers to experience the promise of Jeep commercials. Since only a small proportion of sport-utility vehicle owners ever get a chance to drive off-road, the relationship-marketing event accomplishes several objectives. Chrysler's event allows customers to establish a bond with other customers, the organization, the product, and the brand. Chrysler expects participants in the jamborees to become ambassadors for the brand.

There are many other examples of actions by organizations, particularly services, to increase the social bond with their customers. The banker may host an annual

Christmas party, the hairstylist engages in informal conversation during each visit, and the personal trainer celebrates each gain in fitness achieved. Interpersonal interactions between people within the organization and customers strengthen the linkage and decrease the likelihood that the customer will want to switch providers; thus, efforts that focus on social bonds may increase customer loyalty to the organization itself. However, it does not seem feasible for chewing gum manufacturers to call each buyer with a personalized expression of thanks, does it?

STRUCTURAL-INTERACTIVE RELATIONSHIPS

When a stock broker, such as Charles Schwab & Co., provides computer software so that a client can check stock quotes, evaluate portfolio histories, get information about companies, and trade stocks over the Internet, it has created a structure to enhance interactions with its customers. It provides the solution to an important customer problem. **Structural-interactive relationships** use system design to solve problems, reinforce purchases, and recognize the importance of each customer. Relationships based on structural interactions do not depend on the relationship-building skills of a particular service provider, as in the traditional customer-stockbroker relationship, but on the service delivery system itself.

Many CRM systems use information technology to focus on delivering customized or personalized benefits. For example, an Internet retailer may use its database to send e-mail messages about discounted items to its regular customers. As other examples, consider the receipt of an electronic thank you e-mail from an organization immediately after you have purchased a product, the automatic sign-up to a newsletter or chat room after product purchase, and the reminder message of an imminent birthday a year after you have purchased from an organization on the Web. Structural-interaction is the strategic "so-what" for CRM systems of the financial and social aspects to relationships. However, such interactions are not without their cautions. Consider the following example of questionable ethics within a structural-interaction:

> An example…would be a practice of attempting to make a piece of generally distributed advertising appear to be a word-of-mouth suggestion from a friend. In an envelope that appears to be hand-addressed (although generated as a computer cursive font) is an advertisement that appears to be torn from a newspaper (complete with ragged edges). The advertisement can appear within what appears to be closing stock quotations. Attached to this advertisement is a yellow "sticky" note with the scribbled message, "I thought you might enjoy this. I know I have," signed only with a common first name or maybe only an initial.[4]

The example suggests that the basic tenets of a relationship for social bonding have been violated. While the technology was used effectively to personalize the message, recognize the customer, and offer a solution to a problem in a concise manner, the customer's trust and impression of the organization may not be positive.

THE COMPLETE CRM FOR RETAINING CUSTOMERS

Ideally, a complete CRM system combines the customer benefits of each of these types of relationship strategies: value-added incentives, emotional bonding, an interactive dialog, customized/personalized treatment, and an eye toward the ethics of the situation. A key objective of a comprehensive CRM system is its ability to retain customers at each stage of the customer life cycle.

CUSTOMER LIFE CYCLE

The stages a customer goes through from the time before deciding to do business with an organization until he or she decides to stop being a customer is called the **customer life cycle,** shown in Exhibit 6.2.

When a customer makes an initial purchase, he or she does so to satisfy a need, want, or desire. During the first voluntary transaction, the customer exchanges money, or something of value worth the price of the offering, for something of value—typically the good or service provided by the organization. In other words, both parties benefit because something is given up by each and something is received by each. In Exhibit 6.2, we label this the **acquisition stage**—the customer completes the initial transactional exchange. Notice that even at this stage, the life value of the customer is important in that suspects are qualified to be prospects based on an estimate of lifetime value (to be discussed further in Chapter 8).

In some situations, the initial transaction is the only transaction that ever occurs and the customer is a one-time buyer who is then lost. The benefit of CRM systems is to track

EXHIBIT 6.2   PICTURING THE CUSTOMER LIFE CYCLE

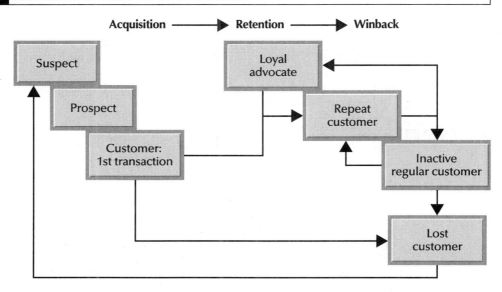

the reasons for losing such initial purchasers and to make corrections to winback strategies where appropriate (a topic for Chapter 7).

However, once an exchange is made, CRM systems stress understanding customers so that the organization can offer them a better product or service and thereby generate additional exchanges. Thus, the CRM objective is to retain profitable customers and ultimately have customers choose to become loyal advocates. In our exhibit, we call this the **retention stage,** implying that the customer is a loyal advocate or at least intends to repeat another exchange with the same organization.

Sometimes, a regular customer becomes inactive or becomes a customer of a competitor. There are a number of CRM winback strategies to regain high-value lost customers. A **winback stage** suggests that the organization will take special steps to have a customer enter into another exchange with the organization. Again, to determine whether or not to engage in winback strategies, organizations first must consider the lost customer to be a "suspect," and ask whether or not the customer should be retained. An effective acquisition strategy is best achieved by having an effective retention strategy. Therefore, we begin our discussion of CRM strategy with retention strategies and wait until the next chapter to discuss customer winback and acquisition issues.

CUSTOMER RETENTION STRATEGY

A plan identifying what basic retention objectives will be pursued and how they will be achieved in the time available is considered to be a **customer retention strategy.** A retention strategy entails commitment to certain courses of action, t. The **attrition rate,** or **churn,** is the percentage of customers lost in a given period, typically a year. The **retention rate** (the percentage of customers expected to keep doing business with the organization) is then 1- the attrition rate.

There are a number of reasons why customers terminate relationships.[5] Some of the most common are shown in Exhibit 6.3. People can seek variety for its own sake. If the organization fails to deliver more than customers expect, disconfirmation and **dissatisfaction** can result. A brand switch may occur if customers perceive that a competitive offering has a relative advantage—a better set of features and benefits to meet their needs. A loss of need can occur as, for example, we grow out of the need for diapers or braces for our teeth.

EXHIBIT 6.3	REASONS FOR LOST CUSTOMERS
Novelty seeking	A need, due to satiation, or a drive, due to thrill-seeking, or an intellectual curiosity that causes people to choose variety over time
Dissatisfaction	The actual performance(s) fell short of expectations
Relative advantage	The customer perceives a higher benefit value associated with an alternative choice and believes it to be more gratifying
Conflict	A disagreement in which the customer's and the company's views seem to be incompatible
Loss of trust	The customer has no confidence that the organization can reliably fulfill its promises
Cease to need	The product or solution is no longer required

Unresolved conflicts and a **loss of trust** may imply that the organization failed to respond to complaints or failed to integrate its feedback process with its customer service and retention staff.

The remainder of this chapter discusses how effective customer retention strategies lessen the chance that these considerations will arise. We begin by discussing the basic needs for a welcome strategy, reliability, responsiveness, recognition, and personalization that should decrease attrition and increase customers' lifetime value.

The Welcome

Fundamental to a retention strategy is the notion that making a sale is the beginning and not the end of the marketing effort. A good first step is to thank the customer for the order.[6] **A welcome strategy** acknowledges the organization's appreciation for the initiation of a relationship or for the exchange. The welcome serves many purposes. The first is the opportunity to create a "delightful surprise." The customer may not anticipate a thank you note, telephone call, or other customer contact. Making a good first impression can have long-lasting value. Second, the welcome may provide the first touch point where additional customer information may be collected. Third, the welcome stage provides the opportunity to reassure the buyer that he or she made the correct choice.

In many post-purchase situations, a buyer may feel uneasy about a purchase. Will the tires be good on snow? Will someone be surprised that I bought this brand instead of that one? Second thoughts can create an uneasy feeling, a sensation that the decision-making process may have yielded the wrong decision. **Cognitive dissonance** is a psychologically uncomfortable post-purchase feeling. More specifically, it refers to the negative feelings, or "buyer's remorse," that can follow a commitment to purchase.

Suppose the car owner has bought the tires and has left the shop; there's no turning back now. She wonders, "Should I have bought Michelin tires instead, even though the price was a bit higher?" Dissonance theory describes such feelings as a sense of psychic tension, which the individual will seek to relieve. Buyers reduce cognitive dissonance by focusing on the advantages of the purchase—by carrying out post-purchase evaluation in a way that supports the choice made. They may mentally downgrade the unselected alternatives and play up the advantages of the selected brand to convince themselves that they made the right choice.

Because they are prone to rationalize choice, buyers may seek reinforcement from friends or from the seller, which explains the need for and the value of supportive information during the welcome stage. Promising good service, telling the buyer to come right back if there's any trouble and "we'll fix it up," and giving a toll-free hot line number help reduce dissonance and encourage repeat business.

At the time of the initial transaction, certain data (item purchased, zip code, etc,) will be entered into each new customer's record. During the welcome stage, other data (preferences for future e-mail correspondence and other do-not-contact information) can be entered into the CRM system. As the following example illustrates, the customer should not be overburdened with data collection at this point in the customer life cycle.

> When you think about it, establishing a relationship online isn't all that different from starting a dating relationship.[7] The problem is that a lot of Internet companies approach their first date with a list of 20 questions: "Could you please fill

out this three-page form about your income, family history, and medical background?" Imagine if that were the first question that a prospective romantic interest asked you! It's absurd to expect people to respond to such questions before you've established a certain level of trust with them.

Instead, what if you started by asking a customer three or four little questions? After establishing that this potential "date" is interested in what you have to offer, you and this customer could begin sharing information back and forth. One of our clients, a San Francisco startup called myplay, is wooing customers with a similar approach. The site is an online personal storage locker for customers' favorite music. When you first sign up, myplay sends you a few preliminary questions. Then, using your answers to those questions, it customizes your locker. The site asks you a few more questions each time it contacts you. Over time, the organization gets to know you, and you get to know, and to trust, the organization.

Thus, a welcome signifies the first hello and is similar to the concept of a continuing courtship. The goal is to ask for the next transaction or date, but only when the timing is right.

Reliability

Retaining customers requires that the products and services that are sold are reliable. From this perspective, **reliability** means the organization can repeat the exchange time and time again with the same satisfying results. Customers expect companies to keep their promises. When they make repeat purchases they expect consistent performance. Loyal McDonald's customers know exactly what they will experience when they go to their local restaurant for lunch. More importantly, when traveling almost anywhere on the planet, the sign of those golden arches implies that the same type of quality, friendly service, and options will be available as well. There are few surprises. Offering the "tried and true" is a means to establish trust and relationship commitment.

Ensuring consistent quality and promoting reliability are fundamental to every customer retention strategy. Consider, for example, the customer who shops at Banana Republic regularly or the consumer who always buys Heinz ketchup. Do the marketers of Banana Republic or Heinz ketchup advertise to this customer? Yes. Is that a waste of money? The answer is no, for the very pragmatic reason that even the most loyal customers must be reminded that a store or product has served them well over time and that it has dependable benefits that make it attractive. This is especially true when competitors tempt loyal customers with their own promotional messages. Sending reminders to existing customers, who are already predisposed to a message, may be a meaningful promotional objective in a retention strategy.

Responsiveness

Customers want to be treated right. **Responsiveness** implies that the organization shows customers it really cares about their needs and feelings. A dentist that finds she is running late may have the receptionist call people with appointments to tell them that they should arrive 15 minutes later than their scheduled appointment. The patients appreciate that the dentist cares enough about them to prevent their spending excess time in the waiting room.

Sometimes customer retention is simply avoiding driving customers away.[8] To lose customers, an organization often has to be apathetic, insensible, impolite, and/or rude. Unfortunately, customers experience uncaring and ill-mannered behavior all the time. How many times have you been in a retail store when the clerk was on the phone talking to a relative about dinner or the clerk was talking to another clerk without a concern about your spending time waiting for them? How many times have you waited over an hour to see your doctor or dentist? It is a simple fact that some companies just are not training their front line employees to be responsive to customer needs. Making it right every time a customer makes contact with the organization is a key to customer retention.

Effective marketers recognize that loyal employees create loyal customers. There is a high correlation between employee satisfaction and customer satisfaction. Employee training can be very helpful in making customer experiences consistent and up to expectations. For example, Radio Shack advertises the slogan "You've got questions; we've got answers." Customers will patronize the store to learn how to solve electronics problems as long as Radio Shack employees remain informative, helpful, and polite.

The term **internal marketing** is often used by marketers, especially those in service businesses, when referring to public relations efforts aimed at their own employees who have contact with the ultimate consumer or who have a direct effect on the ultimate consumer's satisfaction with the product. The objective of internal marketing may be to have employees recognize their role in the organization's effort to be responsive.

Customer-contact employees should have the authority as well as the responsibility for day-to-day operational activities and CRM decisions. When interacting with customers, they may also need to be empowered to act on their own. For example, an employee should be able to grant a refund or adjust an invoice without management approval. An organization with an effective CRM must be responsive to questions, service needs, and complaints. We cover additional aspects of these issues later in this chapter.

Recognition

An effective CRM recognizes relationship anniversaries and shows appreciation for landmarks events. **Recognition** refers to special attention or appreciation that identifies someone as having been known before. For example, the address label on *Sunset Magazine* reads *Sybil Arnold, Valued Reader for over 25 years*. An e-mail is sent informing a retailer that its cumulative purchases surpassed 1,000 cases. A car dealer is notified it is being honored with the *Best Dealer in the State* award. People respond to recognition. Recognition and appreciation help maintain and reinforce relationships.

Personalization

When the organization can use its CRM system to tailor promotions and products to the specific customer, **personalization** is present. In essence, this is the cultivation and development aspect of the CRM approach. The information technology behind personalization is sophisticated. First, we will briefly mention the concept of an **offer engine**,[9] which is a rules-based series of computer algorithms and templates. An offer engine takes customer data after it is analyzed and applies it to create the offer or message that is appropriate to the individual customer. The offer may be a birthday greeting or a special occasion reminder. The offer engine is programmed to be goal oriented. It may offer gift ideas or cross-sell complementary purchases. It analyzes purchase history and schedules, and it can handle event offers. For example, Helzberg Diamonds, which has 191 stores in 28 states, uses CRM to identify customers who responded to special sales promotions in the past. The organization then mails letters and brochures encouraging these customers to visit the store for similar promotions.

Many marketers offer personalized Web sites. Charles Schwab & Company, a stock brokerage firm, offers MySchwab.com to its regular customers. It is a Web site that provides account and portfolio information, current stock market news, financial reports, and other investment tools personalized for individual investors.

Depending on the CRM system, the information technology on a Web site may anticipate and personalize unfolding customer interactions. Amazon.com is more than a bookstore; it is a personalized online shopping experience. Customers are given recommendations based on past transaction data and based on the behavior or opinions of other "like" people who have visited and requested information from the Web site.[10] Someone who purchased the first four Harry Potter books and has given permission to be contacted may get an e-mail that the next book in the series is about to be published.

Likewise, real time personalizations can be incorporated into messages that change as individuals surf a Web site. An individual's clickstream may indicate which goods or services were of most interest to the Web site visitor. For example, if a visitor at Amazon.com searches for "Steve Goodman's recording Go Cubs Go," the Web site might indicate the song is included on the recording *Cubs Greatest Hits: Songs and Live Calls that Rock Wrigley*. The site's clickstream analysis may indicate that a recommendation for the book *Banks to Sandberg to Grace: Five Decades of Love and Frustration with the Chicago Cubs* should also be given to the visitor, who is apparently a Cubs fan. The Web site prints out a message, "Customers who bought [this item] also bought ...."

In many circumstances, the offer engine determines what "free ride" promotions will accompany other messages. A so-called **free ride** is a message that accompanies another message, such as a monthly statement. For example, "The miles you've earned, and the ones you could," is a message on the outside of an envelope containing a Delta Sky Miles statement of total available miles. Inside there are special offers for Earthlink, Nextel, Dollar Rent a Car, Comfort Inn, LendingTree.com, and other Sky Miles partners. The bulk of the marketing costs are associated with the letter that must be sent; therefore, the additional messages get a "free ride."

Recognition, reward, and many of the issues we describe next are interrelated with personalization.

Access Strategy and Customer-Initiated Communication

Customers may need to contact the organization. Marketers must plan an **access strategy** identifying how customers will be able to interact with the organization. How easy is it for a customer to contact the organization? To return a product? To contact technical support? To talk to a human customer service representative? To change a mailing address? Is access to the organization quick and hassle-free? If it is not, the organization may lose customers. An effective retention strategy plans access for its average customers and its high value customers.

Communication is the process of exchanging information with and conveying meaning to others. The traditional communication process is generally thought to be an organization-initiated process. To achieve an effective exchange of meaning, the organization must consider the intended message, channel (medium), and receiver characteristics as shown in Exhibit 6.4. During the traditional communication process, a source encodes a message that is sent through a channel and the receiver decodes that message. For example, suppose Chevrolet wants its customers to know its pick-up trucks are durable, high-quality products that help drivers enjoy driving in rugged terrain. Encoding is the process of translating the idea to be communicated into a symbolic message consisting of words, pictures, numbers, gestures, or the like. Chevrolet uses a magazine advertisement (channel) that has a picture of a pick-up easily negotiating a gravel road in the mountains. The sender's idea is also encoded by using the tag line "Like a Rock." Decoding is the mental process by which the receiver interprets the meaning of the message. In the magazine advertisement, if the receiver interprets the message "Like a Rock" to mean that Chevrolet pick-up trucks are tough, sturdy, and long lasting, the communication has worked.

To ensure that appropriate decoding has occurred, some companies have only a few customer contact (touch) points, while others have many ways to access the organization. An organization may have a mailing address, sales personnel, a customer service telephone call center, an Internet Web site, a fax telephone line, kiosks, in-store contact, and other ways that a customer can access the organization. Suppose a customer initiates communication with an organization by calling a toll-free number or by visiting the organization's Web site. This is a customer-initiated communication, a type of organization access that is growing in importance. One expert believes that "the future of communications will be shifting the transfer of information from the organization and having the customer access the information."[11]

EXHIBIT 6.4   **TRADITIONAL COMMUNICATION PROCESS**

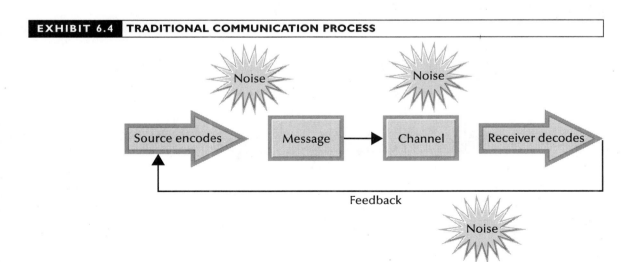

In the **customer-initiated communication** process, the traditional receiver, that is the customer to whom information is to be communicated, begins the process by searching for information. Typically, the customer has a question about product care or usage, a question about account status, or a need to respond to dissatisfaction. In this sense, the communication process begins when the customer recognizes an information need and selects the channel to access.

For example, a credit-card customer who wishes to know an account balance may choose to make a telephone call to the organization. The next step in the process is for the customer to request information by identifying a subject matter. Suppose a telephone call is made and the customer hears a recording that gives a menu of options. The customer selects the appropriate option and then hears the message. Alternatively, the customer may choose to search the organization's Web site and then select the appropriate link to the Web site where the source's message is stored. Exhibit 6.5 illustrates the Customer Initiated Communication process.

Think about a typical 800 number phone call to the supplier of an Internet service. Have you ever received several busy signals, or have you ever heard a recording say, "Please hold for the next available service representative"? Many a customer has been lost while music played and a recorded voice said, "Your call is important to us. Please do not hang up." Companies need to be responsive to the customer's need for time.

> One company that is providing a solution to the influx of e-mail and Web inquiries as well as improved Web self-service is IslandData (www.island-data.com), whose Express Response-hosted application is designed to profile the content, intent, tone and urgency of an inquiry through natural language concept finders. This process helps identify actions that should be taken, such as offering a cross-sell or up-sell opportunity, and helps identify customer profitability as well.[12]

EXHIBIT 6.5   CUSTOMER-INITIATED COMMUNICATION

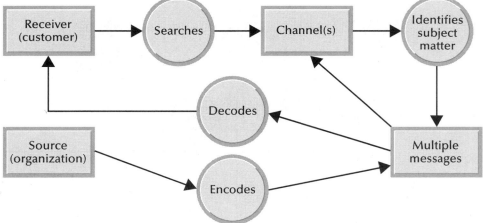

This type of Web site access is a way for an organization to provide customer-initiated interactions with its customers while customers help themselves. Software is now available to facilitate the process. The best customers may be provided with **priority access** so that they have a special number or another channel to gain quick access to the organization. Many airlines provide their best customers with special lines in airports to reduce waiting times and to increase the feeling of special treatment.

An access strategy also establishes what type of information may be gathered at each customer touch point. Use of a "registration" form before initial access is allowed is one means of gathering initial information from customers. For many organizations, a decision that must be made is whether or not the customer should be able to change his or her record. Making decisions about simple changes, such as a new e-mail address, is easier than making decisions that would allow the customer to change more critical information.

Reward Strategy

As we mentioned at the beginning of this chapter, frequent buyer programs (rewards or loyalty programs) were among the earliest efforts to retain an organization's best customers. Typically, frequent customers are awarded redeemable points that can be converted into free services, upgrades in class, and/or exchange of other products and services. The process to redeem points or to obtain rewards should be uncomplicated and easy to administer.

A retention strategy recognizes the need to reward customers for their loyalty. Something as simple as a mint on a pillow or an automatic later check out time may increase a hotel customer's loyalty. Something unexpected, such as a concierge who goes out of the way to secure that hard-to-get restaurant reservation or ticket to a championship sporting event may create an advocate who tells others about the experience.

In its most basic form, a rewards program provides its best customers with preferential treatment or special incentives. Marriott International hotels provide complementary *USA Today* newspapers for their Rewards Plus customers. Several times a year, Foxwoods Resort Casino holds an invitation-only golf tournament for some of its best customers. The casino uses its CRM system to identify people likely to accept the invitation, knowing that once they come for golf, they'll also spend money eating, drinking, and gambling. However, creating a moment that will last forever will have greater benefit than the short-term revenue gained.

Priority access and advanced notification about price deals or special events make it evident to an organization's best customers that they are important. For example, it is a simple reward when Charles Schwab Retail IPO Services tells its signature platinum customers that it is pleased to announce that they are eligible to participate in one of Schwab's client companies' public offerings.

Every organization should recognize that a frequent buyer program offers more than the opportunity to increase an organization's share of a customer's business. A loyalty program is an opportunity to gather information about the customer's shopping and purchase behavior. It is also an opportunity to keep in touch with the customer monthly or quarterly when a points statement is sent. It is an opportunity to customize the services a customer gets each time the customer makes contact with the organization.

We mentioned up-selling and cross-selling in Chapter 1. By marketing customers upgraded products or additional products that will better satisfy their needs, the CRM program can expand the benefits of the relationship. American Express offers its Platinum and Gold Card members advance notice of and access to prime tickets for concerts and sporting events. Value-added incentives such as these can change customer perceptions. The customer will, hopefully, associate added rewards with the organization. At the same time, the customer's value to the organization increases.

Many rewards programs have agreements with partner organizations. Typically, **Partnership Management Programs (PMPs)** are arranged so that customers can earn additional points by making purchases from other organizations. "The miles you've earned, and the ones you could," is a message on the outside of an envelope containing a Delta Sky Miles statement of total available miles. Inside there are special offers for Earthlink, Nextel, Dollar Rent a Car, Comfort Inn, LendingTree.com, and other Sky Miles Partners.

Many rewards programs also build in switching costs for their customers. Companies may build in financial penalties, time loss, or psychological barriers to exit a program—switching costs. These switching costs are a means of retaining customers, or at least of having customers pause before they end a relationship with the organization.

A simple example is a **termination penalty** when a saver must pay a penalty for withdrawing money from a bank's CD account. A more complex situation exists when a marketer creates a continuous, long-term solution to one of its customer's operating problems. For example, a wholesaler offers computer software that controls inventory and automated ordering to its retail customers. Customers trained on this system have extensive switching costs if they wish to do business with a competitor.

A frequent rental car customer who has a minor complaint may be less likely to switch to a competitor if there is a switching cost for doing so. For example, the typical member of a reward program goes through a streamline process when he or she rents a car. To switch to another car company requires entering considerable information (address, credit card number, car preferences, etc.) and perhaps losing the platinum status enjoyed with the current organization. Effective marketers build switching costs into their programs and discretely communicate them to their customers.[13]

PROBLEM IDENTIFICATION AND MANAGEMENT

If a customer has a problem with a product or some aspect of customer service, the organization is better off if the customer tells the company representatives about it than if the customer switches to a competitor or tells someone else about the problem. Negative word-of-mouth communications can cause other customers to be lost.

An effective CRM system should have numerous mechanisms for identifying customer problems. It is essential that the organization understand the voice of the customer. Acting rather than reacting—anticipating changing customer needs—may save many customers from defecting.

Customer satisfaction surveys are an essential ingredient of CRM. They identify problems that are widespread among many customers. Typically, customers are asked questions such as this one: How satisfied are you with technical support? Customers are asked to respond completely satisfied, somewhat satisfied, neither satisfied nor dissatisfied, somewhat dissatisfied, or completely dissatisfied. These measurements are the topic of Chapter 10, which examines the customer satisfaction survey.

In retail and service settings, mystery shoppers may identify problems. **Mystery shoppers** may act as customers and pretend to be interested in a particular product or service in order to observe actions of sales personnel. After leaving the store, the "shopper" evaluates the salesperson's performance and identifies any problems that need to be corrected. As organizations solicit mystery shoppers, they may also create positive opinion leaders for the product or service concept.

At a minimum, Web sites should have a Contact Us feature that allows customers to inform the company of problems, all contact points (i.e. product package, promotional advertisements, brochures, letters, etc.) should contain information on how to reach the organization if a need arises.

CONFLICTS AND CUSTOMER COMPLAINT MANAGEMENT

Customers may be dissatisfied with a product or a service's performance. What can a customer do when he or she is dissatisfied? While there are many alternative actions that can result from dissatisfaction,[14] the most common customer responses are logical. Many people simply do nothing. They take no action and tell no other people, particularly if the purchase is of little value monetarily or psychologically. As the investment in the purchase or the product increases, customers who are dissatisfied may vow to avoid the product and organization in the future, or they may begin to talk to others. If engaging in negative word-of-mouth behavior is insufficient, dissatisfied customers may seek redress from the organization, return the product, or complain to regulatory agencies or the media.

When customers have a problem, they want the solution to be easy and hassle free. The uninformed organization can do nothing if there is no communication about the dissatisfaction. Customer complaints indicate customer dissatisfaction with the purchase or conflicts with the organization. There are several factors that influence a customer's decision to complain.[15] These factors include the level of dissatisfaction, attribution of blame, cost/benefits of actions, and personal characteristics.

There are degrees, or **levels of dissatisfaction,** that can conceivably range from a mild displeasure to raging anger. If the difference between performance and expectations was not great, customers may not be upset or greatly troubled by their dissatisfaction. However, if the product purchase was important or if the situation associated with the consumption of the product was momentous and the customer is greatly disappointed, the likelihood of complaining increases.

Attribution theory holds that people look for explanations for events and occurrences that they experience. "Why did this occur?" they ask. Customers can attribute poor product performance to themselves or they can say, "It's not my fault," and attribute the problem to an external source. If they blame the manufacturer or the store where the purchase was made, they are more likely to complain. Customers also make attributions about the organization's likelihood to repeat poor performance or to respond to a complaint.

Dissatisfied customers are more likely to complain when cost/benefit perception is unfavorable—when the expected benefits of complaining are high and the expected costs are low. If an airline has a Contact Us feature on its Web site, the cost of registering a complaint may be perceived as relatively low. If the customer expects that he or she will receive a free airline ticket by registering the complaint, the likelihood of complaining is quite high.

Personal characteristics are the demographic and personality characteristics of the customer base. Research shows that highly educated people are more likely to complain. Self-confident individuals and aggressive individuals have also been found to be more likely to complain. Anecdotal evidence suggests that older women may be more likely to express dissatisfaction with service than their younger counterparts.

Despite the reasons for dissatisfaction or complaints, the key issue for the organization and for the CRM system is determining the appropriate response to a host of varying circumstances.

WHAT TO DO WHEN CUSTOMERS COMPLAIN

When customers complain, they may be emotional—angry and excitable. They want a simple solution that is hassle free and immediate. Understandably, most of an organization's employees prefer not to deal with customer complaints. It is especially important that customer contact employees have the skill to interact with many different types of people. Some individual's habitual way of interacting with people is assertive, while others are customarily accommodating. Tension may occur when an employee and a customer have incompatible personal styles of interacting.[16] In many situations, customer contact people encounter "difficult" customers, so they must be trained in methods of interacting and in different styles of communication.

When customers complain, the marketer should have a system in place that will enable the organization to do several things. Beginning with preplanning, the organization should be customer-centric as they develop an approach that will (1) express regret, (2) resolve the conflict, and (3) follow-up the situation to assure it will never happen again.

Be Customer-centric

The organization must understand the situation from the customer's point of view—a **customer-centric** approach. First and foremost, the representative should listen carefully and let the customer know that he or she has been understood. Listening attentively and displaying sensitivity to the customer's position conveys a respect and communicates the message that the organization is customer-centric. One customer-centric approach is to rephrase the customer's statements. For example, an organization's representative may say, "If I understand you correctly, you are saying that the product is not functioning properly."

Asking the question, "What can we do to put matters right?" is a potent means to understanding the customer's opinion.[17] As we mentioned in Chapter 5, satisfaction or dissatisfaction is a direct result of confirmation or disconfirmation of expectations. Asking a question like this can discover if the organization built expectations too high. It certainly establishes what the customer's expectations were.

Express Regret

A simple apology can go a long way. Just saying, "I am truly sorry this problem occurred," may turn an angry customer into an appeased customer.[18] Sometimes a gesture of appreciation or an upgrade of service will reinforce the apology. A waitress may say, "I am sorry you had to wait so long for a table. We would like you to enjoy a complementary dessert because we appreciate your patience."

Resolve Conflict

Expressing regret and making amends is certainly appropriate when the organization is clearly wrong, but what should occur when the situation is not as obvious? In some circumstances the customer attributes the blame to the organization, but the organization attributes the blame to the customer. This situation is characterized by conflict. **Conflict** is a disagreement in which the views of the customer and the organization (e.g., customer service representative) appear to be incompatible. One outcome of conflict may be that the customer unilaterally chooses to end the relationship. However, from the organization's perspective, there are several ways to resolve conflict.

- *Accommodation* is a settlement of a conflict that emphasizes cooperative behavior. When the customer (or the customer's lifetime value) is more important than the issue under dispute, accommodation can be a goodwill gesture. It increases the customer's commitment to the relationship.

  A good CRM identifies the complaining customer's value to the organization. There may be a standard "script" or answer given to the typical customer. However, premium customers should be given a different script. Suppose an online hotel booking service gets a call from a customer who says he arrived at a hotel and the hotel had no reservation. The customer service representative, who has had a CRM system identify that this is a high-value customer, may provide a free room. Delighting high value customers with surprises can turn them into advocates who tell their friends, relatives, and associates about their experience.

- *Compromise* is an attempt to find a mutually acceptable middle ground that is somewhat satisfactory to both parties. Mutually beneficial compromises usually involve careful negotiations. For example, one week after the purchase of a new car, a sensor failed to work. When the repair was complete, the service manager stated, "That'll be $120.00." The customer, one of the authors of this book, said, "I thought this was under warranty." The representative said, "Well, there's a $100 deductible on all warranty work." The compromise was for the customer to pay $50 and for the organization to prevent an onslaught of negative word-of-mouth from occurring.

- *Termination* occurs when the organization or the customer ends the relationship and sees no hope of resolving the conflict. There are some customers an organization does not want. For example, a non-regular customer arrives at the veterinarian's office with a dog who is so covered in fleas that the dog dies before the veterinarian can take action. The customer proceeds to yell and scream at employees and other customers in the waiting room. For the veterinarian, asking that customer to leave and to never return is a viable option. Some customers need to patronize competitive organizations.

Follow-Up and Prevent Recurrence

It does not do much good to apologize to a customer for a problem that will reoccur. Preventing recurrence is essential for customer retention. The organization must deal with every legitimate problem and provide a means of incorporating the information into the CRM system and into the minds of customer contact employees.

Shortly after the problem has been resolved, it is a good idea to learn if the solution was acceptable. An automated follow-up might be for the CRM system to send a short satisfaction survey a month (or other appropriate period) after the incident. In business-to-business situations, a telephone call is a simple way to follow up. There are many alternatives, but the outcome should be the same: The feedback should indicate whether or not the customer's problem has been resolved. Customers who complain, experience a hassle-free resolution process, and are given a reasonable solution to their problems are likely to be among an organization's most loyal future customers. Resolving conflict, especially with unexpected positive outcomes, is an effective way to create loyal customer advocates.

Keep in Touch and Listen to Customers

The quote, "There is nothing permanent except change," by pre-Socratic Greek philosopher Heraclitus, has meaning in today's information age. If an organization intends to retain customers, it must understand that other offerings and customers' needs change over time. Yesterday's solution may not apply today. Thus, it is important for companies to keep in touch with customers. It is equally important to know what competitors are doing differently and how customers perceive these changes. For example, competitors often offer "Me Too" products with similar package designs, brand marks, or promotions in order to gain a generalization effect.[19] Each touch point should provide an opportunity to interact and to learn more about the individual customer. Rejuvenation of lapsing customers and reestablishing lost customers are crucial aspects of customer retention. We deal with customer winback in the next chapter.

SUMMARY

Strategies of organization-customer relationships have evolved to include financial, social, and structural-interactive aspects. Frequent buyer programs (also called rewards programs and loyalty programs) are based on financial incentives. Social relationship programs attempt to form a social bond. Structural-interactive approaches are based on a system, usually computer-based, designed to enhance interactions. A complete CRM system combines the customer benefits of value-added incentives, emotional bonding, interactive dialog, and customized/personalized treatment.

Customer life-cycle is defined as the stages a customer goes through from the time before the customer first does business with an organization until he or she stops being a customer. From the organization's perspective, there is an acquisition stage, a retention stage, and, in many cases, a customer winback stage for lost customers.

A customer retention strategy consists of a plan identifying what basic retention objectives will be pursued and how they will be achieved in the time available. The attrition rate, or churn, is the percentage of customers lost in a given period, typically a year. The retention rate (the percentage of customers expected to keep doing business with the organization) is 1- the attrition rate.

There are a number of reasons why customers terminate relationships, including novelty seeking, dissatisfaction, relative advantage, conflict, loss of trust, and cessation of need. The welcome stage provides the opportunity to thank the customer for an order, to reassure the buyer that he or she made the correct choice, and to collect data. Cognitive dissonance is a psychologically uncomfortable post-purchase feeling which may be reduced with communication.

Retaining customers requires that the products and services that are sold are reliable. Ensuring consistent quality and promoting reliability are fundamental to every customer retention strategy. Responsiveness is also important as customers want to be treated right. The objective of internal marketing may be to have employees recognize their role in the effort to be responsive to customers.

A retention strategy recognizes the need to reward customers for their loyalty. Recognition, personalization, and easy communication access help maintain relationships. Companies may build in financial penalties, psychological barriers to exit a program, or other switching costs to retain customers.

An effective CRM system should have mechanisms for identifying problems and for handling customer complaints. Customer complaints indicate dissatisfaction with the purchase or with the organization. There are several factors that influence a customer's decision to complain: level of dissatisfaction, attribution of blame, cost/benefits of actions, and personal characteristics. In general, when a customer complains, the marketer should (1) express regret, (2) manage the conflict, and (3) follow up to ensure that it will never happen again.

KEY TERMS

access strategy
accommodation
acquisition stage
attribution theory
attrition rate
cognitive dissonance
communication
compromise
conflict
cost/benefit perception
customer life cycle
customer retention strategy
customer-centric
customer-initiated
   communication

dissatisfaction
financial incentives
free ride
internal marketing
levels of dissatisfaction
loss of trust
mystery shoppers
novelty seeking
offer engine
partnership management
   programs
personal characteristics
personalization
priority access
recognition

relative advantage
reliability
responsiveness
retention rate
retention stage
social bond
structural-interactive
switching costs
termination
termination penalty
welcome strategy
winback stage

QUESTIONS FOR REVIEW AND CRITICAL THINKING

1. How did relationship marketing programs develop?
2. Outline the stages in the customer life cycle.
3. What is the purpose of a customer retention strategy?
4. What is churn? What impact does it have on a business?

5. Why do customers terminate relationships? Provide some examples.

6. Comment on the CRM implications of the following quote, "Making a sale is the beginning, not the end, of the marketing effort."

7. What is internal marketing?

8. What factors should be taken into account when planning reward and recognition programs?

9. What factors influence a customer's decision to complain to an organization?

10. What actions should the organization be prepared to take when customers complain or express conflict?

NOTES

1. Adapted from Doug Carroll, "Avis Has a License to Celebrate," *USA Today*, (30 October 1991), sec. E, p.10. Reprinted with permission.

2. Richard G. Barlow, "Relationship Marketing—The Ultimate in Customer Services," *Retail Control* (March 1992): 29–37.

3. Tom Collins, review of *Loyalty.com Customer Relationship Management in the New Era of Internet Marketing,* by Frederick Newell, *Digital Direct Newsletter,* <http://www.mrmworldwide.com /digital_3438.html>.

4. Michael K. Rich, "Are We Losing Trust through Technology," *Journal of Business & Industrial Marketing* 17:2/3 (2002): 215–222.

5. Jagdish N. Sheth and Atul Pavatiyar, "Relationship Marketing in Consumer Markets, Antecedents, and Consequences," *Journal of the Academy of Marketing Science* (fall 1995): 263.

6. Paul R. Gamble, Merlin Stone, and Neil Woodcock, *Up Close and Personal: Customer Relationship Marketing at Work* (London: Kogan Page, 1999).

7. Lucy McCauley. Hans Peter Brondmo, "How May I Help You?" Reprinted from the March 2000 issue of *Fast Company,* All rights reserved. To subscribe, please call 800-688-1545.

7. Reprinted with permission from Lucy McCauley. Hans Peter Brondmo,"How May I Help You?" *Fast Company,* March 2000, all rights reserved. To subscribe call 800-688-1545.

8. David Aaker, *Managing Brand Equity* (New York: The Free Press, 1991): 50.

9. Paul Greenberg, *CRM at the Speed of Light* (New York: Osborne/McGraw-Hill, 2001): 138.

10. Joseph A. Konstan, John Riedl, and Bradley N. Miller (all of the University of Minnesota), position paper presented at the CHI 97 Basic Research Symposium, Atlanta, Ga., 22–23 March 1997.

11. Don E. Schulz, "Marcom Model Reverses Traditional Pattern," *Marketing News* (1 April 2002): 8.

12. Erik Lounsbury, "Help Yourself, Stay Informed and Help Me," *Customer Inter@ction Solutions* (April 2002): 50.

13. Tony Cram, *Customers That Count* (London: Financial Times-Prentice Hall, 2001): 219.

14. William L. Wilkie, *Consumer Behavior* (New York: John Wiley and Sons, 1990): 626.

15. Ibid., and Jagdish N. Sheth, Banwaari Mittal, and Bruce I. Newman, *Consumer Behavior* (Ft. Worth, Tex.: Dryden Press, 1999): 550–551.

16. Patricia M. Fandt, *Management Skills: Practices and Experience* (St. Paul, Minn.: West Publishing Company, 1994): 435.

17. Tony Cram, *Customers that Count* (London: Financial Times-Prentice Hall, 2001): 104–107.

18. Ibid.

19. Frederick D. Sturdivant et al., *Managerial Analysis in Marketing* (Glenview, Ill., Scott Foresman, 1970): 174.

CHAPTER 7

Winback and Acquisition Strategies

It wasn't that long ago when Cingular Wireless was marketed in the Southeast under the BellSouth Mobility name. The company had 1 million subscribers in its 28 cellular systems. Even though the company was growing at an annual rate of 45 percent, and adding more than 2,500 customers each day, it was also losing 500 customers each day.[1]

Why were these people leaving? BellSouth wanted to know. In order to achieve its goal of winning back 10 percent of its lapsed customers, BellSouth conducted focus groups among switchers. These lapsed customers revealed that they preferred BellSouth's call coverage, customer service, and billing system. However, these customers were also denied credit for dropped calls, given no free gift promotions, and were denied "free airtime" promotions—all of which contributed to their decision to drop BellSouth.

BellSouth addressed the defection drivers head on in carefully designed promotions. BellSouth sent 3,500 switchers a direct mail reactivation offer for free phones, free airtime, and credit for dropped calls. However, this offer was met with disappointing results: a 3 percent response rate and a 1 percent reconnection rate. Additional research revealed that although respondents rated the offer as strong, current contracts with other cellular companies, misplacing the direct mail card, or never receiving the direct mail card prevented them from switching back.

When BellSouth sent its offer out to 3,500 former customers, it did not pay attention to the date on which the customers had actually left the company. They did not anticipate that contractual agreements with other cellular companies would serve as a barrier for switching back. Thus, BellSouth repeated the offer to 1,000 former customers who had left 11 months before, lapsed customers who would soon be free to switch. BellSouth followed up the letter with a phone call. The results were much improved. The second letter produced an 8 percent response rate and a 3 percent connect rate. When the company followed up with a phone call, it had a 10 percent connect rate.

It is a simple fact of business that some customers stop doing business with the organization. Some are brand switchers. Others do nothing. All are lost customers. This chapter focuses on strategies for customer winback and customer acquisition.

WINBACK STRATEGIES

A recent study showed that every year a typical business enterprise loses 20-40% of its customers.[2] Organizations should identify how many defections there have been each year, but many do not. **Winback** strategies make an effort to reactivate and revitalize relationships with high-value, lost customers. Recovering lost customers who have defected to competitors or rejuvenating lapsed customers who have simply stopped doing business in the product category provides a major opportunity for most organizations.

Winning back lost and lapsed customers can be one of the most profitable aspects of a company's CRM strategy. As shown in Exhibit 7.1, Winback consists of identifying which customers have been lost or are about to terminate their relationships, reasons for losing high value customers, effective methods for re-contacting lost customers, and offers that communicate the benefits of reactivation.

IDENTIFY WHO IS ABOUT TO TERMINATE

The best time to winback a customer is before the customer terminates the relationship. In the best winback strategies, the company acts rather than reacts. The sooner a company

EXHIBIT 7.1	CRM QUESTIONS OF WINBACK

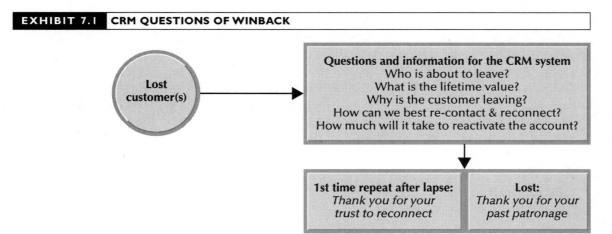

realizes that a customer is about to defect, the better able the company is to winback the lapsing customer.

In many customer-company relationships, customers must formally state their intentions to terminate the relationship. For example, a customer may notify a tennis club that membership is being canceled. In other situations, customers never make it known that the relationship has been terminated. Customers may buy less and less or they may abruptly stop buying.[3] A restaurant may never know what happened to the regular customer who is lost. Establishing a process that requires customers to notify the company in advance that they intend to terminate the relationship provides the company with some time to figure out what went wrong and to then initiate a winback action. By using analytical programs in the CRM system, it may be possible to identify patterns that signal a customer is about to defect.

In many CRM systems, the process will automatically initiate an action to retain customers before they lapse. In some industries, such as the magazine subscription industry, it is fairly easy to detect lapsing customers. This is evident, for example, when a subscription to *Fortune Magazine* is expiring and the customer has yet to respond to notices for renewal.

In an effective CRM system, an automatic trigger may be set off if a customer is identified as having a high risk of defection to a competitor and if a customer is determined to be of high value. A winback strategy would use a proactive approach to try to rekindle the flame. The customer would be offered some special consideration or sent a message via e-mail, a letter, a brochure, a telephone call, or a personal visit to "bond" the relationship.[4]

Many retail companies use analysis of RFM (recency, frequency, and monetary) data to predict who is about to terminate. This topic is discussed in Chapter 9.

Consider Lifetime Customer Value

Remember that some customers have a low lifetime value and the organization may not want to reestablish relationships with those who demand too much service without a corresponding amount of revenue. Thus, an initial aspect of a winback strategy is to profile customers by lifetime future value. A winback strategy should identify and focus on high value customers who show the greatest potential to respond to winback efforts. It is not worthwhile to try to winback low-value customers.

There are many types of customers a company simply does not want. We will give some examples in this section. In many cases low-value customers buy strictly on price. These price sensitive buyers always pit one company's bid against a competitor's offer and are highly likely to switch brands or companies. If there is a sale elsewhere, their business follows. Bad credit risks and customers who pay late, like price sensitive buyers, are, as a rule, undesirable as customers. Of greater concern is the chance of ignoring a declining value to a key customer base. Consider, as one example, the 51 percent share of market held by Cadillac in the late 1980s in the luxury car segment and its problem with lifetime value.

> Unfortunately, the average customer lifetime value among Cadillac's customers was not particularly high because Cadillac's buyer population tended to be older (i.e., averaging age 60). Many of the older Cadillac buyers were on their last car.... Now compare that to BMW. Its youthful and vigorous image could not immediately win the market share war, but it ensured a younger customer base with a higher customer lifetime value. Ultimately, BMW surpassed

Cadillac even in current market share. Cadillac's share now is about 15 percent, down from 51 percent.[5]

Some customers will never be satisfied, and some customers are unacceptable because they don't respect proper business behavior. The old saying that "the customer is always right," must be judged with respect to the cost to employees of caring for people who are more trouble than they are worth.

ESTABLISH WHY CUSTOMERS TERMINATE

Some customers switch brands for variety, some find a competitor has better relative advantage, such as a lower price, and some are dissatisfied because the brand or product falls short of expectations. Some are unhappy with customer service, perhaps because of a conflict that was inadequately resolved. Some customers relocate and are no longer in the trading area. Before an organization can establish an effective winback strategy, it needs to understand why a customer is no longer loyal.

If the CRM system does not identify a reason for losing high-value customers, a common first activity is to contact the customers and verify that they are indeed inactive or lost customers. If they indicate that they are, some attempt should be made to learn why the relationship has soured.

When an employee quits a job, it is common for the departing employee to go through an exit interview. Exit interviews offer a final chance to gather information from personnel that otherwise might be difficult or impossible to obtain. Often bombshells of unexpected information are disclosed.

The **customer exit interview** is an attempt to ask, "Why are you leaving us?" When a cable TV subscriber cancels service, the exit interview may be a single question. However, in business-to-business markets, a senior executive may visit the lost customer a month or two after the relationship has been terminated. The interviewer explains that the purpose of the interview is to learn, rather than to appeal for the return of the business. Although the executive may indicate that the business would be warmly welcomed back, it should be made clear that the exit interview is not a sales call. The purpose is to listen well. The predetermined questions should seek real reasons for the defection and uncover if there was a particular triggering incident that caused the business to be lost.[6]

Consumer goods companies and providers of consumer services may conduct focus group interviews with lapsed customers. A **focus group interview** usually involves 8 to 12 people, former customers in this case, who are paid a fee to talk with a moderator about the reasons for leaving the organization or for failing to purchase from the organization. Focus groups are noted for providing quick results. Organizations may also conduct surveys to identify what factors drive customers to defection. These topics are further discussed in Chapter 10 along with survey research and the measurements needed for CRM.

A company can also establish formal **listening posts** on the frontline to learn what customers are thinking. Customer-contact /frontline personnel, who have direct communication with customers, are in a unique position to gauge customer response and to learn why customers terminate their business with a company. In their day-to-day activities, the sales representatives, cashiers, and customer service employees hear about the problems customers are having. It is important that frontline employees at listening posts keep some record of problems and complaints and that these records are available in the CRM system to trigger improvements.

Other listening posts are designed to solicit customers' comments in their own words. Suggestion boxes and free-form comment boxes on Web sites are examples. A professional baseball team established a video listening post at its ballpark. All a customer had to do was stand in the right spot, push a button, and record a message.

RE-CONTACT LAPSED CUSTOMERS

In a survey of senior managers from America's largest corporations, managers were asked, "How often do you contact lost customers?" One-half of the respondents said that they either never contacted lost customers or only contacted them once or twice.[7] While it seems that re-contacting lost customers should be a key element of any winback strategy, winback, obviously, is not at the forefront in many organizations.

Re-contacting may be as simple as telephoning the lost account. The call may begin with a question to determine why the customer stopped buying. It may be something like, "Our records show that you recently cancelled your account with us. We are very sorry to be losing your business. May I ask why you made your decision to close your account with us?" If a problem with the brand or company is indicated and the sales person can offer a solution to it, the contact-sales person then attempts to reestablish the lost account.

In some organizations a designated cast of salespeople with good communication skills is assembled into a **winback team** to perform the re-contact and reactivation tasks. This approach can be effective if the lost customer group contains people who are of high value to the organization and if the organization is still learning how to prevent lost customers. However, winback teams can be costly if the organization loses its best salespeople to talking with unhappy former customers all day every day.

Depending on the sophistication of the customer and the nature of the product being sold, there may be some "scripted" material for the various scenarios. When a customer gives a particular reason for defection, the contact-sales person enters this information into a computer. The CRM then provides a **situational script** containing a "canned presentation" or talking points for the contact-sales person. In essence, a situational script is written by marketing experts in a conversational style to allow new or less experienced employees to provide a clear and concise response to the customer. (This issue is dealt with further in the next chapter on Sales Force Automation and Automated Customer Service and Support.)

If it becomes clear that the customer has made the decision to keep on buying from a competitor, the sales person should let the customer know that the company has appreciated the customer's past business and that at any future time the company is ready to earn back the business.[8] Typically, the proven principles of personal selling apply in the re-contact situation. For example, it is a good idea for every re-contacted lost customer to received a follow-up thank you letter or e-mail expressing appreciation for the time spent talking with the organization.

PROVIDE A REACTIVATION OFFER

Customers must benefit from reestablishing a relationship with an organization. The **reactivation offer** is the motivation an organization gives customers to return to the fold. If a particular customer wasn't treated right, the offer should be to fix the problem. If a customer received a better deal from the competition, the offer should be sweeter. In many cases, the reactivation offer is tailored to customers lost to a particular competitor or tailored to a specific customer segment. In its analysis of the marketplace, a company should learn which actions, such as price deals, a competitor took that caused customers to switch brands. It should learn competitor weaknesses and barriers to exit. Knowledge of a competitor's deficiencies should be incorporated into reactivation offers to lost customers.

A company that does its homework should know what techniques and offers are most successful at re-establishing lost customers. If the CRM system is designed, as it should be, to process reactivation offers and lost customers and identify which to re-activate, then the organization can learn, over time, which approaches work the best for its key customers.

The effectiveness of different reactivation efforts can be tested. *Sports Illustrated* conducts experiments to test its creative strategies and renewal materials and to reveal the promotions that generate the highest response rates. For each renewal cycle, *Sports Illustrated* researchers include several control variables (source, price, amount paid, etc.) that are used to test the efficacy of renewal methods. These variables include such things as payment methods offered (bill me later, credit card, installment, etc.).

ACQUISITION

An effective acquisition strategy is best achieved by having an effective retention strategy. The organization must understand who among its customers is most loyal and why. It must know the characteristics of loyal customers and how to generate loyalty within different segments. It must apply that knowledge to acquisition strategies that concentrate resources directed at the best prospects. (See Exhibit 7.2.)

OBJECTIVES: CHOOSING GOALS THAT FOCUS ON LIFETIME VALUE

Acquisition programs begin with the setting of objectives. Setting objectives should take into account the cost of customer acquisition. The following steps can be taken to identify the investment required to win a new customer and to track the return on investment.[9]

1. Establish a system to enumerate all costs for acquiring new customers.
2. Divide the total cost of acquisition by the number of new customers gained in a given time period to determine the average cost of acquiring a customer.
3. Determine the number of months the organization must keep a customer in order to provide a payback on the investment.
4. Evaluate the average new customer profitability and set customer acquisition objectives.

Marketers with the goal of customer acquisition should determine which prospects are to be targeted and how much can be spent on acquiring them. Effective customer acquisition is grounded in the concept of an appropriate marketing strategy that selects the right target market and provides a tailored marketing mix to meet identified needs or wants.

STRATEGY: SELECTING TARGETS AND DESIGNING MIXES

Chapter 2 discussed the importance of market segmentation. An analysis of existing high-value customers may reveal that they have certain geographical, demographic, or other

| EXHIBIT 7.2 | CRM ASPECTS OF ACQUISITION |

traits in common. The customer segments considered by analysts to contain high-value potential customers for an organization are likely to become target markets.

After analyzing several potential market segments and selecting a target market, marketing managers position the brand in that market and then develop a marketing mix to accomplish the positioning objective.

The celebrated 4 Ps that comprise the marketing mix—product, price, place, and promotion—are the basic elements of the benefit package designed to meet the needs of the target market. Each of these elements must be planned and integrated when the marketing objective is to acquire a new customer. In many business situations, organizational objectives will be to apply the principles of mass marketing (e.g., broadcast advertising, product sampling, price deals, etc.) to acquire new customers. For other targets, the benefits inherent in the marketing mix must be personally explained to each potential customer.

However, explaining the details for planning and executing an entire marketing mix strategy is beyond the scope of this book. Nevertheless, it is appropriate to mention that within a CRM strategy, marketing research and data analysis may be used to determine the appropriate competitive position and offer/price for each customer segment. The optimum content, timing, frequency of promotional messages, and selection of media to reach customer segments may also be based on CRM analysis of these markets.

In the rest of this chapter, we focus on six particular aspects of the marketing mix that directly relate to the relationship management and the information technology dimensions of CRM systems.

NATURAL REFERRALS: EVERYBODY IS TALKING ABOUT IT

eBay Motors, the used-car section of eBay, started by focusing on unusual cars. But soon it reached out to owners and dealers of mainstream cars. Its acquisition strategy devotes few people to finding sellers. The company's chief executive says, "It's far better for a car dealer to hear about eBay from another car dealer than for our sales force to call on them. Buyers attract sellers, who in turn attract buyers, and so on. That's been the success formula in every category on eBay so far."[10]

The best way to acquire new customers is through the sincere and heartfelt recommendations of satisfied, loyal customers. **Natural referrals,** through word-of-mouth advertising, are the foundation of some of the best acquisition strategies.

Why should a customer make the effort to refer someone to an organization? In many cases it is because the customer is an advocate. Customer acquisition for Harley-Davidson motorcycles is based on referrals because the emotional bond of existing customers with the brand is so strong. It only seems natural to such customers to want their family and friends to experience the same good feeling or to find the same superior service. Most of us enjoy offering free advice to our friends, neighbors, and acquaintances. Have you ever suggested strongly that another person see a movie that you liked, or avoid wasting money on a movie that you detested?

Natural referrals suggest that the organization has maximized a **unique selling proposition (USP).** Other names for USP include competitive edge, determinant attribute, relative advantage, or differential advantage. When customers see something special in an organization's offer and personally refer others to the organization, life is very good for the organization. The CRM system should be tracking such instances by asking new customers why they selected the organization. As these answers are compiled, many organizations discover just what it is that makes it special to the target market of loyal customers.

AFFINITY PROGRAMS: INCENTIVES FOR REFERRALS FROM GROUPS

Another reason customers may make referrals is because the company makes it worthwhile for the customer to do so. An effective CRM plan incorporates a plan for generating referrals. Creating an affinity marketing program is a means to gain access to thousands of potential new customers. **Affinity marketing** is a strategy that is based on marketing to group memberships or associations, such as the University of Colorado Alumni Association, the World Wildlife Fund (WWF), or local Parent Teacher Associations (PTAs). An affinity marketing strategy develops frequent buyer programs or other programs with customer value in exchange for a membership group's or an association's endorsement and/or co-branding. **Group-purchasing programs** leverage the collective buying power of association members. **Co-branding,** the use of two individual brands on a single product, targets consumers who are inclined to participate because they share a common interest or background with others in the membership group. Affinity marketing works best when the group has common interests and cohesive values that reinforce long-term relationships. Typically, the company gives a contribution or a small percentage of revenue to the affiliated group. For example, every time a member of the University of Colorado Alumni Association uses a co-branded credit card, a small donation is made to the university.

AFFILIATION NETWORKS: PAYING COMMISSIONS FOR REFERRALS

The technology of CRM systems combined with the Web provides the power to pay people for building traffic to sites. During the early days of Amazon.com, the organization paid five percent on any sale that occurred due to a referral. Thus, one enterprising student created six web pages per week by accessing information provided by Amazon.com, describing books of interest, attaching his affiliate information, and collecting his $3,000/month income from driving customers to the Amazon.com site.

An **affiliate network program** is a process to reward people who act as sales agents for the organization and who receive a commission on each sale based on their referral. This type of selling may be particularly effective for small Web sites that are unable to attract advertising dollars for banner ads.[11] A quick search of the Web yields opportunities to refer others to Christian material, casinos, adult sites, and may others. This mass marketing concept is based on mass personalization and the assumption that of 1,000 click throughs, some proportion will stop and buy.

RELATIVE ADVANTAGE: GIVE THEM SOMETHING TO TALK ABOUT

Finding a new use for a product or service or improving/reformulating a product can be a means to acquire new customers. Strong relationships with innovative customers and with dissatisfied sources can both be valuable sources for new product ideas.

In business-to-business markets, **lead users** are innovators and early adopters of new technologies. Studies of lead users can predict what the future will be like. Lead users face needs that will be general in the marketplace, but they confront these needs long before the vast majority of customers do so.[12] The theory of lead users suggests that these innovative customers develop the ideas for new technological applications of existing products and for the development of new products. Some companies equip customers with "tool kits" to design and develop their own products.[13] In terms of CRM, a good relationship with lead users may lead to the discovery of new uses for existing products or new ways to approach service design and delivery. This knowledge can be shared and used to attract new customers. Companies like to do business with organizations that understand their business.

Another source for new product ideas is tracking **customer complaints.** Customer complaints represent the organization's first opportunity to prevent a customer from becoming lost. If the CRM system is designed to track, compile, and report on problems that customers face, and if listening posts or other sources are trained to input that information, then the organization is planning to improve its products and services. Unfortunately, without an appropriate concept of the CRM system, the correct information may not get into the hands of the engineer or customer service person who needs it in order to fix the problem. The Express Response software package from IslandData is an example of one such CRM approach that is designed to track and compile complaints.

> The Response Fusion technology, the underlying platform for Express Response, has the ability to automatically re-use new responses created by contact center agents as the core self-help knowledge that addresses previously unanswerable questions through the automatic identification, creation, capture and reuse of knowledge. Clusters of common unanswerable inquiry concepts are developed, with each cluster being identified as a knowledge gap that must be filled. These gaps, along with customer feedback, can then be automatically sent to customer service operations personnel to be addressed.[14]

Thus, the technology is available to foster the concept of the seamless organization, where frontline personnel, customers, and line officers can all have access to the information that is necessary to create new products to meet the needs of defined target groups.

SWITCHING COSTS: ELIMINATE EXCUSES TO STAY WITH THE COMPETITOR

At the beginning of this chapter we used an example about BellSouth. The company recognized that its lost customers had signed 12-month contractual agreements with other cellular companies, which served as a barrier for switching back. Recognizing this barrier to exit the competitor, BellSouth made an offer to former customers who left 11 months before. By doing this, they recognized and countered the customer's switching cost associated with breaking a contract with a competitor.

Similar strategies that attack competitors' barriers to exit can be used to acquire new customers. For example, an offer can be made to transfer or convert a competitor's reward program's redeemable points if the customer switches loyalties. **Promotional offers** for customers who switch from competitive firms typically ease the transfer task for the customer and take a customer-centric focus on barriers.

The key element of many offers is to make switching from a competitor easy. A MSN advertisement uses the headline: "With new hassle-free switching tools, leaving AOL is, well, hassle-free." The offer indicates that subscribers who change over will get free switching software that allows the customer to move his or her AOL Address Book, notify his or her contacts of the new e-mail address, and forward e-mails from the old address. In addition MSN offers $50 back after three paid months.

Product sampling is another way to reduce the perceived cost of switching from a competitor. A trial sample of a product or free trial of a service is given to consumers to stimulate brand awareness, to provide information, and to allow customers to gain first-hand experience with the product. There is no barrier to trial. People who satisfactorily experience a previously untried brand have less perceived risk than those who must purchase an untried brand. A **money-back guarantee,** particularly with the stipulation of a certain length of time, is another common means to reduce barriers to entry and to ensure that the money spent to acquire customers from competitors will result in a return on that investment. Money-back guarantees promise to refund the purchase price of a product or service if it fails to perform as the customer expects.

POINT OF ENTRY: THE INITIAL CONTACT FOR ACQUISITION

For many products it is possible to predict the **point of entry** when a never-before-consumer becomes a customer or user of the service. Identifying and interacting with these customers when they approach the point of entry is a fruitful acquisition strategy. The transition from nonuser to customer often coincides with a particular life event or lifestyle change.[15] Consider the following example:

> At 1:58 P.M. on Wednesday, May 5, in Houston's St. Luke's Episcopal Hospital, a consumer was born. Her name was Alyssa J. Nedell, and by the time she went home three days later, some of America's biggest marketers were pursuing her with samples, coupons, and assorted freebies. Procter & Gamble hoped its Pampers brand would win the battle for Alyssa's bottom. Johnson & Johnson offered up a tiny sample of its baby soap. Bristol-Myers Squibb Co. sent along some of its Enfamil baby formula.[16]

The logic underlying customer acquisition at point-of entry is as follows: 1) develop a system to identify who is most likely to enter the product category, 2) determine when entry is most likely, and 3) be the first to establish a relationship with the first time buyer.[17] As mentioned in an earlier chapter, once people make a choice to purchase a product or service, **cognitive dissonance** rears its ugly head. Customers will attempt to reduce this uncertainty over choice and, if they are successful, they assume they have selected the best solution to their problem. This is the time for organizations to reinforce the logic of that outcome—Yes, customer, you did do the right thing in choosing us. A firm confidence that the decision was correct forms a psychological barrier to switching to a competitive offer for quite some time.

SUMMARY

Winback strategies make an effort to reactivate and revitalize relationships with high-value, lost customers. Winback consists of identifying which customers have been lost or are about to terminate their relationships, identifying reasons for losing a high value customer, and re-contacting lost customers to communicate the benefits of reactivation.

The best time to winback customers is before they terminate the relationship. The sooner a company realizes that a customer is about to defect, the better able the company is to winback the lapsing customer. Using analytical programs in the CRM system, it may be possible to identify patterns that signal a customer is about to defect. If the CRM system does not identify a reason for losing a high value customer, some attempt should be made to learn why the relationship has soured. Exit interviews, focus groups, surveys, and listening posts may serve this purpose.

Re-contacting lost customers should be a key element of any winback strategy. During re-contact, lost customers must perceive a clear benefit from reestablishing a relationship. The reactivation offer is the reason the organization provides the customer to reconnect.

An effective acquisition strategy is best achieved by having an effective retention strategy. The company must understand who among its customers are most loyal and why. It must know their characteristics and how to generate customer loyalty within different market segments.

The 4 Ps of marketing—product, price, place, and promotion—are a company's marketing mix. Each of these elements must be planned and integrated when the marketing objective is to acquire a new customer. However, there are six special aspects of the marketing mix that directly relate to the CRM system: natural referrals, affinity programs, affiliate networks, relative advantage from new or improved products/services, eliminating switching costs, and reinforcing customers at the point of entry.

KEY TERMS

affiliate network program
affinity marketing
co-branding
cognitive dissonance
customer complaints
customer exit interview
focus group interview

group-purchasing
   programs
lead users
listening posts
money-back guarantee
natural referrals
point of entry

product sampling
promotional offers
reactivation offer
situational script
unique selling proposition
winback
winback team

QUESTIONS FOR REVIEW AND CRITICAL THINKING

1. When is the best time to winback a customer?
2. How can analytical programs in the CRM system be used in a winback strategy?
3. How can an organization identify reasons for losing a customer?
4. What is an exit interview?
5. What are the characteristics of an effective acquisition strategy?
6. What is a marketing mix? What elements of a marketing mix are the most applicable to a CRM acquisition strategy?
7. What is an affinity program? What are the benefits of an affinity program?
8. Provide examples of affiliate networking programs.
9. How can customer complaints be used to create a relative advantage?
10. Identify and describe points of entry for three different consumer products or services.

NOTES

1. Reprinted with permission from Jill Griffin, "Lost Customers Can Be Returned to Your Fold," *Austin Business Journal* (19 February 1999).
2. Jill Griffin and Michael W. Lowenstein, *Customer Winback—How to Recapture Lost Customers and Keep Them Loyal* (San Francisco: Jossey-Bass, 2001): 5.
3. Ibid, 54.
4. Gene M. Ferruzza, "Enterprise-Wide Customer Relationship Management," *DM Review,* (May 1999). <http://www.dmreview.com/master.cfm?NavID=215&EdID=19>.
5. Roland T. Rust, Katherine N. Lemon, and Valarie A. Zeithaml, "Where Should the Next Marketing Dollar Go?" *Marketing Management* 10:3 (September/October 2001): 26.
6. Tony Cram, *Customers that Count* (London: Financial Times-Prentice Hall, 2001): 232.
7. Jill Griffin, "Lost Customers Can Be Returned to Your Fold," *Austin Business Journal* (19 February 1999).
8. Anthony Urbaniak, "Keep Their Business—Winning Back Lost Customers and Increasing Sales to Existing Accounts," *American Salesman,* March 2002, sec. i3, p. 24.
9. Tony Cram, *Customers that Count* (London: Financial Times-Prentice Hall, 2001): 35.
10. Saul Hansell, "Meg Whitman and eBay, Net Survivors," *New York Times,* (5 May 2002).
11. Judy Strauss and Raymond Frost, *Marketing on the Internet: Principles of Online Marketing* (New Jersey: Prentice Hall, 1999).
12. Michael D. Hutt and Thomas W. Speh, *Business Marketing Management* (Fort Worth, Tex.: Dryden Press, 1998): 329–330 and Eric von Hipple, *The Sources of Innovation* (New York: Oxford University Press, 1988).
13. Stefan Thomke and Eric von Hipple, "Turn Customers into Innovators," *Harvard Business Review* (April 2002): 74.
14. Erik Lounsbury, "Help Yourself, Stay Informed and Help Me," *Customer Inter@ction Solutions* (April 2002): 50–51.
15. Dawn Iacobucci, ed., *Kellogg on Marketing* (New York: John Wiley and Sons, 2001): 8.
16. David Leonhardt and Kathleen Kerwin, "Hey Kid, Buy This!: Is Madison Avenue Taking "Get 'em While They're Young" Too Far?" *Business Week,* (30 June 1997), 62.
17. Dawn Iacobucci, ed., Kellogg on Marketing (New York: John Wiley and Sons, 2001): 8.

CHAPTER 8

Sales Force Automation and Automated Customer Service Centers

Once business cards were stacked on desks, bound with a rubber band, or filed in a Rolodex.[1] Then technology companies digitized the cards, moving them off desks and onto computer desktops, using small scanners that sorted the information into neatly organized databases.

Now the founder and chief executive of Corex Technologies in Cambridge, Massachusetts, one of the companies that first offered the scanners, has come up with a service that increases the function and accuracy of its product, the CardScan, and of business cards in general.

Jonathan Stern, 47, who designed the CardScan in 1993, got the idea for the new AccuCard Service after talking with users of CardScan and watching several companies introduce virtual business cards, which had the benefit of never being out of date. AccuCard Service automatically updates information so that a user knows, for example, when a sales associate has become vice president of sales.

When setting up AccuCard Service, users send a database containing scans of business cards to the AccuCard server. For each new entry, the server sends an e-mail message to the contact asking for updated information, and then seeks additional updates every three months. The computer automatically synchronizes the information in its server with applications like Microsoft Outlook and Palm Desktop. Users can log on to www.cardscan.net and retrieve information from any location.

Mr. Stern said he designed CardScan, which costs from $249 to $299 (the AccuCard Service is free) because he believed that consumers wanted to be able to slide in a business card, push a button, and have the software do the rest. "My feeling was that we can take this technology and trim it down," he said. "The thinking is that people don't buy technology, they buy solutions. It kind of runs counterintuitive to other competitors who think people want more options."

Many aspects of CRM have already been discussed. However, there are two applications that deserve additional attention: sales force automation and automated customer service and support.

SALES FORCE AUTOMATION

In personal selling, the creation and maintenance of mutually beneficial long-term relationships with customers is called **relationship selling,** or **consultative selling.** One of the fundamental aspects of relationship selling involves maintaining regular contact with clients and being familiar with each customer's circumstances and needs.

The application of digital and wireless technologies to personal selling is known as **sales force automation (SFA).** CRM's beginnings stem from SFA attempts to increase sales productivity, elevate customer service, increase customer satisfaction, and create loyal customers. Today, mobile phones, voice messaging systems, fax machines, and e-mail can be efficient media that field sales representatives use to communicate with prospects and clients. Laptop computers, Personal Digital Assistants (PDAs), Interactive Web sites, wireless data transmission, and CRM databases continue to dramatically change the administrative activities of sales people and, hopefully, reduce the time spent completing "paperwork."

The **sales process** is a logical sequence of selling stages that occurs between the time an opportunity is recognized—a prospect is identified—and the time of follow-up activities after a sale is closed. In the broader sense of CRM systems, the process is a **sales cycle**— a circular process with all but the initial stages being cyclical. The typical sales process varies by industry and is tailored to harmonize with the customer's buying expectations.

SFA software organizes and manages data about sales touch points and the customer's history with the company. Automation tools describe where prospects/customers are in the sales cycle, which in sales automation terms is often called the **sales pipeline,** depicted in Exhibit 8.1. For example, records should show whether a lead is qualified, contacted, developed, or closed (won or lost).[2] SFA may use data mining to integrate the pipeline data with other CRM data and make suggestions about specific activities to a sales representative.

Fully explicating the steps of the sales pipeline is a topic for a sales management text. But consider, briefly, the steps shown in Exhibit 8.1. **Leads** are prospects who may or may not be interested in the organization's offering. **Qualified leads** have been shown to have a positive expectation of lifetime value and an ability to purchase. While the first contact of a sales representative with the organization may be with a purchasing manager, interactions should quickly expand to include contact with other participants in the buying center (influencers, users, deciders, etc.). As the salesperson develops the relationship with the prospective organization, negotiations over terms and product specifications occur where the buyer is comparing the offer to those available from competitors. Once the representative attempts to **close the sale,** or ask for the order, the buyer either agrees or rejects the offer leading to another round in the sales pipeline. At this point the salesperson either acknowledges the sale with

EXHIBIT 8.1   THE SALES PIPELINE

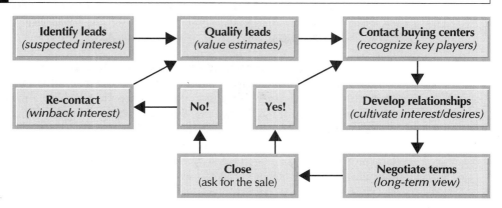

a thank you to the buying center participants or plans how and when to re-contact the organization with an offer designed to winback interest. CRM systems are critical aspects that can facilitate each step of this process.

SFA tools also have risks and costs associated with their adoption. The promise of SFA includes more efficient workers who are empowered to establish close relationships with customers. The reality is that the organization must be willing to invest in SFA equipment and in the people who will be responsible for using it. SFA tools can cause conflict in the salesforce due to fear of disintermediation, fear of being replaced, as well as an irritation in changing traditional approaches to the job. In essence, SFA forces people to change their perceptions of how the sales job is done.[3] Salespeople may be excited over the promise of SFA but fail, months later, to really blend the technology with their traditional concepts of how the sales job should be implemented. These problems may then increase conflict, absenteeism, and voluntary turnover. Thus, without proper attention to the people as well as the technology, the tasks that should be eased with SFA may actually be more difficult to accomplish.

TASKS FOR SFA

SFA consists of many tasks. We will focus on: 1) contact and time management, 2) lead management, and more broadly, opportunity management, 3) knowledge management and intranet access, 4) price quotes and order configuration, 5) follow-up management, and 6) analysis and reporting tools.

Contact and Time Management

Selling requires that an organization get in touch with prospects and existing customers. Contact management involves organizing data about organizations and about customers and prospects within these organizations. Basic information such as name, job title, mailing address, billing address, phone numbers, and e-mail addresses may be integrated with software that displays more complex information, such as the organization chart, the chain of command, and each individual's decision-making level. Contact management applications typically allow a sales representative to enter information about previous contacts and notes about facts—such as a client's birthday, hobbies, or favorite restaurants—that can help the salesperson personalize the sales call. Contact management data may be enhanced with external data such as MapQuest driving directions to the customer's location or corporate financial information from Dun & Bradstreet, Hoover's, or some other data provider (www.hoovers.com).

Typically, contact management software enables the user to automatically dial phone numbers. Most contact managers are integrated with e-mail software (such as Microsoft Outlook) so letters can be sent to contacts. Often they include e-mail templates (e.g., "Thank you for your time" letters) that can easily incorporate personalized customer information or tailor messages to address customers' specific needs.

Most contact managers have a **collaborative communication** feature that allows contact information to be shared with others. Sales team members can be in constant communication and immediately informed about recent activity. Contact managers may also schedule appointments with contacts.

Most SFA applications include a personal calendar that helps the sales representative with time management. The salesperson is able to schedule travel, entertainment, and other activities. The software allows the salesperson to remember to make important phone calls, appointments, and meetings. Appointments and tasks can be associated with contacts and shared with team members.

Lead Management and Opportunity Management

Identifying potential customers who may be interested in the organization or its products is called **prospecting.** Referrals, advertising inquiries from postcards, records of visitors to company Web sites, and other sources may provide the names of prospects or "leads." Consider the case of Tom Hertig, owner of a mergers-and-acquisitions business in New Jersey called Saddle River.

> Hertig logs onto Zapdata.com, a provider of online sales leads, to create
> prospect lists based on very specific criteria such as sales volume, public or

EXHIBIT 8.2 **SFA TASKS**

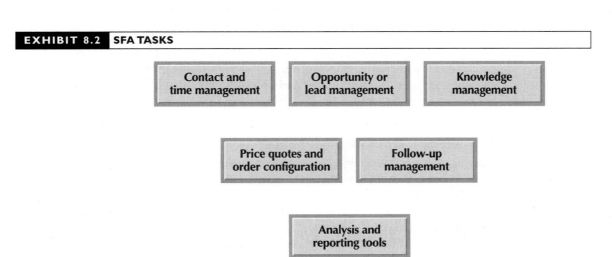

private status, industry, and number of employees. After choosing the parameters, he downloads the list onto his personal computer and imports the information into his own database. Hertig has achieved response rates as high as 2.5 percent (in the industry, 2 percent is considered excellent) and a close rate of 18 percent for respondents. He estimates that 85 to 95 percent of his business is generated from Zapdata leads.[4]

To be classified as a qualified lead, prospects must need the product, be in a position to place an order of sufficient size, be able to pay for it, and be in a position to make—or at least contribute to—the buying decision. **Lead management software** helps determine if a lead is a qualified prospect or not. Once a lead is qualified, the software may automatically direct the lead to the most appropriate field sales representative. In fact, the lead management software may analyze the lead data to provide the sales representative with a recommendation that the prospect should be visited in person, should receive a phone call, or should receive a letter and brochure.

A lead is a company's initial opportunity. However, the nature of the company's opportunity changes as the sales cycle progresses. **Opportunity management** is a comprehensive process that not only includes lead management, but also includes the management of other activity and information throughout the entire sales pipeline. For example, a sales representative who has called on a customer at least once should be able to look at a record and know what e-mails, faxes, and brochures have been sent. A customer's history of dealing with certain competitors may indicate the level of opportunity or threat that competitors represent. Competitive information may be used during the proposal development stage to generate competitive comparisons as well.

As the selling cycle progresses, the sales representative enters information, such as when a prospect was contacted, whether an offer was made, or the likelihood of closing a sale for a certain number of units, into the opportunity management system. This data may be automatically transferred to sales forecasting software. A **sales forecast** is a best guess projection of the unit or dollar volume of sales expected from a customer. Accurate sales forecasts are among the most useful pieces of planning information an organization can have. Complete accuracy in forecasting the future is not possible because change is constantly occurring in the marketing environment. Nevertheless, timely information from the opportunity management system can help make more objective forecasts.

Knowledge Management and Intranet Access

The process of creating an inclusive, comprehensive, and easily accessible organizational memory, often called the organization's intellectual capital, is termed **knowledge management.** [5] Many companies make a significant effort to capture, organize, and share what the organization and its employees know. An **intranet** is a company's private data network that uses Internet standards and technology. Company documents, data, graphics, video, and other information on an intranet are available only to company employees and those specifically authorized to enter the system. Thus, if a sales representative who is out of town needs an expense form, a contract template, sales histories, product literature, or a press release, the representative can access the company information via an intranet. While access via laptop computers is most common, access to intranets is increasingly via mobile handheld devices, such web-enabled mobile phones or PDAs.

An **extranet** is an intranet that is shared with outside parties, such as customers. Often extranets are used as order-entry systems that allow customers to place their own orders. These are especially beneficial for customers that have loyal relationships with a company.

> General Electric this quarter will expand auction, invoicing and demand forecasting capabilities on its private Web exchange in an effort to cut administrative costs and increase supplier participation. With some 36,000 supplier members, GE's Global Supplier Network (GSN) already is one of the largest private Web marketplaces, eclipsing Wal-Mart's 30,000-supplier exchange. But GSN's roster still represents only a quarter of the companies that trade online with GE's 25-plus business units, and about 40 percent of the company's $50 billion in annual spending.[6]

GE and many other firms use extranets for B2B interactions and intranets to maintain contact with the salesforce and to increase the efficiency of placing orders, checking on their status, or pricing repetitively purchased items.

Price Quotes and Order Configuration

SFA systems typically will include data from product catalogs, price lists, discount schedules, and other order information necessary to provide price quotes. **Product configurators** are very important for sales representatives who sell complex products that have to be custom-tailored for a particular customer's situation. Product configurator software programs (often available on an organization's intranet) configure and price products on the spot, reducing the time a sales representative spends working on a proposal.

Some configurators, in addition to telling salespeople how to tailor products to order, can be used to suggest cross-selling companions. In many systems, configurators are programmed on an extranet to allow the customers to place orders at their convenience. As more organizations order from the Web, interact with salespeople by e-mail, and track orders themselves, it becomes more important for selling organizations to ensure an appropriate level of personal contact and effective methods for following up on each sale.

Follow-up Management

Follow-up management, usually as a part of the contact management software, is of great importance to SFA. The CRM system at headquarters may send an e-mail to the sales representative on the road to indicate that a shipment has been sent on time. Or, the SFA software may indicate that a delay should be expected and a computer-generated letter has already been sent explaining the problem.

Analysis and Reporting Tools

SFA within an effective CRM system allows sales representatives to easily generate call reports and other sales reports. It allows sales managers to analyze sales figures and activity levels by

data integration, assignment management, problem resolution, and several other tasks. Many of these activities are highly technical, so we will focus on the basic issues of call center management.

Guiding each customer's call to the customer service representative who is most capable of helping is the concept of **call routing.** In many instances, the call routing software directs the call to an interactive voice response system rather than to a person to allow the computer to handle the entire call.

Interactive Voice Response (IVR) is a convergence of computer telephone integration and voice messaging. IVR can be thought of as a computer talking to a person.[13] The most common input device is a touchtone telephone, and the common CRM system response is a human voice. (A widespread use of IVR is the typical bank-by-phone system in which a customer presses number *1* for option *A,* number *2* for option *B,* etc.) Some systems incorporate voice recognition as input. FedEx's system asks, "Is you package over 100 pounds?" and the caller merely responds "yes."

Information technology with **caller ID systems** has been developed to send incoming phone numbers to the data warehouse, where the caller is instantly matched to a customer record. Simple caller ID systems, such as those in households, provide the name, number, date, and time of the call. Sophisticated caller ID systems trigger information about the entire history of interactions and purchases of the customer with the organization. The call and record are passed to the "next available" customer service representative or another level of the IVR via an **automatic distribution system (ACD).** At the next level calls can be prioritized making it possible to segment customers as they enter the system and handle them as individuals rather than as members of a group. The least desirable customers might never exit the IVR, those in the middle might at least get an option to speak to a human, and high-value customers might get to bypass the IVR altogether.[14]

> The telephones at Capital One Financial Corp. ring more than one million times a week. Here's what happens: Before a caller hears the first ring, the computers identify who is calling and predict the reason for the call. After reviewing 50 options for whom to notify, the computers pick the best option for each situation. Tim Gorman, for example, is a retention specialist who answers the call when the customer's statement is, "I want to close my account." Gorman knows better. Most of them just want a better deal or a lower interest rate. Capital One has enough information on consumers to fill the hard drives of more than 200,000 personal computers. It uses that information much as a physicist uses a particle accelerator: to make scientific decisions that provide mass customization.[15]

Many call center operations begin the CRM process by creating a **trouble ticket,** also known as a **caller note.** The system immediately issues an identification number to the customer when the customer makes the initial call.[16] The identification number is then associated with the customer account number and a log of activities. Thus, information from each contact point can be accessed by subsequent customer service representatives working to resolve the problem or handle the customer's requests. Regardless of the level of automation, customer satisfaction often rests on the characteristics of the personnel hired and trained to interact with customers.

CHARACTERISTICS OF CUSTOMER SERVICE PERSONNEL

Typically, customer service personnel should have the following qualifications: a good phone voice, proper phone etiquette, a positive attitude, self-motivation, and grace under pressure. Customer service personnel, especially technical support workers, should also have highly developed listening and problem-resolution skills, and have in-depth knowledge of the company's products and services.[17]

A company that offers "round-the-clock-support" may hire service personnel in several geographical locations that have been selected because they are indifferent to time zones. For example, a company that uses the "follow-the-sun" concept may have workers in California answering the 9:00 P.M. calls from New York.

Data mining and advanced statistical techniques (see Chapter 9) can be used to analytically derive which answer should be given to certain types of customers who call with particular questions. **Call scripting** is a prearranged and written response to varying, usually repetitive, problems from customers. The script used is often called a situational script. Once a customer service representative enters key words associated with the reason for the call into his or her computer, a situational script appears. Such scripts, when they appear on the monitor, eliminate the need for representatives to make assumptions about what response should be given and allow the organization to hire less experienced personnel to work the phones. Scripts also allow a company to present consistent responses when having a uniform image is desirable.

Scripts may be developed based on the following factors:[18]

- Reason for contact
- Customer's behavioral preferences
- Lifetime customer value
- Cross-selling opportunities and propensity to buy
- Current sales promotions or price deals

For example, when Tim Gorman at Capital One answered the phone to hear that Nancy from North Carolina wanted to close her account, the system identified Nancy as a valuable customer (four year duration, no annual fee, no late payment within 12 months). Further, the monitor displayed three counteroffers that Tim could make in an effort to keep her business.[19]

Evaluation of Call Center Data

CRM software can be used to analyze the effectiveness of the call center's operations. The system should have built-in tracking features that allow the company to evaluate the performance of individual agents and the unit as a whole.[20] The organization should be able to monitor the number of calls, call type, time waiting on hold, abandonment rates (how many calls result in a hang up), time-to-resolution, and average length of call. Many call center systems allow the organization to tape and review calls for quality-control purposes. (The customer should be informed if the call is being recorded.) These issues will also be discussed in Chapter 10 with the measurement of CRM system effectiveness.

WEB-BASED SELF SERVICE

At the outset, it should be noted that the cost of interacting with customers on a Web site is miniscule compared to that of a live person interacting with customers. Nevertheless, many aspects of call center management, such as situational scripting, also apply to customer service and support via the Internet. Yet, the self-service on a company Web site offers some unique opportunities.

Given the lower costs of the Web site in comparison to the people who staff a call center, neophyte managers may be tempted to send all complaints to the Web. What, in that case, is the role of the call center? Effective organizations try to channel traffic to the Web, but they also maintain a call center to help customers who cannot manage the Web or who cannot find an answer to their problems at that location. Then, as unanswerable issues are collected within the call center, the Web site technicians should receive information on how to up-date the FAQs feature or the Web site itself—again, a circular process.

FAQs are frequently asked questions. Most companies can better serve customers if a list of common questions and answers is available on the Web site. If the customer service personnel are doing their jobs and information technology is configured appropriately, FAQs are updated over time and used as input to improve manufacturing processes, delivery options, and instruction sheets.

A web site should have information indicating how to contact the company by letter, telephone, or e-mail. A "contact us" link and an easy to use email response for feedback are essential for a company serious about creating good customer relationships. Organizations should indicate that they read every message and appreciate customer input by building in abilities to respond quickly to an unusual problem or request. Giving tardy responses to e-mail questions is a sure way to cause customer dissatisfaction.

One of the most prevalent complaints about buying products over the Internet is the lack of immediate, personalized help with what are often simple questions. **Live person chat software,** such as that offered by LivePerson.com, allows live customer service agents to interact with Web users when customers make an inquiry. The software allows Web site visitors to engage in a real-time text conversation with customer service support staff who can answer questions. Because consumers often ask similar questions, many of the answers are pre-formatted, and scripted answers are given. That way, customer service representatives can click on an icon and send what appear to be personalized answers to frequently encountered questions.

As we discussed in the section on sales automation, customers may also prefer to order online from a Web site. Consumers can shop from their homes or offices by using personal computers to interact with retailers on the Internet called e-tailers. For example, Travelocity.com, Expedia.com, and many other sites allow owners of personal computers to book airline flights and hotel reservations online. While the number of Internet Web sites, or "store fronts," where products can be ordered has been growing rapidly, the proportion of buyers varies.

While it is estimated that about 34 percent of people have access to the Internet, up from 31 percent in 2001, a stagnant 15 percent actually make purchases. "Almost one-third of users who have not shopped online said they were reluctant to give their credit card details, and more than a quarter felt that it was safer to buy goods and services in a store."[21]

This hesitancy on the part of buyers to conduct e-business is understandable. As we have stressed throughout this chapter, SFA and automated calling centers face risks. People do not automatically accept technological innovations and change. Organizations must be prepared to understand the change process and invest in the people as well as in the equipment of SFA and automated calling centers.

SUMMARY

The application of digital and wireless technologies to personal selling is known as sales force automation (SFA). Mobile phones, voice messaging systems, fax machines, and e-mail can be efficient media that field sales representatives use to communicate with prospects and clients. Laptop computers, PDAs (Personal Digital Assistants), interactive Web sites, wireless data transmission, and especially CRM databases continue to dramatically change the administrative activities of salespeople. In addition to the costs of the equipment, SFA may also incur personnel costs as people attempt to incorporate the technology into their working lives.

The sales process is a logical sequence of selling stages that occur between the time an opportunity is recognized and a prospect is identified and the time of follow-up activities after a sale is closed. SFA applications are designed to help the sales representative during each stage of the sales process. Records may indicate that potential customers are in various stages of the sales pipeline, including prospects, qualified leads, developed, negotiated, or closed (won or lost).

SFA consists of many tasks, including contact management; lead management and, more broadly, opportunity management; knowledge management and intranet access; price quotes and order configuration; follow-up management; and sales analysis and reporting tools.

Customer service and support issues can be resolved through multiple media where the customer can visit a store, telephone a call center, e-mail the company, interact with the company on its Web site, fax the company, write a letter, or make other arrangements. CRM automates and makes many customer service operations self-service.

A company's call center is an organizational unit that supports direct customer interaction via telephone, well-configured information technology, and capable service personnel. Interactive Voice Response (IVR) is a convergence of computer telephone integration and voice messaging. IVR can be thought of as a computer talking to a person. Call routing software is used to guide each call to the customer service representative who is most capable of resolving the specific problem. In many appropriate instances, call routing directs the call to an interactive voice response rather than to a person.

A trouble ticket, or caller note, with an identification number is sometimes associated with the customer account number and a log of activities. Thus, information from each contact point can be accessed by subsequent customer service representatives working to resolve the problem or handle the customer's requests. Data mining and advanced statistical techniques can be used to analytically derive what "situational script" or answer should be given to certain types of customers who call with particular questions. FAQs, live person chats, and many telephone call activities, such as situational scripting, also apply to customer service and support via the Internet.

A key issue is for managers to understand that their job is to supplement sales representatives and customer service personnel with technology as opposed to erroneously believing that all problems can be resolved with self-service systems.

KEY TERMS

automatic distribution system (ACD)
call center
call routing
call scripting
caller id systems
close the sale
collaborative communication
consultative selling
contact management

extranet
FAQS
interactive voice response (IVR)
intranet
knowledge management
lead management software
leads
live person chat software
online incentive programs
opportunity management

product configurators
prospecting
qualified leads
relationship selling
sales cycle
sales force automation
sales forecast
sales pipeline
sales process
trouble ticket (caller note)

QUESTIONS FOR REVIEW AND CRITICAL THINKING

1. Define SFA. What are its major purposes?
2. Identify potential problems with SFA. What are the possible barriers to its successful implementation?
3. What is contact management?
4. How are lead management and opportunity management related?
5. It has been said that "Calls aren't calls, they're people." How does this apply to call center management?
6. What are some tactics associated with Interactive Voice Response (IVR)?
7. What is the purpose of a trouble ticket?
8. What types of calling scripts might an airline have for its call center employees?
9. What steps should organizations take to help employees accept SFA?
10. Provide positive and negative examples of your own interactions with automated customer service operations.

NOTES

1. Reprinted from Judy Tong, "Business Cards Get Automatic Update," *New York Times*, (5 May 2002), sec. BU, p. 2.
2. Paul Greenberg, *CRM at the Speed of Light* (Berkeley: Osborne/McGraw-Hill, 2001): 71–92.
3. Cheri Speier and Viswanath Venkatesh, "The Hidden Minefields in the Adoption of Sales Force Automation Technologies," *Journal of Marketing* 66 (July 2002): 98–111.
4. Julia Chang, "Click Here for Sales Leads," *Sales and Marketing Management* 154:8 (August 2002): 24.
5. Thomas H. Davenport and Lawrence Prusak, *Working Knowledge of How Organizations Manage What They Know* (Boston: Harvard Business School Press, 1998).
6. Tim Wilson, "GE Expands Private Hub to Woo Users," *Internetweek* (7 January 2002): 1, 38.
7. Cheri Speier and Viswanath Venkatesh, "The Hidden Minefields in the Adoption of Sales Force Automation Technologies," *Journal of Marketing* 66 (July 2002): 98–111.
8. Mark McMaster, "Gadgets for the Sales Force," *Sales and Marketing Management* 154:8 (August 2002): 23.

9. Mark McMaster,"Help Desk: Desktop Incentives," *Sales and Marketing Management* 154:8 (August 2002): 25.

10. Stewart Deck, "Three Companies Zero in on Exactly What They Need from CRM—and Then Make It Happen," CIO, <http://www.cio.com/research/crm/>.

11. Jerre L. Stead, "Call Center Services and Technologies: Changing the Way Businesses Operate," *Telemarketing* 10:12 (June 1992): 84.

12. Reprinted with permission from Paul Greenberg, *CRM at the Speed of Light: Capturing and Keeping Customers in Internet Real Time* (Berkeley: Osborne/McGraw-Hill, 2001): 179.

13. Atlantic IVR found at <http://atlanticivr.com/>.

14. Jim Quiggins, "The Route Less Traveled: Conflicting Trends and Interesting Opportunities in Contact Routing," *Customer Interface,*15:4 (April 2002): 13.

15. Charles Fishman, "This Is a Marketing Revolution," *Fast Company* 24 (May 1999): 2, 3.

16. Jill Dyche, *The CRM Handbook: A Business Guide to Customer Relationship Management* (Boston: Addison-Wessley 2002): 54.

17. Diane Gerstner, "Higher Calling: Here Are Five Steps That a Bank Can Take to Develop a Call Center Strategy to Improve Customer Outreach and Enhance Sales," *ABA Banking Journal* 34:3 (April 2002): 22.

18. Jill Dyche, *The CRM Handbook: A Business Guide to Customer Relationship Management* (Boston: Addison-Wessley, 2002): 63.

19. Charles Fishman, "This Is a Marketing Revolution," *Fast Company* 24 (May 1999): 2, 3.

20. Diane Gerstner, "Higher Calling: Here Are Five Steps That a Bank Can Take to Develop a Call Center Strategy to Improve Customer Outreach and Enhance Sales," *ABA Banking Journal* 34:3 (April 2002): 22.

21. Taylor Nelson Sofres, "Cyber-Nervous," *Marketing News* (19 August 2002): 3.

The Basics of Data Mining, Online Analytical Processing, and Information Presentation

Joan, the head nurse of the operating room (OR) at a medium-sized, private hospital was concerned—revenues were down but the number of cases handled each day was higher than it had ever been before. Thus, the nursing staff was stretched to the limit, but the hospital continued to show large losses.

Joan began to drill into the data warehouse in search of answers. She started by clustering doctors based on volume, profitability, and time of day for procedures. She ended the first phase of her search with a much clearer idea of the situation. A few of the clusters of physicians she discovered included:

- **Baby Trenders:** The OR lost money on each baby delivered but made money on each hysterectomy performed. Physicians from three clinics in town seemed to be very balanced in performing both procedures, a break-even concept for the hospital. Physicians from two clinics performed births occasionally but performed hysterectomies at a competing facility, resulting in a net loss for the hospital.

- **Boneyard Bluesers:** The OR lost money on any orthopedic procedure— spinal fusion, hip or joint replacement—due to the limited reimbursements allowed by Medicare, the high costs of the hardware used, and the flat rate fee provided for the procedure regardless of complications. Joan's predecessor had been heavily recruiting orthopedic surgeons, purchasing special equipment to satisfy their needs, and scheduling operations at prime times for this group.

- **Suburban Sneakers:** The greatest loss of money occurred after 3 P.M., when a group of physicians would schedule elective surgeries. These surgeons performed their profitable procedures in the morning at other hospitals in the city, held office hours, and then wanted to schedule a few operations at Joan's OR on their way to their suburban homes. Given that Joan then had to pay overtime for her nursing staff, the hospital lost money on each surgery performed. While we may be uncomfortable with the concept of considering profits in association with hospitals, Joan was faced with real dilemmas. If the hospital could not at least break even and had to close its doors, the west portion of town would be without medical care. The data mining process yielded ideas for Joan to reverse the trend and still maintain the ethical standards of health care.

First, Joan asked the OB-GYN doctors from the two clinics to use her every now and then for hysterectomies. They were pleased to do so. Joan then asked the orthopedic surgeons to use her OR whenever they needed to but to consider using other facilities for the majority of their procedures. The larger facilities were more able to absorb the losses from orthopedic procedures with the gains made from cardiologists, urologists, and other operations. For the suburban sneakers, Joan implemented a policy of no elective procedures past 3 P.M. and carefully explained to each physician the need for the policy. While some of these surgeons were not pleased, others began to use Joan's OR in the morning hours. By summer 2002, the hospital was showing enough of a profit to remain open, and the surgeons had a new respect for the head of OR and for the hospital.

DATA MINING

Firms often classify their customers so that data mining can be used to aim the most effective marketing strategies at specific groups. A good example of a systematic approach to customer classification is RFM, which stands for recency, frequency, and monetary.[1] RFM enables customers to be arrayed in terms of recent purchases, frequent purchases, and average purchase amount. The data warehouse is queried to obtain the data on each customer, and then a quantitative analysis is conducted to arrive at the classifications.

For each of the three measures (recency, frequency, and monetary), customers are assigned codes of 1, 2, or 3. For example, a scoring system such as the following would be used for recency:

- Code 1 = Customer made the most recent purchase a year or more ago
- Code 2 = Customer made the most recent purchase more than a month ago but less than a year ago
- Code 3 = Customer made the most recent purchase within the past month

When each measure is treated in this manner, each customer is assigned a three-digit code, ranging from 333 (the best) to 111 (the poorest). In all there are 27 such codes, allowing for 27 classes. If the firm wants fewer classes, the codes can be grouped in some manner, such as assigning the top 20 percent to a Top group, the middle 60 percent to a Middle group, and the bottom 20 percent to a Bottom group.

Although a classification of this type could be accomplished using a database for a transaction processing system, the availability of rich historical data from the data warehouse provides a more stable basis for the classification.

In our model of the CRM system in Exhibit 4.1, we identified three basic components—the data gathering system, the data warehouse system, and the information delivery system. The purpose of the gathering and storing is to make the data available to CRM system users for analysis when it is needed. The warehouse data repository represents a valuable corporate resource, but in order for its potential to be realized, three basic functions must be performed:

- Retrieval of the data from the warehouse data repository
- Transformation of the data into information
- Presentation of the information to the CRM system users

The term data mining has been coined to describe the retrieval of data from the warehouse. Some data mining software can also perform the transformation and presentation of data, or those functions can be performed by other software. A special class of data mining software called OLAP, for online analytical processing, is tailored to the needs of the data warehouse user. In this chapter we present the basics of data mining and OLAP, and conclude with a discussion of information presentation.

A natural resource resides in the ground; if the resource is to be used, it must be mined. Benjamin Franklin supposedly said,

"Genius without education is like silver in the mine."

If Ben was with us today, and if he was a data warehousing enthusiast, he might well say,

"Genius without education is like data in the warehouse."

The view that the warehouse data must be mined is an appropriate one. The resource is there somewhere, but an effort must be made to find it, retrieve it, and refine it for use.

Data mining is not a blanket term that covers *all* types of information retrieval from a data warehouse. Rather, data mining refers to the retrieval of previously unknown information. We can define **data mining** as the collection of processes that enables a data warehouse user to learn of patterns, relationships, and trends in data not previously known to exist. Applied to CRM, data mining is performed on customer data in an effort to better understand customers and their behaviors.

DECISION SUPPORT

We have recognized that, unlike transaction processing systems, the data warehouse system is intended for use in decision making. The idea of using the computer as a decision support system (DSS) can be traced back to an article in the *Sloan Management Review* by two MIT professors, G. Anthony Gorry and Michael S. Scott Morton, in 1971.[2] The authors described an approach for using the computer to support managers that contrasted with the then popular **management information system (MIS)** approach. Until that time, firms had sought to develop large, comprehensive information systems—MISs—to meet the information needs of all managers in the firm. This task had proven to be overly ambitious, and there were many failures. Managers didn't really know what information they needed, and information specialists didn't understand management.

Gorry and Morton decided to scrap the shotgun approach of the MIS and take a rifle approach, building information systems to support particular decisions that managers made. They coined the term **decision support system,** or **DSS,** to describe a system that assists a problem solver in making the decisions that are necessary to solve a problem. The approach has proven to be a successful, and therefore popular, use of the computer ever since. DSS users typically make database queries and use mathematical models to simulate phenomena in the process of obtaining the information that they need.

CRM system users can use the CRM system as a DSS. We have described how the users make repeated queries of data in the data warehouse. The users can also enter decisions into a mathematical model that uses warehouse data and see the effect of the decisions—a process called "playing the what-if game." Exhibit 9.1 illustrates this modeling process. The user enters decisions into the client workstation and the decisions are transmitted to the data warehouse server, which retrieves data from the data warehouse for use in the modeling. The results of the modeling are transmitted to the client workstation. If the user is not satisfied with the results, the user can modify the decisions and initiate another simulation. As with repeated querying, the modeling is repeated until the user is satisfied with the results.

Since mathematical models typically project historical data into the future, the use of a data warehouse can offer substantial advantages over the use of transaction processing system databases for data support. The data warehouse represents a much richer description of historic performance and, hence, can increase the accuracy of the modeling effort.

HYPOTHESIS VERIFICATION AND KNOWLEDGE DISCOVERY

The querying and modeling activities are examples of a type of data mining called **hypothesis verification.** The user has a preconceived notion of a situation that is thought to exist and uses the CRM system to either support or negate that hypothesis.

Data mining also enables a second type of use to be performed—**knowledge discovery.** This occurs when the user leaves it up to the CRM system to identify certain patterns that exist in the data. The user may suspect that certain types of patterns exist but not know what they are or how to describe them. For example, the user may suspect that customers buy products in a certain sequence but not know what the products are or the sequence in which they are purchased.

Hypothesis verification is a *user-driven* application in that the user guides the retrieval process. Knowledge discovery, on the other hand, is *system-driven* in that the system determines the types and sequences of the processes to be performed.

EXHIBIT 9.1	AN EXAMPLE OF MINING FOR DECISION SUPPORT

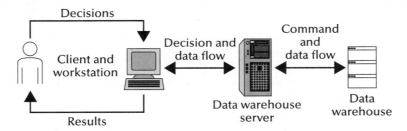

DATA MINING FUNCTIONS

Regardless of whether the CRM system is being used for hypothesis verification or knowledge discovery, data mining can be used to perform four basic functions—determining classifications for the data, forming clusters from the data, determining whether certain associations exist in the data, and determining whether any sequences exist. All of these functions have particular relevance for CRM users.

Classifications

We saw at the beginning of the chapter that businesses often classify their customers based on the customers' behavior so that special products and services can be offered to the more valuable classes—the best customers. A credit card company, for example, will offer a special type of card to its customers who use their card often and pay their bills promptly. An industrial marketing firm will group its customers into credit classes based on purchase and payment habits and offer greater amounts of credit to the better risks.

Clusters

Marketers like to be able to identify clusters of customers with similar characteristics. Recall from Chapter 2 that the PRIZM system describes clusters of lifestyles such as the *shotguns* or *grays*. Armed with such information, organizations can aim particular marketing programs at specific clusters. Data mining software can base the clustering on all types of data—demographic, geographic, activity, psychographic, and behavioral—for a potentially more accurate clustering algorithm than could be achieved by any other means. An **algorithm** is a mathematical routine that can be incorporated into software to enable the computer to accomplish a particular function. Algorithms are frequently based on historical data, and the data warehouse provides a rich source.

Associations

Associations are relationships between such entities as products. Marketers want to know whether such associations exist, and their strength, so that they can make decisions based on the related products. For example, a manufacturer of breakfast muffins can attach a coupon entitling the buyer to a discount on butter to each package. Or, when deciding on store layout, a food store retailer can locate items in the same area if the items are frequently purchased together. The process of identifying associations among products or behaviors is called **associations discovery.** In Chapter 3 we described how Osco Drugs learned that a man buying diapers between 6 and 8 P.M. sometimes also purchased a six-pack of beer. The association of those two products could be strong enough to locate the beer section next to the baby products section. In making the association, no distinctions are made between dependent and independent variables. In other words, no effort is made to determine which product causes the other to be purchased.

Patterns or Sequences

Marketers are also interested in any patterns or sequences in a customer's purchase behavior. Perhaps certain behaviors occur in a certain sequence. This type of data mining is called **sequential pattern discovery.** It includes time as a variable. We discussed this application in Chapter 3 and illustrated it with Exhibit 3.10 to show how TV, computer, and CD/Tape/Radio products are purchased in sequences. The strength of the sequence can be measured quantitatively with the support factor, which is based on the percent of observations that exhibit a particular sequence.

Another approach to discovering patterns or sequences is **similar time sequence discovery.** It not only discovers a sequential pattern, but it also identifies other behaviors with similar patterns. A customer cluster may make purchases in a certain sequence and similar time sequence discovery could be used to identify other clusters that follow similar sequences. For example, football fans purchase catered products, picnic supplies, and other products during football season every year. Each data mining software system is designed to perform one or more of these functions.

How Harrah's Applies the Functions

A good example of how these functions enable a firm to better manage its customer relationships is the way that the Harrah's gambling casino organization mines its data warehouse of customer data.3 Harrah's offers its customers a "frequent gambler" magnetic stripe card, called Total Rewards, that they use when they patronize the various gambling machines. Harrah's is therefore able to build customer profiles based on the machines used, the number of wagers placed, the average bet, and the total amount of money wagered. Twenty-five million Harrah's customers are motivated to use their cards as a way to earn such awards as free trips, meals, and hotel rooms. The benefit to Harrah's is in its ability to better understand customers and to then develop appropriate marketing strategies.

The casino learned that 30 percent of its customers who spent between $100 and $300 per visit accounted for 80 percent of the revenues and almost 100 percent of the profits. Using these profiles, Harrah's was able to group its customers into 90 demographic segments and tailor direct-mail advertising to each. The organization learned that the main determinants of being a repeat customer are age and distance from the customer's home to the casino. The organization could additionally have developed projections concerning the machines used and the number of coins entered. As an example, the "ideal" customer is a 62-year-old woman who lives within 30 minutes of Kansas City, Missouri (where their riverboat casino is located), and plays dollar video poker.

By mining the detailed data, Harrah's is able to cluster their customers into demographic groupings, identify associations among gambling machines, and even project sequences in which the machines will be used.

KNOWLEDGE DISCOVERY METHODOLOGIES

In order for the CRM system to discover patterns in the warehouse data largely independent of user direction, the system must exhibit some type of intelligence. Several methodologies have been employed. Among the more popular are decision trees, genetic algorithms, memory based reasoning, and neural networks.

Decision Trees

A **decision tree** is a network that provides a map for use in drawing conclusions about an entity based on its attributes. Such a network is simply a series of logical paths that can be followed to lead to some conclusion. Usually there is a single starting point and multiple ending points, depending on the paths taken. Exhibit 9.2A is a table of self-reported churn probability data, provided by a store's customers. The table considers three variables in predicting churn rate—whether the customer has a store credit card, whether the customer has any credit card, and whether the customer's home zip code area is the same as that of the store. Exhibit 9.2B is the decision tree that was produced from the data. The base of the tree is called the root, and the ends of the branches are called the leaves. Usually the root is at the top or the left-hand side of the diagram, and the logical progression moves from top down or from left to right. The example shows how a customer can be classified in terms of churn probability based on his or her

---

EXHIBIT 9.2   A DECISION TREE

Customer number	Store card	Any card	Zip code	Churn probability
1	N	N	Same	Good
2	N	N	Different	Good
3	N	Y	Different	Good
4	Y	Y	Different	Poor
5	Y	Y	Same	Good
6	Y	N	Same	Poor
7	Y	N	Different	Poor

A. Self-reported customer loyalty data

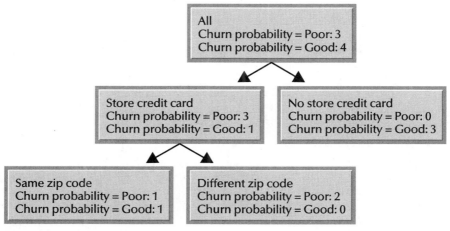

B. Decision tree

attributes by using the table data. In this example, the decision tree modeling algorithm determined that the two best predictors of churn were whether a customer has a store credit card and whether the customer lives in the same zip code area that the store is in. The algorithm determined that having just any credit card was not a factor.[4]

Genetic Algorithms

A **genetic algorithm** is another type of network that can be followed to reach a conclusion. This network has its origin in biology, and it duplicates how a species evolves over multiple generations. The evolution is based on the idea of the survival of the fittest, and it culls out extreme cases for each generation. Exhibit 9.3 shows the first three generations of a proposed advertising strategy. The strategy requires that a decision be made concerning the number of ads to be used in order to maximize sales. Too few ads will fail to make an impact and represent lost revenue potential. Too many can turn the customer off and cause ill will. The number of ads evolves generation by generation, from left to right. In this example, the algorithm simulates additional generations to determine the optimum number of ads.

Memory Based Reasoning

Memory based reasoning is based on the idea of remembering something that has happened in the past and using that memory to make predictions of what might happen in the future. Applied to marketing, this is the essence of brand loyalty—customers remember satisfaction from previous product purchases and predict that such satisfaction will continue in the future.

EXHIBIT 9.3   **AN EXAMPLE OF GENETIC ALGORITHM GENERATIONS**

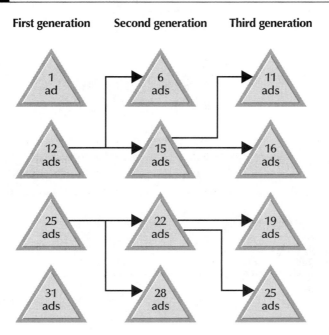

In data mining applications, data records for entities that have a known behavior pattern are grouped to form a test case. For example, data records for customers who make exceptionally large purchases can be grouped and their attributes analyzed to produce a profile of a loyal customer. Then, records for customers with unknown purchase habits can be matched to the profile to determine whether they are potential loyal customers. The same logic can be applied to projecting sequential purchase behavior. A profile of purchase patterns or sequences can be developed from known activity and then used to predict what purchases will be made by customers who have yet to display the activity.

RFM is an example of memory-based reasoning. The customer's past behavior in terms of recency, frequency, and monetary level is remembered and used as a predictor of future behavior.

Neural Networks

Neural networks are another knowledge discovery approach based on biology. In this instance, the basis is the human brain. The neural network, or neural net, is a mathematical model that simulates the interconnected neurons of the human brain. A neuron has the same basic construction as a computer—input, processing, and output. Inputs from other neurons are called dendrites, and outputs to other neurons are called axons. The central processor is called the soma, and it compares the input electrochemical signals to a threshold level to determine whether the neuron will fire and send an impulse to other neurons. Exhibit 9.4A shows these basic neuron components. A neural net consists of layers of nodes connected in one direction as shown in Exhibit 9.4B. Through continual exposure to input values, the network can be trained to discover relationships among the inputs. For example, a neural net can be trained to identify a particular kind of car or bird based on its attributes. Applied to marketing, a neural net can be used to identify a customer who is a good credit risk.

Exhibit 9.5 is a table that shows how the various methodologies are especially well suited to perform the four basic data mining functions.

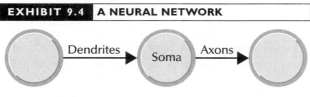

EXHIBIT 9.4   A NEURAL NETWORK

Dendrites   Soma   Axons

A. Neuron components

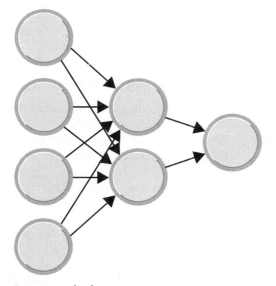

B. A network of neurons

BASICS OF OLAP

OLAP is geared to the needs of the data warehouse user, enabling the interactive user to perform multidimensional analyses and obtain

| EXHIBIT 9.5 | KNOWLEDGE DSCOVERY METHODOLOGIES PERFORM THE BASIC FUNCTIONS |

Methodology	Classifications	Clusters	Associations	Patterns or sequences
Decision trees	X			
Genetic algorithms		X		
Memory based reasoning	X		X	X
Neural networks	X	X		X

quick responses. The user can interact with the system using either a graphical or Web interface and can obtain information outputs in a variety of formats, including graphics.

OLAP is capable of making such popular calculations on the data as moving averages and time series. OLAP also supports drill down, roll up, drill across, and drill through. We discussed these operations in Chapter 4 and illustrated them with Exhibit 4.10. OLAP also can rotate the data in the multidimensional hypercube, enabling the user to view the data from different perspectives. The rotation is called slicing and dicing, and it is illustrated in Exhibit 9.6.

In this example, the three dimensions of the hypercube are customer, product class, and time. The three dimensions can be displayed in a tabular format by assigning a page to one dimension and using rows and columns for the other two. In Exhibit 9.6A, each customer is displayed on a separate page, and rows and columns are used for months and product classes respectively. This display permits the viewer to see how a customer's product class purchases vary by month. Exhibit 9.6B facilitates an analysis by time, showing each customer's purchases by product class. Exhibit 9.6C shows how a customer's purchases of a particular product class vary by month.

This is a simplified example, limiting the analysis to three dimensions. In practice, the number of dimensions can be much greater. Dr. E. F. Codd, in laying out the OLAP guidelines in his 1993 white paper, specified that the number of dimensions should be unlimited.[5]

BASIC ONLINE ANALYTICAL PROCESSING ARCHITECTURES

OLAP can obtain its data from either relational or multidimensional databases. When the data warehouse consists of data stored in relational tables, the architecture is called **ROLAP (relational online analytical processing).** When data in the data warehouse is stored in multidimensional tables, the name **MOLAP (multidimensional online analytical processing)** is used. These architectures are shown in Exhibit 9.7.

In this illustration, both architectures feature servers on two tiers. In the ROLAP architecture, a data warehouse server retrieves the data from the data warehouse, and a ROLAP server performs the functions of a relational database management system on the retrieved relational data. In the MOLAP architecture, the data warehouse server retrieves the data, and the MOLAP server performs the multidimensional database management functions and downloads a multidimensional database (MDDB) to the client workstation.

The structure of the data—relational or multidimensional—has dramatic influences on the capabilities of the two architectures.

EXHIBIT 9.6 **HYPERCUBE ROTATION PRODUCES MULTIPLE VIEWS**

Customer: Lynette Brandon

Month	Shoes	Coats	Sweaters	Skirts/Slacks
January 2003	145.00	279.95	118.29	.00
February 2003	.00	.00	79.95	.00
March 2003	239.50	.00	.00	391.50
April 2003	49.95	.00	.00	129.95

A. Sales by customer by product class by month

Month: January 2003

Product	Millie Hyde	Lynette Brandon	Pat Rector	Ben Varner
Shoes	.00	145.00	89.95	234.68
Coats	234.68	279.95	.00	434.50
Sweaters	112.19	118.29	.00	.00
Skirts/Slacks	141.12	.00	217.92	.00

B. Sales by month by product class by customer

Product Class: Shoes

Customer	January 2003	February 2003	March 2003	April 2003
Millie Hyde	.00	.00	.00	238.92
Lynette Brandon	145.00	94.25	.00	.00
Pat Rector	89.95	122.34	89.95	119.35
Ben Varner	234.68	.00	112.92	.00

C. Sales by product class by customer by month

Relational Online Analytical Processing (ROLAP)

Databases of all sizes consist of relational tables. These databases are well supported by such standard DBMSs as DB2, Oracle, and Access—all of which have proven capabilities in terms of managing databases of virtually unlimited size. However, when put in a data warehousing setting, they suffer the limitation of being unable to perform all of the necessary analysis.

Exhibit 9.8 is an example of a type of report that could be produced by ROLAP. It is an analysis of sales by store region, product class, and quarter. Separate pages can be used for each product class for each region. Using separate pages is a good way to handle more than two or three dimensions.

Gross sales, returns, and net sales are shown for each quarter, with final totals for each. These amounts can be calculated from data of a fine granularity in the warehouse data repository. This example illustrates how information outputs can be generated from detailed warehouse data.

EXHIBIT 9.7   **ROLAP AND MOLAP ARCHITECTURES**

A. ROLAP architecture

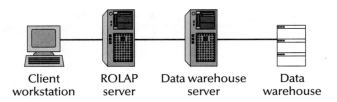

| Client | ROLAP | Data warehouse | Data |
| workstation | server | server | warehouse |

B. MOLAP architecture

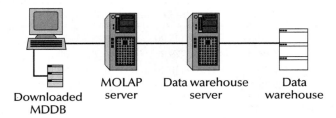

| Downloaded | MOLAP | Data warehouse | Data |
| MDDB | server | server | warehouse |

EXHIBIT 9.8   **AN EXAMPLE OF A REPORT THAT COULD BE PRODUCED WITH ROLAP**

Product Class by Store Region by Quarter
2001 Through 2003
In Dollars

Store region: West
Product class: Video

Quarter	Gross sales	Returns	Net sales
1/2001	16,525	765	15,760
2/2001	7,280	0	7,280
3/2001	11,310	1,108	10,202
4/2001	12,445	1,829	10,616
1/2002	16,418	2,314	14,104
2/2002	1,320	725	595
3/2002	6,694	890	5,804
4/2002	12,310	2,555	9,755
1/2003	11,927	3,719	8,208
2/2003	5,423	1,429	3,994
3/2003	2,764	960	1,804
4/2003	15,329	4,320	11,009
Total	119,745	20,614	99,131

Multidimensional Online Analytical Processing (MOLAP)

Multidimensional databases are an outgrowth of data warehousing and are not typically used as commercial databases. Therefore, such commercial DBMSs as Access and DB2 are not available. Instead, vendors such as IBM and Microsoft have developed multidimensional database management systems (MDBMSs). The MDBMSs are well suited to OLAP in being able to perform complex analyses on multidimensional data, but a shortcoming is the fact that database size is limited. This is the reason for downloading the MDDB to the client workstation. The MDBMS, therefore, must only manage a subset of the data in the data warehouse.

An example of a report produced with MOLAP appears in Exhibit 9.9. It is a report of year-to-date product sales by store and customer gender. The totals for gender and age group are carried as summary totals in the downloaded MDDB. This example illustrates how outputs can be produced from preprocessed summary data and used to develop marketing strategies. Here, males aged 21 through 31 represent the cluster that is the best target for promotional or other activity.

A decision that CRM system designers must make is whether to use ROLAP or MOLAP. A determining factor is the type of analysis to be performed. When the database is large and analysis is modest, ROLAP can do the job and is well supported by off-the-shelf software systems. When the database is smaller and analysis is complex, MOLAP is much preferred. In those cases where user needs tap into strengths of both ROLAP and MOLAP, a hybrid approach such as the HOLAP option of the Microsoft SQL Server 2000 Analysis Services can solve the dilemma.

OLAP SOFTWARE

Two examples of OLAP software systems are the Microsoft SQL Server 2000 Analysis Services and the IBM DB2 OLAP Miner.

The Microsoft product creates multidimensional cubes from the dimension and fact tables in the warehouse data repository, and, as the cubes are being prepared, summarizes quantitative values. Availability of this summarized data along with the detailed data provides both a flexible and a rapid reporting capability. The detailed and summarized data can both be stored in a relational or a multidimensional OLAP database, or in a hybrid combination, called **HOLAP.** In HOLAP, the detailed data is stored in a relational database and the summary data in a multidimensional database.[6]

IBM DB2 OLAP Miner supports hypothesis-driven data mining by providing simple navigation and quick query response. It also provides an opportunity-discovery feature that consists of an analysis of multidimensional data with interesting values being presented to a data analyst for further hypotheses-driven exploration.[7]

INFORMATION PRESENTATION

In addition to obtaining the data from the data warehouse and transforming it into information, the data mining software can also format the information and present it to the users. Conversely, the formatting and presentation can be accomplished by other software—database query languages, report writers, or decision support systems.

INFORMATION USERS

We recognized earlier that the CRM system is not restricted to users in the marketing area, but it is a resource to be used by problem solvers and decision makers throughout the firm. Within each business area, users can be novices, analysts, and power users.

A **novice** is someone with no special computer training, who typically wishes to obtain information without the need for a great deal of analysis. Executives are examples of novices; they usually prefer highly distilled summaries that can be preformatted and downloaded from the server to their workstations.

An **analyst** is someone who is skilled in the use of analysis and statistical tools and transforms data into a form that is usable by someone else—an executive or manager. Analysts are typically members of a manager's staff.

The most sophisticated CRM user is the **power user,** who can perform the work of the analyst plus perform more advanced operations such as importing data from other systems and writing macro commands that prewritten software does not perform. Power users are information professionals, such as marketing researchers, financial analysts, and industrial engineers.

In designing an interface for use by such a wide range of users, a good technique is to design it so that it can be tailored to a particular user's needs. For example, extensive online help would be available to the novice user but not the power user.

INFORMATION DELIVERY SOFTWARE

CRM system users can obtain information from the data warehouse by means of report writers, database query languages, decision support systems, and online analytical processing.

Report Writers

Users often receive reports according to some schedule, without having to request them. The reports are prepared by the server and consist of predefined content and format. Although they are the traditional way to distribute information, reports are an inflexible output

---

EXHIBIT 9.9   **AN EXAMPLE OF A REPORT THAT COULD BE PRODUCED WITH MOLAP**

Product Sales by Customer Gender
Year-to-date 2003
In Units

Store type: Drug
Product: Electric razor 599234

	Age= 15-20	Age= 21-30	Age= 31-40	Age= 41-50	Age over 50	Total
Female	23	97	87	111	79	397
Male	97	235	192	204	111	839
Total	120	332	279	315	190	1,236

medium since their content might not be what the users need and changes may be difficult to achieve. Users cannot drill down to lower levels of detail and cannot modify the presentation by switching rows and columns to obtain different views.

Database Query Languages

When database query languages came along in the early 1970s, they immediately became popular. Database management systems have query languages that enable users to specify what information they would like to receive from the database and what format to use. Whereas reports are system-driven, queries are user-driven. In obtaining data or information from a data warehouse, metadata guides the user in formulating the query.

Decision Support Systems

Some decision support systems consist of custom software, with information outputs an integral part. As with report writers, these systems can be inflexible and difficult to change. Other decision support systems utilize packaged software, such as electronic spreadsheets. These systems usually are constructed so that users can request the information that is needed. For example, an executive information system enables the user to easily flip-flop between graphic and tabular displays.

Online Analytical Processing

Users can mine data using report writers, database query languages, mathematical models, and OLAP. Exhibit 9.10 is an overview of the information delivery topology showing how OLAP encompasses both a querying and modeling capability. All of the data mining systems take data from the warehouse data repository, perform the necessary analysis to transform the data into information, and deliver the information to the CRM system users.

SUMMARY

Data mining involves the retrieval of detailed and summary data from the data warehouse, transformation of the data into information, and presentation of the information to the users.

The information that is mined is intended for use in decision making. Decision support systems originated in 1971 and have focused on database query and mathematical modeling as the means of obtaining the information needed to make decisions to solve problems.

There are two basic types of data mining—hypothesis verification and knowledge discovery. Hypothesis verification is user driven, and in it the system provides information that either supports or fails to support the user's hypothesis. Knowledge discovery is system driven in that the system determines the paths to follow in analyzing the data and informs the user of the findings. Both types of data mining tell the user something that the user did not previously know about the data.

Data mining performs four basic functions. It makes classifications, forms clusters, makes associations, and determines patterns or sequences. Four methodologies are used in performing these functions—decision trees, genetic algorithms, memory based reasoning, and neural

EXHIBIT 9.10 INFORMATION DELIVERY TOPOLOGY

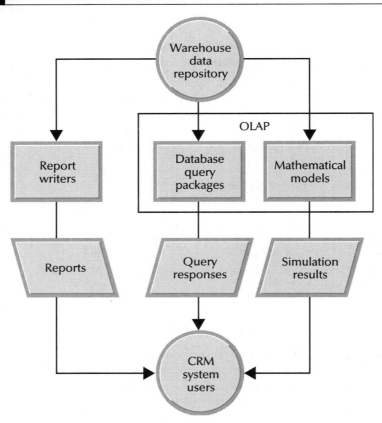

networks. Decision trees, genetic algorithms, and neural networks are all types of networks that form logical paths that can be traversed in the process of reaching a conclusion.

OLAP is a querying capability designed especially for mining data in data warehouses. Relational online analytical processing (ROLAP) uses a relational database management system and can handle data warehouses of practically any size. The main limitation is that ROLAP frequently cannot perform all of the processes that the user requires. Multiple online analytical processing (MOLAP), on the other hand, can perform the processes but is restricted in terms of data warehouse size. In MOLAP, the practice is to download a subset of the data warehouse to the user's workstation. The subset contains much summarized data and simplifies the preparation of summary outputs.

Data warehouse users include novices, analysts, and power users. The challenge is to design the interface so that each level of users is accommodated. The information is delivered to the users by means of report writers, database query languages, decision support systems, and OLAP.

KEY TERMS

associations discovery
data mining
decision support system (DSS)
decision tree
genetic algorithm
hybrid online analytical processing (HOLAP)

hypothesis verification
knowledge discovery
memory based reasoning
multidimensional online analytical processing (MOLAP)
neural networks

relational online analytical processing (ROLAP)
sequential pattern discovery
similar time sequence discovery

QUESTIONS FOR REVIEW AND CRITICAL THINKING

1. Is data mining a term that can be correctly used to describe the retrieval of any types of information from a database or data warehouse? Explain.
2. What does mathematical modeling offer that reports and database querying do not?
3. If hypothesis verification is a data mining technique, how does it tell the user something that he or she did not previously know?
4. What is the difference, if any, between classifications and clusters?
5. Which knowledge discovery methodologies are based on biological networks?
6. If a manager prefers summaries, would the manager use ROLAP or MOLAP? Explain.
7. If a manager prefers to work with detailed data, would ROLAP or MOLAP be the best choice for providing data? Explain.
8. Does OLAP function as a report writer? A database query language? A decision support system?

NOTES

1. Mark Sakalosky, "RFM, Part 1: Analyzing Customer Data," *WebTrends*. (January 2002); www.clickz.com
2. G. Anthony Gorry and Michael S. Scott Morton, "A Framework for Management Information Systems," *Sloan Management Review* 13 (fall 1971): 55–70.
3. Joe Ashbrook Nickell, "Welcome to Harrah's. You Give Us Your Money. We Learn Everything About You. And Then You Thank Us and Beg for More. How's That for a Business Model?" *Business 2.0* (April 2002).
4. This example is based on Sanjay Soni, Zhaohui Tang, and Jim Yang, "Performance Study of Microsoft Data Mining Algorithms" (white Paper), Microsoft Corporation, 2001: 5.
5. E. F. Codd, "Providing Online Analytical Processing to User Analysts" (white paper), E. F. Codd and Associates, 1993.
6. "Microsoft Corp. SQL Server 2000 Analysis Services," *Datapro Application Development Software Report 3054* (November 2000).
7. "IBM DB2 OLAP Miner: An Opportunity-Discovery Feature of DB2 OLAP Server," *IBM Business Intelligence Solutions* (November 2001).

In a scene similar to the Cathy cartoon, the 2002 television advertisement for Circuit City shows a young man searching frantically through his wallet for the receipt for an item he is trying to return. As he unfolds several scraps of paper, the Circuit City sales associate says, "Don't worry. We save your information—the date, dollar amount, and the item purchased—just in case you lose the receipt." Finally, a retail store is putting a bit of satisfaction into the warranty process.

THE VALUE OF MEASURING CUSTOMER SATISFACTION

Delighting the customer by doing a bit more than just satisfying the customer's expectations is an important first step for an organization to take to build a positive relationship. Measuring customer satisfaction over time allows a company to determine whether customers believe the organization is continuously improving, losing ground to a competitor, or stagnating.

A more subtle reason for measuring customer satisfaction is to communicate a "We Care" message to customers. When organizations contact customers and ask, "How are we doing," this simple act tells customers that the organization is committed to a long-term relationship.[1] Satisfaction measures declare that the organization wants an individual's business.

There are many ways to measure customer satisfaction. Surveys of customer perceptions are the most common. However, objective measures of operational activities are often used as surrogate measures that substitute for talking with customers. An **objective measure** is considered to be hard data, such as number of units sold or time that customers spend in a queue waiting for service, that is not affected by perceptions of people. For example, a hotel might record the waiting time for guest check-in and the waiting time for checkout at the front desk. An airline might measure on-time flight arrival and percentage of baggage mishandled. Registering the number and nature of customer complaints and recording product returns are also common activities in many organizations that provide an objective measure for the causes of dissatisfaction.

As mentioned in Chapter 8, call centers should automatically be tracking the number of calls, time that customers spend waiting on hold, abandonment rates, and the average length of the call. CRM systems, by definition, should be designed to warehouse data on objective aspects of the organization, particularly for customer touch points with the organizations. Since it does not require sophisticated computer algorithms to understand that the longer people must wait the less happy they are likely to become, managers and organizations should try to find objective measures of operational effectiveness. Objective measurements use the CRM system most effectively and are the most cost effective to apply. Objective measures can, however, miss an understanding of the details of the exchange or of customer expectations.

Subjective measures of satisfaction attempt to measure people's perceptions of a brand, process, or experience with the organization in relation to competitive offerings. If done well, satisfaction surveys can be conducted quickly and inexpensively, and the organization benefits from the direct communication with customers or key constituents. How better to eliminate problems than to ask customers why they are dissatisfied? Further, survey results can be used as benchmarks for making comparisons over time.

CONDUCTING A CUSTOMER SATISFACTION SURVEY

Organizations can hire internal personnel whose skills will develop over time to conduct satisfaction surveys, or organizations can subcontract the measurement task to external suppliers. Many organizations and college professors make a living by designing and administering surveys. However, it is important for managers to be aware of the basic elements involved in satisfaction surveys if the CRM system is to be designed to benefit from this feedback over time.

A customer satisfaction survey, or any survey, is a systematic and objective inquiry in which information is gathered from a sample of people through a questionnaire.[2] Customer surveys typically, but not necessarily, follow a generalized pattern of eight stages: (1) defining the problem and objectives, (2) planning the survey design, (3) designing a questionnaire, (4) selecting a sample, (5) collecting data, (6) analyzing data, (7) drawing conclusions and preparing a report, and (8) following up. See Exhibit 10.1.

The steps in the survey process are highly interdependent. These stages overlap and affect one another. For example, a decision to sample customers of low educational levels (Stage 3) will affect the wording of the questions posed to these customers (Stage 2). Though survey research methods should be learned from a marketing research text, a brief review of the steps will be helpful.

Stage 1: Defining the Problem

Problem definition is the starting place for a customer satisfaction survey. Surprisingly, this fact is not evident to all, and its importance is often overlooked. Managers should

EXHIBIT 10.1 **A SURVEY RESEARCH PROCESS**

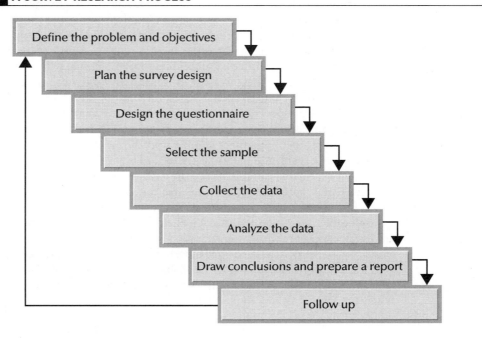

- Define the problem and objectives
- Plan the survey design
- Design the questionnaire
- Select the sample
- Collect the data
- Analyze the data
- Draw conclusions and prepare a report
- Follow up

expend a great deal of effort answering the question "Why are we conducting a customer satisfaction survey?"[3] Getting "closer to the customer" is a generalized objective, but one that is not very precise. Understanding customer expectations, evaluating critical performance attributes, determining if there have been any recurring problems, assessing performance of a brand relative to its major competitors, and learning if customers have noticed continuous quality improvements are examples of some specific answers to the question, "Why are we doing this?"

An informal study to provide background information, **exploratory research,** is usually needed to clarify the nature of a customer satisfaction problem. A symptom, such as declining sales, signals the need to clarify the issue. Sometimes, checking secondary sources—magazines, journals, or information on the Internet—may be appropriate. In other cases, a short series of interviews with a few customers or sales representatives may be in order. Library information, search engines, interviews with employees, and focus groups are all commonly used to help managers understand the basic issues involved.

One example of informal studies, **focus group interviews,** are loosely structured discussions with groups of 6 to 12 people who "focus" on a product or some aspect of the buying process. During a group session, individuals describe problems or explain why they quit doing business with an organization. The organization typically must reimburse each participant in the group, hire a focus group moderator, rent a facility, and provide a meal. Thus, focus groups can provide quick reactions but are conducted at a cost.

Managers may also obtain exploratory insights online from customer chat rooms. **Community complaint rooms** are Web sites designed to allow customers to complain about specific products, organizations, and services. For example, www.PlanetFeedback.com is designed to collect complaints from customers to forward to specific organizations. A quick browse on the Internet may save the organization money and offer clear insights as to the nature of dissatisfaction for similar products or services.

The culmination of Stage 1 of the survey process is a formal statement of the problem(s) and the research objective(s). Research objectives outline the information needed to solve the dissatisfaction problem. In essence, the research objective formally states the purpose of conducting the study.

Stage 2: Planning the Survey Design

After the problem and purpose are stated, a formal **survey design** specifies the specific techniques and procedures that will be used to collect and analyze data relevant to the satisfaction issue. The three basic *research* designs are exploratory, descriptive, and causal. Exploratory research is used to define the problem. The goal for a **descriptive research** study is to measure the characteristics—who buys, what do they buy, how much do they spend, when do they buy, where do they shop/purchase—of defined segments. **Causal research** studies use carefully controlled experiments to isolate reasons for behaviors or outcomes. Although direct observation of behavior can be beneficial, most satisfaction studies use surveys in a descriptive research design and collect data by means of telephone interviews, personal interviews (door-to-door, shopping malls, or some other public place), mail, or an electronic medium such as a fax, e-mail, or the Internet. Telephone, mail, and Internet surveys are currently the most common.

How does the researcher choose the appropriate survey technique? The definition of the problem itself generally suggests which technique is most appropriate. The researcher and manager may need to answer some additional questions, such as "Is the assistance of an interviewer necessary? How willing will customers be to cooperate? How closely do we need to represent the views of the population?" The survey design may be affected by the design of the questionnaire, the types of questions that need to be asked, the time available for the study, the level of accuracy needed, and the budget available for the research.

Stage 3: Designing the Questionnaire

Wording survey questions appropriately is a skill in which the goal is to ask relevant questions that respondents can answer. The researcher should avoid complexity and use simple, accurate, conversational language that does not confuse or bias the respondent. The wording of questions should be simple and unambiguous so that the questions are readily understandable to all respondents. **Double barreled questions** have two subjects or nouns (i.e., How satisfied are you with the *cost* and *quality* of the product?) and can be difficult to interpret. If the respondent is dissatisfied, the researcher has no way of knowing if the cause is the price paid or the quality delivered. Examples of a few questions related to automobile tires are shown in Exhibit 10.2.

Stage 4: Selecting a Sample

The next step is to select a sample of people, organizations, households, or other group of interest. The methods for selecting the sample are important for the accuracy of the information provided by the study. **Sampling** is any procedure in which a small part of the whole is used as the basis for conclusions regarding the whole. A sample is simply a portion, or subset, of a larger population. A survey of all the members of a group is called a **census.** Sampling requires answers to three types of questions—who will be sampled, the size of the sample, and how the sample will be selected.

Who Will Be Sampled?
Specifying the target population, or the total group of interest, is the first aspect of sampling. The manager must make sure the population to be sampled accurately reflects the needs of the organization. Suppose a nursing home wishes to measure customer satisfaction. Should residents, family members, insurance providers, legislators, or all of these groups be sampled? Lists of telephone numbers, club memberships, utility customers, or automobile registrations are a few of the many population lists from which a sample may be taken. If the list is not accurate, the sample may not be representative of the larger population of interest.

What Is the Sample Size?
The conventional, tongue-in-cheek response to this question—"big enough"—suggests the true answer. The sample must be large enough to properly represent the characteristics of the target population. In general, bigger samples are better than smaller ones. Nevertheless, if appropriate sampling techniques are used, a small proportion of the total population can give a reliable measure of the whole. A general rule of thumb is to select at least three respondents for each question on the survey. With higher needs for accuracy, a researcher may suggest attempting to obtain up to ten respondents per item on the survey.

| EXHIBIT 10.2 | EXAMPLES OF TYPES OF SATISFACTION QUESTIONS FOR TIRES |

A. Instructions: *Please circle the number which best describes your level of satisfaction with the tires you recently purchased. Notice that a 1 indicates you are very dissatisfied and a 5 indicates you are very satisfied.*

How satisfied would you say you are with:	Very Dissatisfied				Very Satisfied
Appearance/Looks of the tires	1	2	3	4	5
Performance of the tires	1	2	3	4	5
Speed rating for the tires	1	2	3	4	5
Dependability of these tires	1	2	3	4	5
Price of the tires	1	2	3	4	5
Brand name of the tires	1	2	3	4	5

B. Instructions: *Now please compare the aspects of the tires you just purchased in terms of your expectations when you walked into our store. Notice that a 1 indicates you feel performance is much worse than you expected and a 5 indicates the performance is much better than you expected.*

How would you rate each issue in terms of your expectations?	Much worse than expected				Much better than expected
Performance of the tires on the road	1	2	3	4	5
Physical appearance of the tire store	1	2	3	4	5
Appearance of the personnel	1	2	3	4	5
Promptness of the service provided	1	2	3	4	5
Courtesy of the employees	1	2	3	4	5
Knowledge of the employees	1	2	3	4	5
Individualized attention of the service	1	2	3	4	5

C. Instructions: *This section asks you to compare these tires to competitive brands (1=better and 3=worse), including the last set of tires you purchased.*

How would you rate these tires in comparison to:	Better		Worse
The last set of tires that you owned	1	2	3
A set of Michelin tires	1	2	3
Your ideal set of tires	1	2	3

Sample Selection

The way sampling units are selected is a major determinant of the accuracy of customer satisfaction research. There are two major sampling methods: probability sampling and nonprobability sampling.

With a **probability sample,** each element or person in the population has a known and non-zero chance of being selected for the sample. A **simple random sample,** perhaps the best known of these procedures, means each element has an equal chance. If you were to sample students at a university by using class lists, then students registered for three classes would have a greater chance of being included in the sample than those registered for only one class—a probability sample. For a simple random sample, a list of students from the registrar would be needed, where each person is listed only once to equalize the chance of selection. **Sampling error** is the difference between the sample results and the results you would have gotten if you had been able to poll the entire population. In other words, there is a risk that your sample doesn't accurately represent the entire population. The major benefit of a probability sample is the ability to use statistics to calculate sampling error and to then generalize the results with a given level of confidence to a larger population.

When sample units are selected on the basis of convenience or personal judgment, the result is a **nonprobability sample.** In one type of nonprobability sample, a **convenience sample,** data are collected from the people who are most conveniently available. A restaurant that puts a questionnaire on each table, an organization that stops people in the mall, and a researcher who gives a survey to one class of students are all examples of a convenience sample. It is easy and economical to collect information this way, but unfortunately, this type of sampling often produces unrepresentative samples. **Unrepresentative samples** mean that the organization can use the results for exploratory ideas but should not base costly decisions on the results since the sample does not necessarily represent the views of the larger population. It is not possible to estimate sampling error with nonprobability samples, thus, it is not possible to know how likely it is that the results represent the views of the population. As you can see, the type of sample clearly affects the methods for collecting the information, costs of the study, and the resulting accuracy in the information obtained.

Stage 5: Collecting Data

Once the research has been designed, the researcher must actually collect the needed data. Whether a telephone interview, mail survey, Internet survey, or another collection method is chosen, it is the researcher's task to minimize errors in the fieldwork process—and errors are easy to make. For example, interviewers who have not been carefully selected and trained may not phrase their questions properly or may fail to record respondents' comments accurately. Worse, if the fieldworkers are poorly paid, they may be tempted to fill out the forms themselves creating a fraudulent set of data for analysis. **Field service firms** are organizations that specialize in the collection of data. A **computer assisted telephone interview (CATI)** is perhaps the most often used method for collecting survey data from a random sample of people. With this procedure, field workers enter the respondent's answer directly into the database, minimizing translation errors. Most organizations use field service firms to collect data as opposed to supervising the process themselves.

Stage 6: Analyzing the Data

Data processing ordinarily begins with jobs called editing and coding, in which surveys or other data collection instruments are checked for omissions, incomplete or otherwise unusable responses, illegibility, and obvious inconsistencies. Coding assigns numbers to subjective responses. For example, the reasons for switching to a competitive product may need to be given numerical identification numbers such that 1=cheaper price,

2=better value, 3=coupon, and so on. Data analysis is next. Data analysis may involve statistical analysis, qualitative analysis, or both. The type of analysis used should depend on the research objectives, the nature of the data collected, and who will use the findings. Of course, if a nonprobability sampling procedure is used, then statistical procedures will not be needed as there is no basis to estimate sampling error. The purpose of the statistical test is to estimate levels of sampling error and accurately judge how different the sample results may be from the population totals.

A review of the many statistical tools that can be used in customer satisfaction research is beyond the scope of this book. They range from simple comparisons of numbers and percentages ("100 people, or 25 percent of the sample of 400 people, were completely satisfied") to complex forms of analysis, such as multiple regression. Again, field service firms will provide many of these services, particularly for initial editing and coding of responses.

Stage 7: Drawing Conclusions and Preparing the Report

Remember that the purpose of customer satisfaction research is to aid managers in making effective marketing decisions. The researcher's role is to answer the question "What does this mean to our CRM strategy?" Therefore, the culmination of the survey process must be a report that usefully communicates research findings to management. Typically, management is not interested in how the findings were derived. Except in special cases, management is likely to want only a summary of the findings. Presenting these clearly by using graphs, charts, and other forms of artwork, is a creative challenge to the researcher and any others involved in the preparation of the final report. If the researcher's findings are not properly communicated to and understood by the organization and its managers, the survey process has been, in effect, a total waste.

Stage 8: Following Up

After the researcher submits a report to management, he or she should follow up to determine if and how management responded to the report. The researcher should ask how the study and/or the report could have been improved and made more useful. The output of one study is typically the initial input for defining research objectives for the next one, thus, the ending discussion is also the time to consider the specific issues in need of better description as well as the exploratory steps that should be taken to initiate the next satisfaction measure.

SATISFACTION AND QUALITY MEASURES

There are many ways to define and assess satisfaction as well as quality. In general, satisfaction is viewed as a comparison between what customers expect from a product or service and the actual performance received.[4] If the organization delivers more than what was expected, customers are delighted. If the organization falls short of its promises, customers are dissatisfied. A basic organizational need, then, is to understand satisfaction in terms of the many aspects of a product or service that could be important to different segments.

The current best practice in assessing customer satisfaction may well involve an understanding of the drivers of customer perceptions of brand, value, and relationship/retention equity.[5] A **perceptual driver** is similar to a key performance indicator—it identifies which issues seem to affect satisfaction the most.

> *Value equity* represents the objective appraisal of the brand (things like perceptions of quality, price, and convenience); *brand equity* is the subjective appraisal of the brand (things like brand awareness and attitude toward the brand); and *relationship equity* involves the special relationship elements that link the customer with the brand (e.g., frequent buyer programs).[6]

Satisfaction can be affected by customer responses to tangible aspects of the product or store, intangible perceptions of the product, brand name or image, as well as the drivers of the strength of the relationship with the customer. As shown in Exhibit 10.2 which rates customer satisfaction with tires, some questions ask customers to provide a global judgment of satisfaction (i.e., section A); other questions ask for comparisons to expectations (i.e., section B); while still other questions ask for comparisons of the current performance to competitive products or to an ideal (i.e., section C). Drivers of perceptions are multidimensional indicators of customer satisfaction—the who, what, where, why, and how of the effects.

Consider the automated call center. Objective indicators of the performance of the routing system such as call handling times and number of transfers can be compared to subjective indicators of call center agent performance such as evaluation scores or call outcomes. Organizations should have an interest in assessing the effects of new training programs, improved contact points, or revised routing procedures.

> The ability to roll up, drill down or drill across data at any level—including listening to the actual call recordings underlying the data—gives an unparalleled opportunity to understand reality from the customer's perspective. Detailed analysis can include drilling down through different levels of the organization, across time for trend analysis or comparing departments or product lines against each other.[7]

Objective measures and subjective perceptions can be important when the right data is captured, consolidated, analyzed, and reported as part of a circular process that is used by the entire organization to improve customer experiences.

> Service organizations create value for consumers through performances. All businesses are service businesses to some degree. Computer manufacturers and food retailers create consumer value through a goods–services mix. Commercial banks and hospitals create consumer value largely through services. Service convenience facilitates the sale of goods as well as the sale of services.[8]

Thus, there are tangible aspects of a service such as automobile repairs and intangible aspects to products such as the check-out experience. Both can be important components of the organization's understanding of customer contact points. Two key subjects of interest to organizations include the tangible features of a product and the intangible elements associated with the provision of service.

Quality of Tangible Goods

Organizations used to define quality only by engineering standards and statistical control of defects. While such objective information can be an important indicator of the need to improve, most organizations understand that having a quality product means conformity to customer requirements. Rather than having customers be thankful that nothing went wrong, they should experience some pleasant surprises or reap some unexpected benefits.

In other words, quality assurance is more than just meeting minimum standards. Product quality can be measured using perceptions of the eight conceptual characteristics listed in Exhibit 10.3, as one approach. Questions should be tailored to the specific product offered by the organization as well as include an understanding of competitive offerings.

At this point we should remind you—at the risk of overemphasizing this point—that customer satisfaction surveys tend to become standardized and ongoing so that performance can be compared against previous periods and quality standards. Whatever the nature of the measurement, it is important that standards are developed and incorporated into the operational management of the enterprise—the strategic "so what" of conducting the measurement.

EXHIBIT 10.3	QUALITY DIMENSIONS FOR GOODS
Performance	How well does the product perform its core function? (How well does a shaving razor remove whiskers?)
Features	Does the product have adequate auxiliary dimensions that provide secondary benefits? (Does a sun block lotion come in a convenient package?)
Conformity to specifications	What is the incidence of defects? (How many computer discs will have bad sectors?)
Reliability	Does the product ever fail to work? Does the product perform with consistency? (Will the chain saw work properly each time it is used?)
Durability	What is the economic life of the product? (How long will the motorcycle last?)
Aesthetic design	Does the product's design look and feel like that of a high-quality product? (Is there a discernible difference between the generic disc and the brand name?)
Serviceability	Is the service system efficient, competent, and convenient? (Does a computer software manufacturer have a toll-free telephone number and a technical staff ready to answer questions quickly?)

SOURCE: Based on David A. Aaker, *Managing Brand Equity* (New York: Macmillan, 1991): 90–95 and David Garvin, "Product Quality: An Important Strategic Weapon," *Business Horizons* (May–June 1984): 40–43 and David A. Garvin, "Competing on the Eight Dimensions of Quality," *Harvard Business Review* (November–December 1987): 101–108.

EXHIBIT 10.4	SERVQUAL: FIVE DIMENSIONS OF SERVICE QUALITY

Tangibles	appearance of physical facilities, equipment, personnel, and communication materials
Reliability	ability to perform the promised service dependably and accurately
Responsiveness	willingness to help customers and provide prompt service
Assurance	knowledge and courtesy of employees and their ability to inspire trust and confidence
Empathy	the caring, individualized attention the organization provides its customers.

Quality of Services and Service Components of Products

Services, which are intangible, can be described by a number of attributes. However, customers tend to use the same general criteria to determine the quality of many types of services. A team of service quality researchers developed the SERVQUAL measurement that consists of a set of five dimensions, shown in Exhibit 10.4.[9] The SERVQUAL approach compares expectations to perceptions of actual performance.

The SERVQUAL Gap Analysis Model was designed to identify the possible causes of poor service quality.[10] A **gap analysis model** simply defines potential problems between what customers expect and what the organization delivers. The approach helps managers think of a service, or the service support system, as a process instead of as a series of isolated activities. If customer expectations do not match performance, a gap is said to exist that can cause dissatisfaction. Four gaps that frontline personnel/management activity can influence define interesting aspects of service delivery.

Gap 1: A *management perception-consumer expectation gap* can exist if managers cannot identify or do not understand what aspects of the service encounter are important to customers. Gap 2: When an unfavorable *management perception-service quality specification* gap exists, managers know what customers want, but planned specifications are less than what customers expect. In other words, managers who should know better plan and implement unacceptable standards for service delivery. Gap 3: *Service quality specification-service delivery* gaps occur when frontline contact personnel do not perform their tasks according to guidelines. Service managers may improve these situations with training and closer supervision. Gap 4: A *service delivery-external communications* gap may exist if advertising messages or other external communications promise more than the organization can deliver. Simply put, to achieve customer satisfaction, organizations must deliver more than what they promise.

With this perspective, the organization would measure service expectations with questions designed to assess the five dimensions of the SERVQUAL instrument, shown in Exhibit 10.4, and then measure service performance on those same five dimensions. While the SERVQUAL approach has been used extensively, adaptations and shorter versions of the survey have received mixed results. As an assessment of the perceived quality of the information system infrastructure, for example, the questions seem to lack reliability.[11] When versions were modified to assess perceptions of the information system services, tangible aspects were not included since all interactions were virtual. Thus, the SERVQUAL questionnaire should be viewed as a convenient starting point that can be carefully modified to fit the circumstances of the organization.

MEASUREMENT OF BRAND LOYALTY

We have said many times that customer satisfaction is not the same as loyalty. If they are not the same, how does one measure loyalty to a brand, store, company, or organization? As with most things in life, there are objective and subjective approaches.

In Chapter 5, we said measuring brand loyalty by the proportion of purchases—the number of times the brand is purchased divided by the total number of times the product category is purchased—is a traditional *behavioral measure.* And, as discussed in the last chapter, the CRM system can provide indications of the sequence of purchasing patterns for clusters of customers, thereby offering the needed data to calculate the proportion of times any one brand is purchased by a cluster of customer. Consider the example of the call center and efficiency versus the effectiveness of the agents who deliver that service:

> At the most basic level, measuring efficiency is agent-centric and delivers interaction optimization; measuring effectiveness is customer-centric and delivers business optimization. In a world where costs must be kept in check, too often productivity goals can get in the way of efforts to optimize customers' experiences. When contact centers focus only on agent-centric measurements, other indicators of business success such as customer satisfaction and loyalty, or up-sell success and closure rates, might be ignored.[12]

Customer loyalty is a customer's commitment or attachment to a brand, store, manufacturer, service provider, or other entity based on favorable attitudes and behavioral responses, such as repeat purchase. This definition implies a need for both behavioral and attitudinal (affective) elements. Consider the questions in Exhibit 10.5 designed to measure sports loyalty.

The example measure of sports loyalty focuses on the behavioral aspects of being a fan, but implied in the continuum of answers is the commitment to and *liking* of a sport or sports program—the attitudinal interface. See another example in Exhibit 10.6 that refers to store loyalty. Many researchers who attempt to measure customer loyalty ask about the three components of attitude toward the brand or organization—knowledge, affect, and behavioral intention. Behavioral intention is assessed with surveys by asking about the customer's willingness to *repurchase* and likelihood of *recommending* the brand or organization to a family member, friend, or associate. Questions may resemble these: How

---

EXHIBIT 10.5 **DIFFERENTIATING LEVELS OF SPORTS LOYALTY**

Instructions: We are going to ask you to classify the type of fan you consider yourself to be for different sports and sports programs. Please check the box which best indicates the type of fan you consider yourself to be for sports.

☐	**Diehard**	Watch games, follow-up on scores and sports news multiple times a day
☐	**Avid**	Watch games, follow-up on scores and sports news once a day
☐	**Casual**	Watch games, follow-up on scores and sports news occasionally
☐	**Championship**	Watch games, follow-up on scores and sports news only during championships or playoffs
☐	**Non**	Never watch games or follow-up on scores
☐	**Alienated**	Dislike, oppose, or object to a certain sport

---

EXHIBIT 10.6	AN EXAMPLE MEASURE OF STORE LOYALTY

Instructions: *Please rate your level of agreement (1-Strongly Disagree, 5 = Strongly Agree) with each of the following items.*

	Strongly Disagree				Strongly Agree
I like this store very much	1	2	3	4	5
For this group of products, I have a favorite store	1	2	3	4	5
When buying (product), I always shop at this store first	1	2	3	4	5
In the past 3 months, a majority of my shopping trips have been to this store	1	2	3	4	5
I prefer to shop at this store even if another store advertises the same deal	1	2	3	4	5
I usually divide my shopping time among two or three stores*	1	2	3	4	5

The stronger the agreement the higher the loyalty score.
* indicates reversed coded item.

SOURCE: Jagdish N. Sheth, Banwaari Mittal, and Bruce I. Newman, *Consumer Behavior* (Ft. Worth, Tex.: Dryden Press, 1999): 721.

likely is it that you will repurchase (brand name)? Based on your experience, would you recommend (brand) to a friend who wanted to purchase (product concept)? Of course, organizations with CRM systems have an opportunity to blend the intention measures with actual customer behaviors such as sequence of buying certain brands.

The knowledge, or cognitive, component of an attitude refers to a customer's beliefs about the product features, benefits, or comparative values provided by the brand or organization. Questions can assess the extent to which the organization's brand delivers superior value. For example, which credit card provides the lowest interest rate? Some researchers attempt to measure preference or a favorite choice. For example, which credit card do you prefer to use? What is your favorite restaurant?

While the basic aspects of loyalty should be consistent for all types of products and services, online exchanges may have unique characteristics. Of eight facets of loyalty used to assess the attachment to online retailers, Exhibit 10.7, two were found to be most important: care and character.[13] Care reflects the attention paid to customer contact points and the ease of completing transactions, while character reflects the aesthetics of the Web site and the reputation or image of the organization.

A customer focus implies a need to constantly search for new issues that are important drivers of perceived satisfaction and loyalty. There is no one best solution that will survive forever. The environment is dynamic and measures must evolve with the dynamic marketplace.

MEASUREMENT OF EMPLOYEE SATISFACTION AND LOYALTY

We have indicated that there is a relationship between employees' behavior and customer satisfaction and loyalty. Frontline personnel are internal customers who need to

EXHIBIT 10.7	**EXAMPLE ISSUES TO MEASURE E-LOYALTY**

e-Loyalty: a customer's favorable attitude toward an online retailer

Customization	Tailor products, services, and the exchange environment to customer needs; recognize a customer and then offer options and messages for that customer
Contact interactivity	Foster dynamic and ever-changing exchanges with customers; ease navigation, offer product facts, and answer online inquiries quickly
Cultivation	Offer relevant information and incentives that invite a customer to return to the site; coax a customer by cross-selling relevant items
*Care	Pay attention to long-term aspects of the relationship; avoid breakdowns in service, provide information about the status of orders, allow minimal disruptions
Community	Develop social aspects of the online environment; offer comment links, buying circles, and chat rooms
Choice	Generate one-stop shopping by increasing the range and variety of product options from the organization or its alliance partners
Convenience	Simplify user-friendly contact points; offer a logical format for customers to access information and purchase products easily
*Character	Create aesthetic components; foster a positive reputation, image, and personality—text, style, graphics, colors, logos, and slogans

* most important drivers, in one study, of e-loyalty

SOURCE: Srini S. Srinivasan, Rolph Anderson, and Kishore Ponnavolu, "Customer Loyalty in E-Commerce: An Exploration of Its Antecedents and Consequences," *Journal of Retailing* 78:1 (spring 2002): 41–50.

be motivated and encouraged to deliver the quality service to external customers. Many organizations measure employee satisfaction and loyalty using objective measures, such as staff turnover. Surveys are also frequently used with employees. Questions about job satisfaction and questions about employee motivation (I strive to do my best every day) may be asked and correlated with customer satisfaction or loyalty measures.

Satisfaction with the job can be measured in a generalized manner[14] that reflects how satisfied employees are with the job and the kind of work performed. Satisfaction can also be assessed in regards to specific aspects of the job, such as the employee's motivation, supervisors, level of rewards, or any number of other facets.[15] A key task for managers is to define the drivers of employee satisfaction and improve those components over time.

Mystery shoppers, or mystery callers with a problem, may provide indications of the actual service delivery of frontline personnel. External research providers may conduct focus groups with employees to gather information about potential gaps or problems in the system in a non-threatening manner . A key is to go beyond the traditional "suggestion box" with its contents of gum wrappers and actively solicit information and feedback from the internal customers of the organization—the employees—as well as from external constituents.

SUMMARY

Measuring consumer satisfaction is a means of determining how well a product or service is meeting customer expectations and organizational objectives. Measuring satisfaction over time allows an organization to determine whether consumers believe the organization is continuously improving or stagnating. A more subtle reason for measuring customer satisfaction is to communicate a "We Care" message to customers.

Customer satisfaction is often measured by surveying customers and by recording certain objective measures of operational activity. A customer satisfaction survey is a systematic and objective inquiry in which information is gathered from a sample of people through a questionnaire. Customer satisfaction surveys often follow a generalized pattern of eight stages: (1) defining the problem and objectives, (2) planning the survey design, (3) designing a questionnaire, (4) selecting a sample, (5) collecting data, (6) analyzing data, (7) drawing conclusions and preparing a report, and (8) following up.

Organizations used to define quality by engineering standards and statistical control of defects. Today, the level of quality is the degree to which a good or service corresponds to buyers' expectations. Product quality can be measured using customer perceptions of tangible aspects such as the following eight product characteristics: performance, features, conformity to specifications, reliability, durability, aesthetic design, and serviceability.

The logic behind measuring perceived service quality is based on the discrepancy approach, which states that service quality equals perceptions minus expectations. The five dimensions of the SERVQUAL approach to measuring service quality include tangibles, reliability, responsiveness, assurance, and empathy.

Customer satisfaction is not the same as loyalty. Most complex definitions of loyalty include a need to measure both behavioral and attitudinal (affective) elements. Insight into the connection between objective behaviors and the more subjective, perceptual feelings about brands and organizations provides useful information for improving the organization over time.

KEY TERMS

brand equity	customer satisfaction	perceptual driver
causal research	survey	probability sample
census	descriptive research	relationship equity
community complaint	double barreled questions	sampling
rooms	exploratory research	sampling error
computer assisted	field service firms	simple random sample
telephone interview	focus group interviews	subjective measures
(CATI)	gap analysis model	survey design
convenience sample	nonprobability sample	unrepresentative samples
customer loyalty	objective measure	value equity

QUESTIONS FOR REVIEW AND CRITICAL THINKING

1. Why do companies measure consumer satisfaction?
2. Outline the eight stages of a customer satisfaction survey.

3. What are the advantages of measuring customer satisfaction by recording certain objective measures of operational activity?

4. What are the advantages of measuring customer satisfaction with satisfaction surveys?

5. How can a researcher construct questions that determine whether the product's quality of performance was a delightful surprise, well beyond expected performance?

6. Define and give an example of each of the eight product characteristics used to measure product quality.

7. Outline the SERVQUAL Gap Analysis model. Provide an example of a reason why gaps exist.

8. What is service quality?

9. Give an example of a measure of customer satisfaction.

10. Give an example of a measure of customer loyalty. How does the measurement of loyalty differ for stores and online Web sites?

NOTES

1. Tony Cram, *Customers That Count* (London: Financial Times-Prentice Hall, 2001): 207–208.
2. This section follows the logic of survey research presented in William G. Zikmund, *Exploring Marketing Research,* 8th edition (Cincinnati: SouthWestern, 2003).
3. Earl Naumann and Kathleen Giel, *Customer Satisfaction Measurement and Management* (Cincinnati: Thomson Executive Press, 1995): 20.
4. Richard L. Oliver, "A Cognitive Model of the Antecedents and Consequences of Satisfaction Decisions," *Journal of Marketing Research* 17 (November 1980): 460–469.
5. Roland T. Rust, Katherine N. Lemon, and Valarie A. Zeithaml, "Where Should the Next Marketing Dollar Go?" *Marketing Management* 10:3 (September/October 2001): 25–28.
6. Ibid., 26.
7. Marlene Rosati, "Measuring the Reality of the Customer Experience," *Customer Inter@ction Solutions* (May 2002): 39.
8. Leonard L. Berry, Kathleen Seiders, and Dhruv Grewal, "Understanding Service Convenience," *Journal of Marketing 66* (July 2002): 1–17.
9. Valarie A. Zeithaml, A. Parasuraman, and Leonard L. Berry, *Delivering Quality Service: Balancing Customer Perceptions and Expectations* (New York: The Free Press, 1990): 26.
10. Ibid.; A. Parasuraman, L. L. Berry, and V.A. Zeithaml "SERVQUAL: A Multiple-Item Scale for Measuring Customer Perceptions of Service Quality," *Journal of Retailing* 64:1 (spring 1988): 12–40; A. Parasuraman, L. L. Berry, and V. A. Zeithaml, "Refinement and Reassessment of the SERVQUAL Scale," *Journal of Retailing* 67:4 (winter 1991): 420–450; and A. Parasuraman,V. A. Zeithaml, and L. L. Berry, "A Conceptual Model of Service Quality and Its Implications for Future Research," *Journal of Marketing* 49:4 (fall 1985): 41–50.
11. Christopher L. Carr, "A Psychometric Evaluation of the Expectations, Perceptions, and Difference-Scores Generated by the IS-Adapted SERVQUAL Instrument," *Decision Sciences* 33:2 (spring 2002): 281–296.
12. Marlene Rosati, "Measuring the Reality of the Customer Experience," *Customer Inter@ction Solutions* (May 2002): 38–43.
13. Srini S. Srinivasan, Rolph Anderson, and Kishore Ponnavolu, "Customer Loyalty in E-Commerce: An Exploration of Its Antecedents and Consequences," *Journal of Retailing* 78:1 (spring 2002): 41–50.
14. Alan J. Dubinsky and Steven W. Hartley, "A Path-Analytic Study of a Model of Salesperson Performance," *Journal of the Academy of Marketing Science* (spring 1986): 36–46.
15. See, for example, Harish Sujan, "Smarter Versus Harder: An Exploratory Attributional Analysis of Salespeople's Motivation," *Journal of Marketing Research* 23 (February 1986): 41–49 and George H. Lucas, Jr., A. Parasuraman, Robert A. Davis, and Ben M. Enis, "An Empirical Study of Salesforce Turnover," *Journal of Marketing* 51 (July 1987): 34–59.

Issues for Implementing CRM Systems

While CRM systems for consumers may be the most visible, the fastest growth in successful CRM systems will probably occur in the B2B arena. This prediction is partially based on the fact that only 42 percent of distributors currently exchange business documents with electronic data interchange (EDI) processes.[1] Consider these two examples.

As the manager of Bearing Chain and Supply in Dallas, Texas, Charley Amos spot orders from PTplace.com—a wholesaler for four major power transmission manufacturers. Charley only acquired information and checked parts on the Web site last year, but now he buys from $30,000 to $40,000 per month from PTplace.com and tracks shipments online. He orders for his own business and for his customers. Charley is a case in point for showing the promise of further growth for online B2B interactions. As business customers and suppliers take the process further by exchanging business documents electronically and by standardizing item numbers, the convenience of B2B relationships continues to grow

Newark Electronics, an electronic components distributor, reportedly used EDI to replace purchase orders sent by fax, paper, or e-mail and saved $1.2 million last year by reducing errors in communication. EDI helped Newark reduce duplicated orders, excess inventories, out-of-stock items, and the time spent by sales representatives in correcting problems with orders.

According to Ken Brack at Industrial Distribution, the next language for the Web will be Extensible Markup Language (XML), which will replace HTML and facilitate these B2B transactions. XML tags complex documents and automatically generates an electronic ticket and invoice for exchanges. As the cost for EDI transactions continues to decline and outsource services increase, the growth in B2B CRM systems will escalate, and could reach $38 billion by 2005.

POTENTIAL IMPLEMENTATION PROBLEMS

Implementation of a CRM system can follow the same general systems development life cycle that is followed for information systems of all types. Organizations have been implementing such systems for almost a half-century, and several sound methodologies have evolved based on both the successes and failures that have been experienced.

CRM projects have not been without their failures. Arvind D. Shah, a managing principal of Performance Development Corporation (PDC), has identified ten problems that implementing firms face.[2] Some of these problems are caused by a failure to provide the proper focus for the project, and some are caused by a failure to develop the system in the proper way.

FAILURE TO PROVIDE PROPER PROJECT FOCUS

Both management and the developers contribute to the failure to provide the proper focus for both the project and the CRM system. This failure is derived from the following:

- Management and the developers do not have a clear understanding or definition of the components or purpose of a CRM system
- Management and the developers define the project scope too large
- Management fails to commit an executive sponsor or champion to the project
- Management and developers fail to understand the expectations of key constituent groups in using the CRM system

FAILURE TO DEVELOP THE SYSTEM IN THE PROPER WAY

In a similar fashion, both management and the developers contribute to errors made in developing the system once the project gets underway. These errors take the following form:

- The developers lack the required technical knowledge and skills
- The developers fail to define all of the risks
- The developers begin by selecting development tools rather than by defining functional requirements and system objectives
- The developers fail to recognize the importance of quality
- The developers fail to follow a phased development methodology
- The developers overlook the importance of privacy and security
- Management and the developers fail to perform a post-implementation evaluation

All of these problems can be avoided by following a proven system development methodology in the prescribed way that is based upon a sound understanding of customer expectations and the objectives of the finished product.

PHASED DEVELOPMENT

Prototyping and rapid application development (RAD) are two system development methodologies that have proven successful. Prototyping is well suited for small projects and for use at multiple points during large projects. RAD is best suited for large projects. A third methodology, called the **phased development methodology,** incorporates the best features of both prototyping and RAD and can be used for projects of all sizes. We use phased development as the basis for our discussion.[3]

The phased development methodology consists of six stages. In the preliminary investigation stage the functional requirements of the new system are defined. Then the project is subdivided into modules (or phases), and for each module the analysis, design, and preliminary construction stages are implemented. In the analysis stage the developers gather information to understand the module; in the design stage, they determine how the new module will function; and in the preliminary construction stage, they develop the software and data for the module. After this has been successfully accomplished for each module, all of the modules are integrated in the final construction stage. Then the system undergoes a user acceptance test in the system test and installation stage. At this point the organization cuts over to the new system.

The analysis, design, and preliminary construction loop incorporating a user review reflects the influence of prototyping. A **prototype** is an archetype or sample of a final product. Thus, the software and data for each system module is a form of prototype that is presented to the user for review. User suggestions for improvement cause the loop to be repeated. When the module meets the user's satisfaction, it can be integrated with the other modules during final construction.

A key element in following this methodology is the identification of the system modules. For a data warehouse, a good set of modules would be the **data marts**—they are logical subsets of the data warehouse. Each data mart can be developed as a module and then integrated to form the data warehouse. Exhibit 11.1 illustrates how the analysis, design, and preliminary construction (A-D-C) stages are taken for three data marts— marketing, manufacturing, and finance. This is essentially a **bottom-up approach**—first developing the marts and then integrating them to form the data warehouse.

Another way to define the modules is to take a **top-down approach**—implementing a data warehouse and then subdividing it into data marts. When this approach is taken, a good set of modules consists of the components of the data warehousing system—information gathering, staging, warehouse data repository, metadata repository, management and control, and information delivery.

When the project team includes sufficient resources, work on several modules can be performed at the same time, shortening the life cycle.

EXHIBIT 11.1   **DATA MARTS AS SYSTEM MODULES**

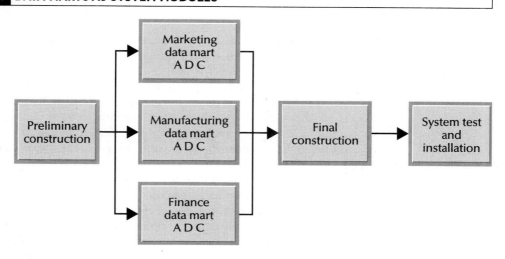

AVOIDING THE IMPLEMENTATION PROBLEMS WITH PHASED DEVELOPMENT

Potential implementation problems may be avoided by properly following the phased development methodology. The problem solutions for each of the major phases of implementation are described in the following section.

Preliminary Investigation

Something triggers interest within the enterprise to develop a CRM system. The trigger might originate with top management or with the information technology (IT) unit. Regardless of the impetus for a CRM approach, the importance of top management support cannot be overemphasized. In organizations where executives believe that CRM systems will offer a strategic advantage, their beliefs serve as powerful signals to the rest of the community about the importance of this process.

Three powerful structuring actions—top management championship, strategic investment rationale, and extent of coordination—act as institutional supports to foster the assimilation of new technologies such as the Web or of new systems such as the infrastructure needed to implement CRM systems.[4] **Top management championship** signals the extent of value placed on the implementation of CRM systems for the organization. A managerial champion sets the tone of value and serves as a liaison between top executives and those responsible for the implementation of a successful system. The **strategic investment rationale** explains the expected organizational benefits to be derived from the commitment of resources toward the implementation of a CRM approach. As such, the investment rationale should outline expected costs and savings from the new system. The **extent of coordination** refers to the need to blend IT knowledge with customer habits and with business manager experiences as the implementation affects functional units throughout the organization. Coordination may include internal and external managers as the organization seeks to use the most qualified people to design and implement the CRM approach. The challenges that these organizational supports must overcome are also shown in Exhibit 11.2 and described later in this chapter.

Once top management gives the go-ahead, a development team is formed, consisting of both users and IT specialists. If it is clear from the outset that sufficient CRM, data warehousing, and data mining expertise does not exist within the organization, outside specialists can be added to the team. A member of top management is designated as the executive sponsor, to oversee the development project and to serve as the intermediary between the developers and top management.

The developers should ensure that management has a good understanding of what CRM is—what it can *and cannot* accomplish, and the level of resources required to implement it across the different functional areas of the organization. This understanding can be achieved by conducting in-house educational programs and by benchmarking efforts.

During the preliminary investigation stage, management and the developers agree on the scope of the project. This determination is influenced by the goals and objectives of the new system, by both system and project risks that the developers face, and by time and resource constraints. System objectives are stated in terms of performance criteria that the CRM system must achieve once it is implemented. The performance criteria are measures of what the users expect of the system in terms of speed, quality, security, and privacy. The developers conduct a feasibility study to consider how feasible the system

---

EXHIBIT II.2 **SUPPORTS AND CHALLENGES OF CRM IMPLEMENTATION**

Top management champion(s)	Strategic investment rationale
Coordination across functional units	

Organizational Supports for CRM Implementation

Challenges of CRM Implementation

Expectations of speed, responsiveness, security, and privacy	
Capital expenditures for infrastructure development and maintenance	Organizational change and employee motivation to alter work flow patterns

and project are in terms of technology, economic justification, legal and ethical issues, and the time schedule. When management gives approval for the project to continue, development moves to the analysis, design, and construction of the system modules.

Analysis, Design, and Preliminary Construction

The developers expand on the functional requirements by gathering information from users concerning their information needs. One approach is to define the customer touch points and the data that should be gathered for each. Another approach is to address each market segment in terms of the problems to be solved and the decisions to be made. With a good understanding of the information that the users need, the developers can then identify the sources that are to provide the data.

During these stages, the developers decide which development tools will be used. The tool selection is based on the functional requirements of the system. Some tools are used in analysis and design to model the system data, processes, and objects. Others are used in construction to produce the software, databases, data marts, and data warehouse of the new system. The database and data warehouse designs incorporate such security precautions as passwords, user directories, and encryption to meet the security performance criteria.

Final Construction

During this stage, the CRM software and data are tested, any required hardware is obtained and tested, any new or additional facilities are built, and user training programs are conducted.

System Test and Installation

When the development reaches this point, the developers have assembled and tested all of the components of the new system. All that is left is for the developers to conduct a user acceptance test to assure the users that the system meets all of the performance criteria. With user approval, the system is installed and is put into production.

During the first few months after cutover, a post-implementation evaluation is conducted to learn the users' perception of the system, the developers' perception of the project, and managements' perceptions of the project management. This information is helpful as the system is maintained, redeveloped, and perhaps, reengineered.

By following a methodology such as phased development in the prescribed way, the organization may avoid many of the problems that have contributed to CRM system failures, and thereby increase the likelihood of success.

CHALLENGES OF CRM IMPLEMENTATION

A phased implementation process with careful planning may minimize many of the nightmares of adopting CRM systems, but the road to implementation will include barriers and problems. Three challenges that have been stressed in different ways throughout this text include expectations, investments, and reactions to change.

Theoretically, the design of a CRM system should begin with a clear understanding of expectations. The key areas that developers and management should know include expectations of the speed, responsiveness, need for privacy, and approach to internal security for the CRM system. Within B2B systems, as the opening example showed, the XML language may replace HTML to facilitate transfer of complicated documents. B2B partners may expect similar forms, standardized item numbers, and systems that can "speak" to each other with a minimal delay. These changes will cause critical needs for high levels of responsiveness and careful design of firewalls to protect internal records while opening other systems to members of the extranet. Given that B2C applications and internal employees also affect established expectations and opinions as to what the CRM system should accomplish and how it should operate, the organization must understand a divergent array of opinions. Thus, the use of focus group discussions for internal and external customers of the CRM system may facilitate implementation before the first dollar is invested. As prototype modules are designed, the developers should once again return to the key constituents—employees, managers, and customers—to check for clarification and for additional ideas.

A significant financial commitment is generally required to implement an effective CRM system. In acquiring and implementing a CRM system from SAP, for example, Brother International Corporation tracked costs for hardware, software, external consulting, and outside training of about $1.7 million.[5] As expectations of various people are gathered, organizations may decide that other investments and changes are also required. For example, the implementation of online incentive programs for the salesforce through linkages within a CRM system may also require changes in ordering, shipping, and in accounting or payroll.

Perhaps the most difficult challenge of implementing CRM systems is in managing organizational change and in motivating employees from various areas to enthusiastically adopt the new approach.[6] The champion from top management can assist in setting priorities, but process changes must be carefully approached and tracked over time. The enthusiasm for a new, perhaps more efficient, approach may well be followed by a type of depression and resistance to implementing changes quickly.

POTENTIAL REWARDS FROM CRM IMPLEMENTATION

As the CRM system is discussed and designed, the organization may experience several unexpected benefits unrelated to the returns from the operational system itself. With discussions among customers, employees, and managers about the expected uses of CRM, the organization may define new opportunities to distinguish its offerings from those of the competition. Given an ultimate goal of growth and increased relationships with customers, the organization should consider the level of investment required for each desired outcome.

> Among the critical inputs is the organization's knowledge of customer behavior, particularly with respect to market segmentation, brand commitment, customer loyalty, and employee commitment. This critical knowledge about your customer landscape is gained through the application of sophisticated market research and analytic CRM. This process input knowledge shapes the firm's CRM vision/strategy (the marketing process), which is then implemented through people, processes, and technology. The process outputs pertain to the

value created for the organization's key stakeholders, including customers, employees, owners, and the community.[7]

Despite the fears of problems with CRM systems, the bottom line for the future success of any organization may well be its ability to manage people within an electronic marketspace that complements or replaces traditional approaches to conducting business. If implemented correctly, the CRM system may well help the organization continue to learn to adapt and change within a dynamic environment.

SUMMARY

Implementation problems occur as failures to provide the proper focus for the project and failures in developing the system happen. In terms of focus, management and developers may fail to understand the purpose of the project, define the scope too broadly, fail to designate a champion, or fail to understand the expectations of key constituent groups. Development of the system may face problems from a lack of technical knowledge, failure to define the risks involved or the quality desired in the system, a process that begins with tools rather than with system objectives, failure to use a phased developmental methodology or to recognize the importance of privacy and security, and failure to conduct a post-implementation evaluation.

The phased development methodology consists of six stages. In the preliminary investigation stage the functional requirements of the new system are defined. Then the project is subdivided into modules (or phases), and for each module the analysis, design, and preliminary construction stages are implemented. Then all of the modules are integrated in the final construction stage. The system undergoes a user acceptance test during the installation stage. At this point the organization cuts over to the new system.

Organizational support for CRM implementation consists of a champion from top management, a rationale for the strategic investment, and a plan to coordinate across functional units. Challenges of CRM implementation include the needs to define divergent expectations for B2B, B2C, and employee constituents, to garner the sizable capital investment usually required, and to manage the organizational change process. Potential rewards of CRM implementation include the discussions that occur about customers, strategic investments, and the need to change over time.

KEY TERMS

bottom-up approach	prototype	top management
extent of coordination	strategic investment	championship
phased development	rationale	top-down approach
methodology		

QUESTIONS FOR REVIEW AND CRITICAL THINKING

1. What are two key problem areas that cause CRM implementation to fail?
2. What are the steps of a phased development methodology?
3. Why is it important to have constituent groups provide feedback about prototype modules of the system?

4. What are the three major supports the organization can provide to facilitate a successful implementation of a CRM system?

5. What are the major challenges the organization faces in implementing a CRM system?

6. What benefits may accrue to the organization from the implementation process for a CRM system?

NOTES

1. Ken Brack, "B2Beyond the Exchanges," *Industrial Distribution* 91:7 (July 2002): 49–50.

2. Arvind D. Shah, "Customer Relationship Management: Practical Tips for Successful Implementation," *DM Direct* (12 July 2002).

3. For more information on the phased development methodology, see Raymond McLeod, Jr. and Eleanor Jordan, *Systems Development: A Project Management Approach* (New York: John Wiley & Sons, 2002).

4. Debabroto Chatterjee, Rajdeep Grewal, and V. Sambamurthy, "Shaping Up for E-Commerce: Institutional Enablers of the Organizational Assimilation of Web Technologies," *MIS Quarterly* 26:2 (June 2002): 65–89.

5. Ali Pirnar, Linda Plazonja, and Robert Scalea, "Brother International Corporation," *The ROI Report* 6:3 (June 2002): 1–22.

6. Mehmer C. Kocakulah, Abbas Foroughi, and Mitchell Lannert, "Streamlining Supply Chain Management with E-Business," *The Review of Business Information Systems* 6:2 (spring 2002): 1–7.

7. Lawrence A. Crosby and Sheree L. Johnson, "High Performance Marketing in the CRM Era," *Marketing Management* 10:3 (September/October 2001): 10–11.

Business Index

Subject Index

DATE DUE